DESCARTI

Descartes' *Meditations*, one of the most influential works in western philosophy, continues to provoke discussion and debate. This volume of original essays by leading established and emerging early modern scholars ranges over all six of the *Meditations* and explores issues such as skepticism, judgment, causation, the nature of meditation and the meditator's relation to God, the nature of personhood, Descartes' theory of sense perception, and his ideas on the nature of substance. The contributors bring new insights to both central and less-studied topics in the *Meditations*, and connect the work with the rich historical and intellectual context in which Descartes forged his thought. The resulting volume will appeal to a wide range of scholars of early modern thought.

KAREN DETLEFSEN is Associate Professor in the Department of Philosophy at the University of Pennsylvania. She has published articles in *Oxford Studies in Early Modern Philosophy*, *Perspectives on Science* and *Philosophy Compass*.

DESCARTES'
Meditations
A Critical Guide

EDITED BY

KAREN DETLEFSEN

University of Pennsylvania

CAMBRIDGE
UNIVERSITY PRESS

CAMBRIDGE
UNIVERSITY PRESS

University Printing House, Cambridge CB2 8BS, United Kingdom

Cambridge University Press is part of the University of Cambridge.

It furthers the University's mission by disseminating knowledge in the pursuit of education, learning and research at the highest international levels of excellence.

www.cambridge.org
Information on this title: www.cambridge.org/9781107463172

© Cambridge University Press 2013

First published 2013
First paperback edition 2014

A catalogue record for this publication is available from the British Library

Library of Congress Cataloguing in Publication data
Descartes' *Meditations* : a critical guide / edited by Karen Detlefsen.
p.   cm. – (Cambridge critical guides)
Includes bibliographical references (p.) and index.
ISBN 978-0-521-11160-7 (hardback)
1. Descartes, René, 1596–1650. Meditationes de prima philosophia.
2. First philosophy.   I. Detlefsen, Karen.
B1854.D45 2013
194–dc23
2012024502

ISBN 978-0-521-11160-7 Hardback
ISBN 978-1-107-46317-2 Paperback

To my mother and father, Joyce and Bill Detlefsen

Contents

vii

Contributors

LILLI ALANEN is Professor Emeritus of Philosophy at the University of Uppsala. She is author of *Descartes's Concept of Mind* (2003) and editor of *Feminist Reflections on the History of Philosophy* (with Charlotte Witt, 2004).

MARTHA BRANDT BOLTON is Professor of Philosophy at Rutgers University. She has written on a wide range of early modern philosophers. Her articles include those in *Studies on Locke: Sources, Contemporaries, and Legacy* (eds. Sarah Hutton and Paul Shurman), *Berkeley's Lasting Legacy: 300 Years Later* (eds. T. Airaksinen and B. Belfrage), and *Companion to Leibniz* (ed. Brandon Look).

DEBORAH BROWN is Associate Professor in the School of History, Philosophy, Religion, and Classics at the University of Queensland. She is author of *Descartes and the Passionate Mind* (Cambridge, 2006).

JOHN CARRIERO is Professor of Philosophy at the University of California, Los Angeles. He is author of *Between Two Worlds: A Reading of Descartes's "Meditations"* (2009) and co-editor with Janet Broughton of *A Companion to Descartes* (2008).

KAREN DETLEFSEN is Associate Professor of Philosophy and Education at the University of Pennsylvania. She has published articles in *Oxford Studies in Early Modern Philosophy*, *Perspectives on Science* and *Philosophy Compass*.

DANIEL GARBER is Stuart Professor of Philosophy at Princeton University. He is author of *Descartes' Metaphysical Physics* (1992), *Descartes Embodied* (Cambridge, 2001), *Leibniz: Body, Substance, Monad* (2009), and *What Happens after Pascal's Wager: Living Faith and Rational Belief: The Aquinas Lecture* (2009). He is also editor of *The Cambridge History of Seventeenth-Century Philosophy* (with Michael Ayers, Cambridge, 1998),

Kant and the Early Moderns (with Béatrice Longuenesse, 2008), and *The Mechanization of Natural Philosophy* (with Sophie Roux, forthcoming).

GARY HATFIELD is the Adam Seybert Professor in Moral and Intellectual Philosophy at the University of Pennsylvania. He is author of *The Natural and the Normative: Theories of Spatial Perception from Kant to Helmholtz* (1990), *Descartes and the Meditations* (2003), and *Perception and Cognition: Essays in the Philosophy of Psychology* (2009).

MICHAEL W. HICKSON is Assistant Professor of Philosophy at Santa Clara University, California. His articles have appeared in journals such as *Journal of the History of Philosophy, History of Philosophy Quarterly*, and *Journal of the History of Ideas*.

THOMAS M. LENNON is Professor Emeritus of Philosophy at the University of Western Ontario. He is author of *The Battle of the Gods and the Giants* (1993), *Reading Bayle* (1999), and *The Plain Truth: Descartes, Huet, and Skepticism* (2008). He is editor of *Cartesian Views: Papers Presented to Richard A. Watson* (2003) and *The Achilles of Rationalist Psychology* (with Robert J. Stainton, 2010).

TAD M. SCHMALTZ is Professor of Philosophy at the University of Michigan. He is author of *Malebranche's Theory of the Soul* (1996), *Radical Cartesianism* (Cambridge, 2002), and *Descartes on Causation* (2008). He is editor of the *Historical Dictionary of Descartes and Cartesian Philosophy* (with Roger Ariew, Demis Des Chene, Douglas Jesseph, and Theo Verbeck, 2003), *Receptions of Descartes: Cartesianism and Anti-Cartesianism in Early Modern Europe* (2005) and *Integrating History and Philosophy of Science: Problems and Prospects* (with Seymour Mauskopf, 2012).

JORGE SECADA is Professor of Philosophy at the University of Virginia. He is author of *Cartesian Metaphysics: The Scholastic Origins of Modern Philosophy* (Cambridge, 2000).

LISA SHAPIRO is Associate Professor of Philosophy at Simon Fraser University. She is the translator and editor of *The Correspondence between Princess Elisabeth of Bohemia and René Descartes* (2007), and co-editor with Martin Pickavé of *Emotions and Cognitive Life in Medieval and Early Modern Philosophy* (2012).

Acknowledgments

I would like to thank the contributors to this volume. They all have been wonderfully patient, and I could not have asked for a more pleasurable and stimulating group of scholars with whom to work. Hilary Gaskin, Anna Lowe, and Joanna Garbutt at Cambridge University Press have been enormously helpful at every stage of this project, and I am grateful for their guidance. As always, Tan Kok Chor and Amalia Tan deserve special appreciation for all the joy.

Descartes' texts

All references to Descartes' texts are by AT number, usually followed by CSM(K) number. For example (7: 84, 2: 58) indicates p. 84 of the seventh volume of AT, followed by the same passage as translated on p. 58 of the second volume of CSM(K). There is variation in citation style among chapters in this volume, and these variants are noted in those chapters.

Descartes, René. 1964–76. *Oeuvres de Descartes*, 11 vols., ed. C. Adam and P. Tannery (Paris: J. Vrin).

    1967. *Oeuvres Philosophiques*, vol. ii, edited by Ferdinand Alquié (Paris: Editions Garnier Frères).

    1983. *Principles of Philosophy*, trans. Valentine Roger Miller and Reese P. Miller (Dordrecht: Reidel).

    1985a. *The Philosophical Writings of Descartes*, 2 vols., trans. John Cottingham, Robert Stoothoff, and Dugald Murdoch (Cambridge University Press).

    1985b. *The Philosophical Writings of Descartes*, vol. iii, *The Correspondence*, trans. John Cottingham, Robert Stoothoff, Dugald Murdoch, and Anthony Kenny (Cambridge University Press).

    2001. *Discourse on Method, Optics, Geometry, and Meteorology*, trans. Paul J. Oscamp, revised ed. (Indianapolis, IN: Hackett Publishing).

    2008. *Meditations on First Philosophy with Selections from the Objections and Replies*, ed. and trans. Michael Moriarty (Oxford University Press).

Introduction

Karen Detlefsen

It is difficult to overestimate the importance to the history of western thought of René Descartes' *Meditations on First Philosophy*. It is the most widely read and best-known text of a crucial figure working in a time of extraordinary intellectual ferment in Europe, a time which included transformations in philosophy, natural sciences, religion, art, and more. Indeed, among those we now characterize as philosophers, Descartes is widely considered *the* key figure in the break from the past and in the birth of modern philosophy; the *Meditations* is seen to capture much of Descartes' new philosophy.

Given the tremendous scholarly attention that has been paid to the *Meditations* over the last centuries, it may seem difficult to write anything new about the text. One way of characterizing the innovative nature of the chapters in this volume is to note the historiographical trends that have marked scholarship on early modern philosophy in recent decades, and to further note the way this volume fits into those trends. For much of the twentieth century, at least in the Anglo-America tradition, scholars tended to take an internalist, analytic approach to philosophy of the seventeenth to eighteenth centuries, analyzing arguments within texts, often with an eye to illuminating problems of contemporary, and not necessarily historical, interest. Recently, the contextualist approach has increased in importance, and texts have thus been read in terms of the intellectual, political, theological, scientific, and other contexts of their own time. This trend has greatly increased the role of *history* in our histories of philosophy, and has sometimes downplayed the role of *philosophy* (taken here as critical engagement with arguments) in studies of the past. This volume draws on both these approaches, showing that taking a contextualist approach to the history of philosophy is not at odds with an analytic approach to that history, and that the two approaches enrich each other. (This will come as no surprise to many scholars of the early modern period, including the authors in this volume, some of whom have been practicing the history of philosophy in precisely this vein for decades.) This commitment to a methodology drawing upon both contextualism and analysis allows the authors new ways of thinking about Descartes' *Meditations*, sometimes offering highly innovative readings of old themes.

The eleven chapters in this volume are grouped in four sections: skepticism; substance and cause (the foundations of metaphysics); the sensations (which deals with aspects of Descartes' new theory of sense perception in light of his theory of substance and mechanism); and the human being (which deals with dualism and the unity of the human, to be sure, but also with normative issues surrounding human freedom and the will, the human's relation with God, and her moral development and self). However, in providing a brief sketch of them, I will treat these chapters in terms of the context upon which they draw.

Some chapters locate the *Meditations* within the context of Descartes' own developing philosophy, drawing upon important Cartesian texts beyond the *Meditations*, and drawing on Descartes' own evolving thoughts on various topics, to elucidate under-appreciated features of the text. Gary Hatfield deals with a number of unresolved issues in Descartes surrounding sensory perception. Among these issues is that of resemblance, and Hatfield concludes that for Descartes, all ideas – even sensory ideas such as color – represent by resembling their objects in the world. Drawing upon Descartes' account of material falsity, and elements from Descartes' broader philosophy, including his physiological work, Hatfield further argues that sensory ideas represent their objects only obscurely. Lilli Alanen discusses Descartes' account of judgment in the Fourth Meditation, with special focus on the will, to argue that the will contributes to belief formation, which in turn has consequences for Descartes' account of the self. Examining Descartes' account of freedom of the will throughout Descartes' broader corpus, and two senses of indifference to be found in Descartes' account of freedom, Alanen argues that we can have self-determining control over our volitions, though in the case of willing to assent to the true and the good clearly perceived, our self-determining control is indirect, namely in making the prior choice whether to pursue knowledge of the true and the good in the first place. Jorge Secada's chapter challenges a standard approach to the *Meditations*, an approach that claims it is a treatise that relies exclusively, or even primarily, upon rational argument. Rather, Secada makes the case that we must take the meditative nature of the text much more seriously than is typical, and that if we do so, we see that the text provides treatment for "a cognitive illness inherent in human beings, resulting from the embodiment of the mind." Secada focuses specifically on the meditation upon God, his nature and existence. Moreover, Secada argues that these exercises are crucial for the transformation of the self that can be brought about by meditation. We can thus read Secada's chapter as one focusing on Descartes' broader – arguably lifelong – project of the human's care for herself. In her contribution to the volume, Lisa Shapiro examines the standard reading of the nature of the Cartesian self as soul, arguing that this conception cannot account for important features of the *Meditations*, including the meditator's "psychological continuity afforded by memory" and her development of epistemic virtue throughout the six meditations. Memory is crucial to the meditator's intellectual progress throughout the *Meditations*. Cultivating virtuous epistemic habits is crucial to moral progress, and on this point, Shapiro draws our attention to the role of the passions and control of the passion in this work, long before Descartes turns to a focused treatment of that topic. Being alert to Descartes' later interests thus allows Shapiro to provide a much richer account of the nature of the self offered in the *Meditations* than is typically allowed by seeing it exclusively as a text in epistemology and metaphysics.

Other chapters draw upon Descartes' interactions with the ideas of his contemporaries and near contemporaries. In his chapter on Descartes' conception of substance and his confrontation with materialists, Daniel Garber aims to make sense of the *Meditations* on its own terms, resisting the temptation to read the conception of substance found in the *Principles* back into the earlier text (on this latter point, Garber also reads the *Meditations* within the context of Descartes' developing philosophy). Garber argues that the well-worked-out account of substance/principal attribute/mode that is found in the *Principles* is not to be found in the *Meditations* itself, and the later text's account of substance as that which is independent makes only a weak showing in the *Meditations*, where the dominant account of substance is rather the "ultimate subject" conception of substance (substance is the ultimate subject in which accidents and faculties inhere). What encouraged the change in the general account of substance between the two works? And what does this change entail? Garber's answer to the first question is that the confrontation with Hobbes and other materialists made clear that Descartes could not hold on to his earlier theory of substance. His answer to the second question is that Descartes' later conception of substance is, metaphysically, extremely thin. Martha Brandt Bolton addresses an equally fundamental question, namely what Descartes' basic account of the

constitution of thinking substance must be. She addresses this problem mindful of Arnauld's and others' concern that since thinking is the
nature of mind (as substance), since passing thoughts are mere *modes*,
and since thinking *qua* substantial nature cannot therefore be those
passing thoughts, then Descartes must give an account of what thinking, as mind's nature, actually *is*. Turning to Descartes' and Arnauld's
extended interaction on this, as well as to other seventeenth-century contexts and tools from Descartes' own philosophy, Bolton offers an interpretation of thinking as a "determinable that collects all and only the
possible determinate acts of thinking … but not causing those states."
Bolton uses this solution to deal with a number of Cartesian difficulties about substances in general and mind in particular, noting that not
all these difficulties can be resolved. Tad M. Schmaltz's chapter examines the three causal axioms Descartes offers in his geometrical account
of the *Meditations* as found in the Second Replies. Schmaltz evaluates
these axioms against a consideration of one of Descartes' immediate
scholastic predecessors, Suárez, noting what remains and what changes
of Suárez's accounts of these axioms in Descartes. Schmaltz thus draws
our attention to the continuities and discontinuities between Descartes
and the most systematic and thorough theorist of causation in the later
medieval period. Schmaltz also looks at the *Meditations* within the context of Descartes' somewhat broader intellectual project, showing how
the axioms as they are outlined in the Second Replies are used in the
Meditations themselves, sometimes in ways divergent from how they are
presented in the Second Replies.

Yet other chapters take a broader contextualist approach, drawing
upon ancient and scholastic texts and concepts to illuminate Descartes'
thought in the *Meditations*. In her chapter, Deborah Brown considers
Descartes' skepticism within the long history of skepticism. While it
is true that Descartes is much indebted to ancient forms of skepticism,
Brown argues, she resists the interpretations that he offers nothing new
and that his innovations are merely to restrict the scope of his skepticism
to theoretical knowledge in order to protect the affairs of everyday life
from it, thus avoiding the skeptic's problem of how to live. In contrast,
Brown argues that there *is* something radically new in Descartes' skepticism, namely a skepticism with respect to the content of one's own ideas,
and so Descartes' solutions to various skeptical challenges must depart
notably from those offered by the ancients and medievals. Brown notes
both continuities and discontinuities between Cartesian skepticism
and previous forms of skepticism, and she also situates the *Meditations*

within Descartes' overall development, arguing that only in the *Passions* do we finally find a solution to the practical challenge of how the skeptic ought to live. John Carriero – building on work in his *Between Two Worlds: A Reading of Descartes's "Meditations"* – turns to the standard reading of Descartes as an indirect realist with respect to sensory cognition, and argues against this reading. While it is true, Carriero argues, that Descartes' conception of sensory cognition evolves from the start through to the end of the *Meditations*, and that Descartes starts with a roughly Aristotelian realist account of sensory cognition, the view that he ends up with is not as distant from his scholastic starting point as typically has been believed. One interesting line of argument Carriero pursues is his belief that Descartes' rejection of the resemblance thesis does not commit him to a "causal covariance" model of sensory representation, according to which bodies cause ideas in the mind; rather, Carriero argues, Descartes means that the reality that we sense exists in our mind, but it exists only obscurely and confusedly. In her chapter, Karen Detlefsen examines the Sixth Meditation passage on the human composite – drawing upon a conceptual apparatus developed from examining Aristotelian and Platonic approaches to teleology – to argue that the passage is first and foremost about the natures of beings, and only secondarily provides a teleological account of the role of the senses in human life. Moreover, depending upon how one interprets Descartes' account of the nature of the composite, one will have greater or lesser difficulties taking into account what appear to be teleological accounts of living beings found in Descartes' biological works. Taking this into account, Detlefsen defends a particular reading of the nature of the mind–body composite, and the teleological account that follows from this.

One chapter manages what might be the most difficult task: saying something new about the *Meditations* while focusing almost exclusively on the arguments of the text itself. This chapter, by Thomas M. Lennon and Michael W. Hickson, addresses Descartes' use of skepticism in the First Meditation, including forms of skepticism he raises only to reject, namely the madman and the evil demon. The chapter provides a fresh reading of Descartes' rejection of lunacy and the evil demon by making clear what it means for a doubt to be methodical and reasonable, and why these two forms of doubt fail to be so. Their conclusions allow Lennon and Hickson to consider anew what is unique about the Second Meditation *cogito*.

The chapters in this volume all offer new interpretations of centrally important elements of one of the most important philosophical texts of the western world. They do so by situating the text both within Descartes' developing intellectual projects and the astonishingly turbulent intellectual age in which he lived. Together, they touch upon many themes that animated Descartes throughout his lifetime, unsurprising given that the *Meditations* occupies such a critical place in Descartes' maturing thought, and in the history of western philosophy.

PART I

Skepticism

CHAPTER I

The skepticism of the First Meditation

Thomas M. Lennon and Michael W. Hickson

INTRODUCTION

Descartes seeks unshakeable certainty about truth by "the apparently opposite course" of deliberately generating uncertainty (6: 31, 1: 127). His premise is that if at some point the attempt to generate uncertainty fails, unshakeable certainty will have been found. For the project to succeed, the reasons leading Descartes to uncertainty at the outset must not be arbitrary; they must be, on the contrary, "powerful and well thought-out" (7: 22, 2: 15): the doubt must be methodic and reasonable. What it means for doubt to be methodic and reasonable rather than haphazard or gratuitous should be a central question for any interpretation of the *Meditations*. In what follows we give an account of reasonable doubt that differs from other such accounts in the literature in several important ways. First, we take the madman and evil demon objections *not* to be reasonable doubts. They are included by Descartes in the *Meditations* precisely for the purpose of contrasting them with what he takes to be reasonable doubts: the madman is contrasted with the dream argument (section I of this chapter) and the evil demon is contrasted with the deceiving God objection (section II). Getting the distinction right between reasonable and unreasonable doubt is crucial, we argue, for understanding what is unique about the particular foundation of knowledge that Descartes settles upon in Meditation Two, namely the thought or assertion that *"I am, I exist"* (section III of this chapter). As we will see, because there is no way of reasonably doubting that proposition, our knowledge of it constitutes a model for all other knowledge.

Descartes begins the *Meditations* by going "straight for the basic principles on which [his] former beliefs rested" (7: 18, 2: 12). We will present Descartes' method of doubt as consisting of various challenges to a series of "models of knowledge" with the aim of finding one that resists every conceivable challenge. We will take M to be a model of knowledge for some person P if (1) P knows M, and (2) for all other things X that are identical to M in some relevant respect R, P knows X. As we will see, Descartes' method of doubt leads him to the discovery that the thought or assertion, "*I am, I exist*" (referred to in the literature and by us as the "*cogito*"[1]), is a model of knowledge for him because (1) Descartes knows that the *cogito* is necessarily true whenever he perceives it, and (2) everything else that is identical to the *cogito* in the relevant respect that it too is perceived clearly and distinctly is likewise known by Descartes to be necessarily true whenever he perceives it.

The first model that comes under attack is sensory experience, which is challenged on the basis of the relativity of its deliverances. In very allusive fashion, Descartes deploys the Pyrrhonian trope that what is perceived is relative to the conditions under which it is perceived and therefore lacks the objectivity that characterizes knowledge of the truth. In particular, size and distance make such a difference: the senses at least occasionally deceive us about very small or distant objects. The prospect is better with respect to proximate, medium-sized objects, especially those belonging to Descartes' own body, such as the hands before his face; but this second model fails when challenged by the possibility that the experience is only one of dreaming. However, knowledge of simpler and more universal things such as arithmetic and geometry, the third model, can still be certain and indubitable, unimpeachable by the possibility of dreaming. But such knowledge is open to doubt on the basis that God might allow deception about such apparently certain things in *all* instances, since He allows deception about them in at least *some* instances. If certainty about them is to be achieved, therefore, proof must first be found that there exists a God who would not allow such universal deception. This proof would also eliminate such other reasons for universal deception as that we come into being through some cause less perfect than God, such as chance, fate, or "some other means" (7: 21, 2: 14).

This three-stage generation of doubt is a fairly standard reading of the First Meditation and is accurate as far as it goes. But it misses two challenges that offer refinement of Descartes' argument there. One is the lunatic, the other is the evil demon. Both tend to be ignored by the literature, or to be melded into one of the other models, lunacy into the dream

---

[1] In following the literature in referring to this thought or assertion as the *cogito* we are not thereby taking the *cogito* to be an inference, a performative, a simple assertion, or anything else. For our purposes, we can also ignore the distinction between the *cogito* as formulated above and the assertion that Descartes cites for his model in the Third Meditation: "I am a thinking thing" (7: 35, 2: 24).

challenge, the evil demon into a deceiving God challenge.[2] The tendency does not necessarily lead to error, but it does foreclose certain refinements of Descartes' argument, especially concerning the methodic nature of his doubt. Although he seems to dismiss uncritically the possibility that the experience of his hands and the rest of his body is that of a madman, he does so on the basis that it would be mad to take that possibility seriously. The lunacy challenge thereby shows that Descartes' procedure of doubting is limited to what can be doubted reasonably. He is thus poised to distinguish, as he soon does, his doubt of mathematics as "not a flippant or ill-considered conclusion, but [one] based on powerful and well thought-out reasons" (7: 21, 2: 15).

For reasons to be discussed below, Descartes further supposes that "not God, who is supremely good and the source of truth, but rather some malicious demon of the utmost power and cunning has employed all his energies in order to deceive me" (7: 22, 2: 15). Is the doubt based on this supposition of an evil demon a reasonable doubt for Descartes? We think that it is not, for the doubt is immediately dispelled, at the outset of the Second Meditation, by the *cogito*: "Let him deceive me as much as he can, he will never bring it about that I am nothing so long as I think that I am something" (7: 25, 2: 17). Narratively, the evil demon at this point disappears from the *Meditations*, never to be referred to again, but not before achieving what, logically, was the purpose of its introduction.[3] For just as the Pyrrhonists in their search for tranquility discovered it "as if by chance" upon their suspension of judgment, so Descartes incidentally discovers in this "first cognition," *I am a thinking thing*, a general rule for truth: whatever I perceive in the way that I perceive this residue of

---

[2] This tendency is to be found even in the most thorough and sophisticated literature. Broughton treats the lunacy argument together with dreaming; both explain "how the meditator could have acquired the belief if it were false" (2002, p. 65). Newman refers to the evil genius "as a kind of mnemonic for the more general doubt about our cognitive nature." He differs from Broughton, as do we, in holding that "what underwrites the doubt is not a specific story about how I got my cognitive wiring" (2005). But we differ from his view that "it's the realization – regardless of the story – that my cognitive wiring is flawed." As we see it, our nature is not flawed, only fallible. Miles sees a distinction between the "deceiving God" and the "malicious demon," but holds that "nothing turns on it since if the malicious demon, though finite, is yet powerful enough to deceive us all the time in matters that we perceive clearly and distinctly, reason itself is in jeopardy ... Given that the finite deceiver has sufficient power to control human reason, and the prospect of delivery from doubt is as remote as that of a reasoned escape from the specter of madness" (1999, p. 140). For more bibliography on the deceiving God–evil genius distinction, see Ablondi (2007, p. 88n.18). Ablondi draws the distinction, but in a way that does not persuade us.

[3] Strictly speaking, the demon survives for two additional paragraphs, since Descartes then allows that the assertion "I am a thinking thing" is immune to the demon's malicious power (7: 26–27, 2: 18). See note 1 above.

the abortive fifth challenge is true (7: 35, 2: 24).[4] This is the model for all other knowledge whose certainty he seeks from the outset.

I

The fullest treatments of the last decade of the madman objection have been given by Janet Broughton (2002, 2005). In her book, Broughton construes the doubts of the First Meditation as a series of four "sceptical scenarios" (2002, pp. 64–67): lunacy, dreaming, God, and fate. On her account, these scenarios have two characteristics: (1) they are all *causal* explanations of how we might have our beliefs, such that (2) if the account is true, then the beliefs are false. These scenarios bear a superficial resemblance to the challenged models of our account, but we have three concerns about them. First, although it certainly is a causal account of false beliefs, Descartes summarily *dismisses* the relevance of the lunacy scenario, a feature that Broughton's 2002 account does not notice and seemingly has no way to explain, for Broughton takes the lunacy objection to be paradigmatic of the structure of Descartes' doubt. That lunacy is not such a paradigm is seen by considering that Descartes requires, but the lunacy challenge fails to provide, valid and considered *reasons* (*validas & meditatas rationes*) for doubt. Descartes has no reason to think that he is mad, and thus to doubt on the basis of the possibility of being mad would be gratuitous and unreasonable. Second, the challenge based on an omnipotent God is not obviously a "causal story" as Broughton makes it out to be. As we learn from the Fourth Meditation, God only allows us to be deceived; He does not *cause* us to be deceived. Our deception lies with our misuse of our will, which is not invoked in the First Meditation. A third concern of ours is that Descartes *accepts* the dream scenario as consistent with truth. Even in a dream we can have a clear and distinct perception that two and three are five, due, perhaps, like the appearance of Jacob Marley to Scrooge, to a bit of uncooked potato. Deviant cause does not by itself entail falsity of belief.

In a later (2005) paper on the madman and the dream objections, Broughton discusses at greater length why Descartes invoked lunacy in Meditation One. She takes lunacy to provide Descartes with reasons for doubt about certain sensible objects, and concedes that the dream argument provides better reasons for doubting, thus leading us to the problem of why Descartes would include the madman objection at all. Broughton's answer is

---

[4] "*in hac prima cogitatione … pro regula generalii … statuere.*"

that that objection "keeps us honest" in a way that the dream objection does not. Her argument is that the madman objection is more jarring, disquieting, and immediately perceivable than the dream objection. To understand that I might now be dreaming invokes memory as I recall vivid, deceptive dreams and compare them to subsequent, waking experiences; to understand the madman objection I have only to look on as a lunatic declares his head to be made of glass, when it clearly is not. But as we will see, there are important differences between the dream and madman objections, such that only the former in fact provides any good reason to doubt.[5]

The most recent treatments of the madman have been given in a paper by Fred Ablondi (2007) and a reply by David Scott (2009). Ablondi largely follows the classic line of Harry Frankfurt (1970): the madman is never taken seriously because it would call into question the logical thought processes required to carry out the project of the *Meditations*, thus putting an end to the work before it had even begun. Scott argues, on the contrary, that the madness hypothesis *is* taken seriously by Descartes, and its skeptical force is subsequently incorporated into the dream argument. The reason Scott gives for why the madman objection is not sufficient on its own without the dream argument involves a point about Descartes' methodology. Scott, following work by Hide Ishiguro, argues that in order for our doubt to be methodic we must assume that we understand the patterns of relations that hold between our beliefs, and between our beliefs and the world. In the case of madness, we do not know these patterns of relations, while in the case of dreaming, we do; hence, the dream argument is more methodic. We cannot agree, however, with either Broughton or Scott that the madman objection is similar to the dream objection or included in some way in the dream objection, for we take the madness objection to be an instance of gratuitous doubt, while dreaming is given as an instance of reasonable doubt, as we will now argue.

---

[5] Still, we take Broughton to be in one sense surely on the right track. For we take Descartes, who is generally regarded as the paradigmatic internalist, to be an externalist, committed to holding that there is knowledge of p just in case there is belief of p and belief of p only if p. But this is as far as the externalism need go. For we do not see Descartes as committed to viewing the condition 'only if' in the usual causal terms. Even this much of the account is difficult to find explicit in the texts; in any case, the importance of it here is its ontological underpinning. The idea of the sun is in a sense non-mental, for it just is the sun itself (7: 102, 2: 75). In another sense, it certainly is mental, for Descartes immediately qualifies the sun as "existing in the intellect." But being in the mind is only what he calls an extrinsic denomination, which might mean nothing more than that the sun is known. To put it in the terms of the Third Meditation, the objective reality in the mind of the sun that exists formally in the sky is not some double existence leading to a representationalist epistemology and a correspondence theory of truth. One just sees the truth when one sees the object, but the cause of the seeing doesn't matter.

The madman objection extends the relativity objection against sense knowledge by considering that our beliefs that our bodies have a certain character, or even that they belong to ourselves, are reliable only to the degree that we are mentally sane (i.e. relative to our sanity). Madmen give us occasion to call into doubt the allegedly indubitable beliefs Descartes mentions ("that I am here, sitting by the fire, wearing a winter dressing-gown, holding this piece of paper in my hands ... that these hands or this whole body are mine") because they possess false beliefs both about their own circumstances ("they firmly maintain they are kings when they are paupers, or say they are dressed in purple when they are naked") as well as about their own bodies ("or that their heads are made of earthenware, or that they are pumpkins, or made of glass"). Yet this extension of the relativity objection is immediately found wanting by Descartes: "But such people are insane, and I would be thought equally mad if I took anything from them as a model for myself" (all quotations in this paragraph: 7: 18–19, 2: 13).

The madman objection is successful in reintroducing a relativity argument in order to call immediate sense data about ourselves into doubt, but this argument does not have the cogency of the objection that called into doubt our beliefs about small and distant sensory objects. The latter doubt made us realize that *all of us, some of the time*, are deceived by the senses. Anybody reading the *Meditations* would be given reason to call some of their beliefs into doubt on account of this reflection. The madman objection, on the other hand, makes us realize only that *some of us, some of the time*, are deceived by the senses. Not all readers of the *Meditations* (in all likelihood, none of the readers) would be given a reason to doubt their beliefs on account of this argument alone. Indeed, as Descartes remarks, "I would be thought equally mad if I took anything from them as a model for myself." In other words, a person could respond to the madman objection by claiming, "that argument serves to call the beliefs of madmen – of which you may be one, Descartes – into doubt; but as for me, I have no reason to believe that I am a madman, and so I will continue to believe that my body is flesh and bone rather than glass or earthenware." The madmen objection does not, without further information, have universal applicability, or even applicability to any individual person.

The madman objection could be made universal, however, by supposing that *everybody* is mad some or all of the time, although most of us do not realize this about ourselves. Then the relativity argument would apply to everybody, for just as we are all sometimes in non-optimal external circumstances for trusting our senses, so too we are all, by supposition, sometimes in a non-optimal frame of mind for trusting our senses. But Descartes never strengthens the argument in this way, nor does he have any reason to do so. To assume that every human being is insane is a gratuitous doubt. As Scott has demonstrated from a number of texts, madness is, for Descartes, a physiological imperfection ("brains so damaged by the persistent vapours of melancholia" [7: 19, 2: 13]) and not in any way a total lack of, or a different kind altogether of, reason. As an imperfection rather than its own nature, therefore, madness implies the existence or at least the possibility of sane minds, and those are Descartes' audience. A world of only madmen would result only through some great accident, not because of anything inherent to rational nature itself. Sane minds are the norm; madness is the exception, by definition. Why suppose, then, that persistent vapours have got to everybody's heads, or the head of any particular person? To suppose something so arbitrary is perhaps, as Descartes says, itself a sign of madness.

Broughton considers an account of Descartes' dismissal of the madness objection similar to the one just sketched by us. She discusses the way in which dreaming is inherent to human nature while lunacy is not and asks whether Descartes could have dismissed the madness objection for this reason. She concludes that he could not have, given that "*nothing we know* about them [madmen] and us shows us that we are constitutionally incapable of having our vapor-balance upset too" (2005, p. 17; our emphasis). While there is a possibility that we might all be mad, or that any given person might be mad, we do not believe that this bare possibility alone provides enough of a reason to doubt one's own sanity. The dream argument, on the other hand, does provide a reason for doubt. It is introduced to supply the relativity argument of the sort that Descartes needs to question sense knowledge about ourselves; an argument that shows readers of the *Meditations* that *all of us*, at least *some of the time*, are deceived by the senses about our very selves. It is a reasonable doubt because sleeping and dreaming form a part of everybody's life, just as viewing small and distant objects does.

II

The concept of a God who allows me always to be deceived even in matters that seem wholly certain and evident (see 7: 35–36, 2: 24–25) and the concept of an evil demon who "has employed all his energies to deceive me" (see 7: 22, 2: 15) are different concepts, described differently and invoked for different dialectical purposes by Descartes. By contrast to the God who is described as omnipotent, literally capable of everything (*qui omnia potest*), a characterization that underlies Descartes' doctrine of created truth, the evil demon is described as only of the utmost power and cunning (*summe potentem & callidum*), all of whose energies are used to make our perceptions "merely the delusions of dreams that he has devised to ensnare my judgment." An omnipotent God would not have to rely on cunning to lead us to deception, nor would he exhaust his power in doing so. An omnipotent God would at most *permit* us to be deceived by failing to create what only appears to exist as we perceive it; he would not *actively* deceive us by seducing our judgment, as an evil demon might.

The demon is introduced not for methodological but psychological reasons. Descartes finds that even with the hyperbolical doubt in play, his former, now dubious belief cannot be relinquished, and therefore he resolves, for theoretical purposes, "to turn [his] will in completely the opposite direction and deceive himself, by pretending that these former opinions are false and imaginary" (7: 22, 2: 15).[6] And he does so with the supposition of the evil demon. As we will later remark, this act of willful self-deceit is the hallmark of unreasonable doubt. The question, therefore, is this: why is the possibility of a deceiving God, then, counted among reasonable doubts?

To reiterate, God is never said, or even hypothesized, to be a deceiver, as the evil demon is, only as *allowing* deception. That God allows deception is not removed by the proof of the existence of a veridical God that culminates in the Fifth Meditation, or by the Fourth Meditation, which absolves God of responsibility for our sins and errors by attributing them to our misapplication of the will to what the intellect does not clearly and distinctly perceive as good or true. Nonetheless, Descartes admits he is at least sometimes deceived about what he takes to be obviously good or true, which is sufficient for the hyperbolical doubt that he is always so deceived if "God has given me a nature such that I was deceived even in matters which seemed most evident" (7: 36, 2: 25).

What kind of nature would he have, always to be deceived even in the most evident matters? The hyperbolical doubt is not that God has given him a corrupted nature, i.e. one incapable of the truth, or of

---

[6] It seems clear that Descartes is referring to the Pyrrhonian skeptics, who doubt not for good reasons, but willfully. When the intended result of this doubt, the possibility of an evil demon, cannot be maintained, the psychological futility of Pyrrhonism is thereby indicated.

distinguishing it from the false; for in that case God would be a deceiver in a sense which Descartes rules out right from the outset of the *Discourse on the Method* when he says that good sense (*le bon sens*), what he also calls "reason," is part of human nature and could not be better for its task of "judging well and of distinguishing the true from the false" (6: 1–2, 1: 111). That we do not have the power of such judgment is of course possible, but to doubt that we have it would not be reasonable, for there is no reason to suspect that we do not have it. As the *Discourse* begins: "Good sense is the best distributed thing in the world: for everyone thinks himself so well endowed with it that even those who are the hardest to please in everything else do not usually desire more of it than they possess. In this it is unlikely that everyone is mistaken" (6: 1–2, 1: 111). That we do err at least sometimes is not because of a defective power of reason, but because of a (culpable) misapplication of it, the elimination of which is the aim of the method proposed in the *Discourse*. But we might always be mistaken if we are created such that although we are capable of distinguishing the true from the false, we never succeed in reaching the truth. And a reason for this is indicated in the First Meditation as the ground for the challenge that results in the hyperbolic doubt: "there is an omnipotent God who has made me the kind of creature that I am. How do I know that he has not brought it about that there is no earth, no sky, no extended thing, no shape no size, no place, while at the same time ensuring that all these things appear to me just as they do now?" (7: 21, 2: 14).[7]

The list Descartes gives of what God might fail to create is long, perhaps designed for heuristic purposes. The key item, extended thing (*res extensa*), which is later revealed as essentially comprising all the others, is only slipped in, apparently en passant. But given what is later revealed, the explanation of how mathematics could always be false for us becomes clear: God might not have created *res extensa*, which is its object; we would have what only appears to be clear and distinct perception of it. Another way to put this possibility of error is that although we are capable of the truth, we just never encounter it. Descartes' method promises only

---

[7] For the opposing view, that the hyperbolical doubt is based on "the hypothesis of a flaw in our cognitive faculties," see Newman and Nelson (1999, esp. pp. 376–77). They provide a "canon" of seven texts in which, according to them, "it is clear that hyperbolic doubt is in every case linked to meta-level questioning of the cognitive faculties by means of which we perceive … for all I know, my cognitive equipment is flawed" (1999, pp. 373–74). But Descartes never mentions cognitive flaw. All he says is that our nature might be such that we are deceived even in what seems most evident. On our reading, one naturally assents to what seems clearly and distinctly true, but that might always lead to error if the object that would make those perceptions true were not (created by God).

the avoidance of error, not arrival at truth, a promise that would be blasphemous.[8] Thus it is natural for Descartes to include in this same ground for the challenge that results in the hyperbolic doubt the possibility of our having been created by fate or chance, whose imperfection would fail to guarantee that there is an object of evident perceptions.[9]

The Sixth Meditation is largely the mop-up operation of providing moral certainty about the immortality of the soul and about the practical reliability of sensory experience insofar as it passes the test of coherence. The search for unshakeable certainty ends, in the Fifth Meditation, with the completion of Descartes' argument for the existence of God, whose veracity insures that He has not created us so as to err even in what seems most evident. The conclusions drawn in the Fifth Meditation are not only that God exists, and that His existence is known as certainly as anything else, but also that the certainty of everything else *depends* on certainty of it (7: 69, 2: 47–48). How so? According to the Fourth Meditation, it is impossible to doubt a clear and distinct perception of the truth as long one has the perception. But when that perception is no longer occurrent – when, for example, attention wanders from the reasons on the basis of which it is perceived as such – other reasons might intrude and shake the certainty of it, unless blocked by knowledge of God, with the result that there would never be "true and certain knowledge about anything, but

---

[8] See the subtitle of Malebranche's *Search after Truth*: "Wherein are treated the nature of Man's mind and the use that he must make of it to avoid error in the sciences." Descartes' first rule of method in the *Discourse*, like the Fourth Meditation's prescription concerning the proper use of the will, is essentially negative, telling us what not to do in order to avoid error.

[9] The full account of this failure would involve an account of Descartes' conception of truth as an object. Like Augustine, and unlike Malebranche, he conceives of truth as a *thing*, not as a *relation* either between ideas or between things and ideas. Thus Descartes claims that God is the total and efficient cause of even eternal truths, which we take to mean that He creates a certain object – *res extensa* – in the case of mathematics. It is this conception of truth, which Locke was later to call metaphysical truth, that leads Descartes to say in a letter to Clerselier of 23 April 1649 that "there is no distinction between truth and the thing or substance that is true" (5: 355, 3: 377). It is also why he says to Mersenne (July 1641 and 22 July 1641) that terms or propositions do equally well in expressing truth (3: 395 and 417, 3: 186 and 187). When Descartes invokes the scholastics' slogan as *adaequatio rei et intellectus*, he does not mean, as the scholastics do, a correspondence between thing and intellect – a shared form, for example. Instead, he means *adaequatio* in the sense of attaining, or reaching, by equaling metaphorically in the sense of being up to the task (of perceiving the object). He seems to say just this to Mersenne:

it is possible to explain the meaning of the word to someone who does not know the language, and tell him that the word "truth", in the strict sense, denotes the conformity of thought with its object, but that when it is attributed to things outside thought, it means only that they can be objects of genuine thoughts [*pensées veritables*], either ours or God's (2: 597, 3: 139; modified).

The thoughts are true only in the sense indicated, namely veritable or genuine; they are not true in the sense things are true (*vraies*). As later Cartesians were to make clear, putative thoughts or ideas without objects are not ideas at all.

only shifting and changeable opinions" (7: 69, 2: 48). So knowledge of God supplies the certainty lacking to clear and distinct perceptions which are not currently attended to. It is not the memory of some previous clear and distinct perception that the knowledge of the existence of God guarantees (namely, that a recalled perception was truly clear and distinct), but the reliability of the clear and distinct perception itself, which is capable of being called into doubt only insofar as it is merely remembered. If the reasons that lead to knowledge of the existence of God are themselves questioned, then they need only be recalled, restoring the clear and distinct perception that God exists, which as such is indubitable.[10]

III

Notice that Descartes says, without making an exception for the *cogito*, that the certainty about *everything* else depends on his certainty of the existence of God. But the certainty of the existence of God comes no earlier than the Third Meditation. (As we see it, in fact, only in the Fifth Meditation is that certainty asserted.) How, then, can the *cogito* be asserted in the Second Meditation? To ask what might be the same question, doesn't the claim that all other certainty depends on certainty about the existence of God undo the unique privileged status of the *cogito* and thereby the whole program of the *Meditations*? We begin to answer these questions by asking still another: does Descartes in the First Meditation doubt whether he exists?

In the Third Meditation, he says that "something very simple and straightforward in arithmetic or geometry" is open to doubt on the ground that "some God [*aliquem Deum*] could have given me a nature such that I was deceived even in matters which seemed most evident" (7: 35–36, 2: 25). In his Objections, Bourdin took this, plausibly enough, to mean that "nothing ... absolutely nothing [is left free of doubt] until we have established for certain that God exists and cannot be a deceiver" (7: 455–56, 2: 305). Bourdin emphatically makes no exception for the *cogito*, with the result, as he saw it, that until he is certain about the existence of God, who would "curb" the evil demon, Descartes cannot be certain

---

[10] Our Frankfurt-style view is thus an instance of what Newman and Nelson call an "on-demand reproducibility" view, which they see as removing doubt only one more step without resolving it. But as we see it, that step is sufficient to end all reasonable doubt, and ensure warranted stability. Their own view is that the ultimate bedrock of Cartesian warrant lies not in demonstration of a veridical God, but in a properly arrived-at perception of His necessary existence (1999, esp. pp. 384–85, 390–93).

that the evil demon is not tricking him, presumably even about the *cogito*. In reply, Descartes explains how Bourdin's paraphrase should be understood, reaffirming what he had said in the Fifth Meditation:

So long as we attend to a truth which we perceive very clearly, we cannot doubt it. But when, as so often happens, we are not attending to any truth in this way, even though we remember that we have perceived many things very clearly, nevertheless there will be nothing which we may not justly doubt so long as we do not know that whatever we clearly perceive is true. (7: 460, 2: 309)

Once again, no exception is made for the *cogito*. Descartes' reply goes on, however, to supply a useful correction in Bourdin's understanding of the universal doubt.

But my careful critic here takes "nothing" quite differently. From the fact that at one point I said that there was nothing that we might not doubt—namely in the first Meditation, in which I was supposing that I was not attending to anything that I clearly perceive—he draws the conclusion that I am unable to know anything certain, even in the following Meditations. This is to suggest that the reasons which from time to time give us cause to doubt something are not legitimate or sound unless they prove that the same thing must be permanently in doubt. (7: 460, 2: 309)

So, the *cogito* is included in the universal doubt, if not explicitly, at least implicitly. But it is included, like all else that is doubted, only because it is not clearly and distinctly perceived. So far, the *cogito* does not differ from the elements of geometry and arithmetic, which also become indubitable only when clearly and distinctly perceived. The difference between the two cases emerges from the ways in which each comes to be clearly perceived. In mathematics, clarity is achieved in the fashion of the wax analysis of the Second Meditation. But the clarity is vulnerable to the "legitimate and sound" hyperbolic doubt when only remembered. The *cogito* becomes clear when Descartes realizes that, even to be deceived by the demon, he himself must exist. Unlike mathematics, the *cogito* is not liable to any doubt, even when only remembered, for there is no legitimate and sound basis for raising doubt. I can see *now* that even *then* in order for me to be deceived I must have existed. The *cogito* must be immune in this way if permanent skepticism at the outset is to be avoided. Still, it is on certainty that God exists that certainty about the *cogito*, like all other certainty, depends. There is a sense in which dependence is more obvious for the *cogito* than for mathematical truths. For certainty is certainty about truth, and there is undeniably a time at which Descartes did not exist, and, as the Third Meditation argues, he would not exist, and would not exist with his idea of God, unless God had created him, whereas the dependence of mathematical truth on God requires more metaphysics of a less obvious sort.

The privileged status of the *cogito* over other clearly perceived truths such as those of mathematics can be put as follows. Although certainty of its truth depends no less than theirs on the certainty of the truth of God's existence, there is no "legitimate or sound" reason, not even the hypothesis of an evil demon, for doubting it. To see this unique character of the *cogito*, we might consider what unsound and illegitimate reason there might be for doubting his own existence. Ultimately, perhaps the only reason would be that even if the *cogito* were clearly and distinctly perceived – indeed, even if the rejection of the demon hypothesis were clearly and distinctly perceived on the basis of the *cogito* – he could doubt, contrary to these good reasons for believing, just by an act of the will. This is the extreme case Descartes describes in correspondence. Although it is "hardly" possible for us to do so, "absolutely … it is always possible for us to hold back from admitting a clearly perceived truth, provided we consider it a good thing to demonstrate the freedom of our will by so doing" (4: 173, 3: 245).[11] Epistemologically, however, such doubt would be utterly gratuitous; it would amount to the willfulness of Satan.[12]

Such a doubt of the *cogito* would in fact be the doubt of the skeptics for which Descartes expresses contempt because it is a doubt for the sake of doubting. The gratuitousness of such a doubt is why Descartes allows himself the apparently cavalier dismissal of Mersenne's objection that there is no need to suppose that God is a deceiver in order for there to be deception about what is thought to be clearly known, which might instead lie just with him (7: 126, 2: 90). In reply, Descartes allows the possibility of a cleavage between what we can determine to be true by our best efforts and what is in fact true, but also states that it is irrelevant. He begins by reiterating the irresistibility of a clear and distinct perception, and concludes from it that the possibility of it being absolutely false does not detract from its affording perfect certainty. "If this conviction is so firm that it is impossible for us ever to have any reason for doubting what we are convinced of, then there are no further questions for us to ask: we have everything that we could reasonably want." To willfully doubt as the skeptic does is *unreasonable*. "Why should this 'absolute falsity' bother

[11] To Mesland, 9 February 1645. The text referred to here is authentic, but its date, intended recipient, and even its status as a letter, are open to question.
[12] Thus Gouhier, for whose designation of "ce Satan épistémologique" we provide more justification than he does (1962, p. 119).

us, since we neither believe in it nor have even the smallest suspicion of it?" (7: 144–45, 2: 103). Doubt about the *cogito* and doubt based on the cleavage between ultimately warranted assertibility and absolute truth is like doubt based on the possibility of lunacy. The possibility can never be excluded, but there is and can be no reason to believe that it is ever realized for any given subject, and hence no reason to doubt on the basis of it. This contrasts with both sensory doubt on the basis of relativity and dreaming, which are experienced by everyone, and instances of error even in what seems most obvious in mathematics, which Descartes himself admits to.

We are now in a position to offer a general characterization of a "legitimate and sound reason" for doubting, through the conversely unreasonable ground for doing so. An unreasonable ground for doubt is the willful representation of doubting as by itself a "good thing," with no other reason for doubting.[13] All other reasons, however contrived, are legitimate and sound; they are reasonable and available in the search for certainty. To be sure, doubt about mathematics and even doubt that there is a coherence to be found among sensory perceptions turn out to be unreasonable in just this sense, that is to say, that doubt is possible only through willful representation as good. But the unreasonableness of this doubt is only *after* the existence of a veridical God has been established; previously, the doubt is perfectly reasonable for the reasons given in the First Meditation. In this distinction between what is reasonable before and after the proof of a veridical God, doubt about mathematics and doubt about the availability of sensory coherence differ from doubt about the *cogito*, which is unreasonable from the outset.

At this point, a pair of interesting, related questions intrudes upon us. First, if all knowledge depends as it does for Descartes on knowledge of the existence of a veridical God, why doesn't he begin the *Meditations* with the hyperbolic doubt, since it would comprehend the doubts based on relativity and dreaming? Why aren't the latter doubts just distractions? That is, why not immediately cut to the chase? Second, why doesn't the *cogito*, suitably directed, refute at least the hyperbolic doubt?

One obstacle to including sensory knowledge in an omnibus hyperbolic doubt is that the reason for doubt must be equilibrated to what is

---

[13] This formulation captures what is needed here, though it might be tightened for other purposes. It might be required further that the doubter have been previously mistaken about what is now in doubt. Appeal to previous mistakes is made in the opening sentence of the *Meditations*: "Some years ago, I was struck by the large number of falsehoods that I had accepted as true in childhood" (7: 17, 2: 12).

being doubted. If the reason for doubt is stronger than what it calls into question, then it might be taken simply as a reason for accepting the *denial* of what is intended only to be doubted. On the other hand, a second reason for withholding the hyperbolic doubt from sensory perception is that while the hyperbolic doubt must be overcome if there is to be any certainty at all, there is a sense in which doubt about the senses is never overcome. To be sure, the conclusion of the Sixth Meditation announces that "the exaggerated doubts of the last few days should be dismissed as laughable. This applies especially to the principal reason for doubt, namely my inability to distinguish between being asleep and being awake" (7: 89, 2: 61). But this confidence over the "vast difference between the two" that he has come to see does not apply to every individual perception taken in isolation, but only to the larger coherence of such perceptions. More importantly, this coherence itself, while an objective fact guaranteed by divine veracity, does not always provide a guarantee about the objective world beyond sensation. In fact it never does, and is always deceptive if taken to do so. The senses are designed for survival value, not for truth. "Sensory perception does not show us what really exists in things, but merely shows us what is beneficial or harmful to man's composite nature" (8A: 39, 1: 224).[14]

The answer to the second question, as to why the *cogito* is not applied directly in response to the hyperbolical doubt, is that such application would be question-begging. Despite its unique status as discussed above, certainty about the *cogito*, like certainty about all else, depends on certainty about the existence of a veridical God. The upshot of Descartes' *cogito* is that the evil demon cannot deceive him, which is sufficient for the derivation of his truth rule, but not that the *cogito* is somehow more certain than anything else. The truth rule, especially with its injunction to accept only what cannot be denied, is analogous to the Stoics' criterion the satisfaction of which "grabs us by the hair" and makes us believe. But the truth rule generalized from the *cogito* is a criterion only in the sense of being a model for the apprehension of all other truth. (Accept

---

[14] This is the title of *Principles* II.224 (CSM I, 224). The text says that sensory perceptions are related exclusively to the mind–body connection, and inform us of the harm or benefit that other bodies might do to it, without showing us, "except occasionally and incidentally," what external bodies are like in themselves. The exception might relate to the epistemological shot in the dark envisaged by the Fourth Meditation, when the will by chance lights upon the truth when unconstrained by the illumination of the intellect. If so, then because, according to Descartes, such lucky encounters with truth are a misuse of the will, even a chance revelation of objective truth by sensory coherence is deceptive. For more on teleology in Descartes' account of the senses, see Simmons (2001).

only what cannot fail to be accepted in the way the *cogito* cannot fail to be accepted.) In particular, it is not an identifying label that attaches to it, as "clarity and distinctness" are usually taken to be, so that it is not liable to the skeptics' challenge to identify the label without begging the question, arguing in a circle, or resorting to an infinite regress.[15] The *cogito* construed as a truth rule or model is not liable to such challenges because there is no conceivable ground on which it can reasonably be challenged. But the inconceivability of its being false does not exempt our certainty of it from depending on the certainty of the existence of God.[16]

---

[15] For the fuller account of the truth rule in these terms, see Lennon (2008, section 15).

[16] Quite apart from the usual syllogistic rendering of the *cogito*, Descartes has interesting ways of illustrating the inconceivability of its being false. In the Third Meditation, after insisting that "if I do not know [that God exists and is not a deceiver] it seems that I can never be quite certain of anything else" (7: 36, 2: 25), but before proving that the veridical God exists, he says that "whatever is revealed to me by the natural light—for example from the fact that I am doubting I exist, and so on—cannot in any way be open to doubt. This is because there cannot be another faculty both as trustworthy as the natural light and also capable of showing me that such things are not true" (7: 38, 2: 27). Also, in the Second Replies, he says, in what might be a reiteration, or continuation, of the same argument, that "we have a real faculty for recognizing the truth and distinguishing it from falsehood, as is clear merely from the fact that we have within us ideas of truth and falsehood. Hence this faculty must tend toward truth, at least when we use it correctly" (7: 144, 2: 103; see also the opening of the *Discourse on the Method*).

CHAPTER 2

Descartes and content skepticism

Deborah Brown

I INTRODUCTION

Obtaining clarity on what, if anything, is new in Descartes' use of skeptical arguments is an important exercise both for revealing the nature and scope of his skepticism and for revealing something about his historical relationship to the ancient skeptical traditions. A prevailing view is that while there are no new skeptical arguments in Descartes' corpus, his purely "methodological" interest in skepticism is new, a fact which enables him to avoid the problem of *apraxia* (the problem of how to live as a skeptic) which befuddled the ancient skeptics.[1] A "methodological" approach to skepticism seems to imply that it is narrower in scope, applying only to knowledge (certainty) claims rather than to beliefs, especially those we use in everyday affairs. Others deny that there is any significant difference between the scope of ancient and modern skepticism. Some, for example, argue that both forms of skepticism extend to belief as much as to knowledge, to the practical realm as much as to the theoretical, and that both solve the *apraxia* problem in much the same way, namely, by accepting appearances as a criterion for action but not for truth.[2] If "methodological" is supposed, by contrast, to pick out a difference in the *nature* of skeptical reasoning between the ancients

---

I am deeply indebted to the editor of this volume, Karen Detlefsen, for her truly insightful comments, and to Calvin Normore for many fruitful discussions about Descartes' philosophy.

[1] Descartes writes: "I know that no danger or error will result from my plan (to doubt everything I have previously taken to be highly probable), and that I cannot possibly go too far in my distrustful attitude. This is because the task now in hand does not involve action but merely the acquisition of knowledge" (7: 22, 2: 14). For interpretations allowing that Descartes' skepticism is more radical because it is methodological, see, for example, Curley (1978), Williams (1978 and 1983), Burnyeat (1982, pp. 30–31 and 1983), Grene (1999, p. 555), and Broughton (2002). Broughton (2002, ch. 3) develops an interesting argument that Cartesian skepticism targets certainty but not reasonable belief. I also do not do justice here to the subtle differences between Pyrrhonian and Academic skepticism. For a more thorough treatment, see again Broughton (2002, ch. 2).

[2] See Gouhier (1962, p. 35), Groarke (1984), and Fine (2000).

and Descartes, the claim seems simply confused. The arguments and methods of reasoning seem much alike.³ My own view is that there is something new in Descartes' skepticism but it isn't (or isn't just) that its approach is methodological. It is rather that unlike ancient skepticism, Descartes' skepticism extends to the very content of ideas themselves. What it means to "accept appearances for the sake of action" is, therefore, a very different kind of epistemic attitude for a Cartesian than it is for an ancient skeptic.

If the view to be advanced here is correct, what I am referring to as Descartes' "content skepticism" is thus more radical in its scope than any of the preceding forms of skepticism, a fact which determines the kind of cure which is possible for the "disease" which skepticism is (7: 172, 2: 121; 7: 547, 2: 373–74). More precisely, it is crucial to recognize that once skepticism is defeated, we cannot simply go back to believing that the world is the way it appears. Appearances will not, in other words, be restored as a criterion for truth.

II DESCARTES AND ANCIENT SKEPTICISM

Descartes himself does much to contribute to the impression that there is nothing new in his skeptical arguments, telling Hobbes that while it is distasteful to him to "reheat this old cabbage," nothing is more conducive to acquiring firm beliefs, particularly regarding the distinction between intellectual and corporeal things, than engaging in skeptical reasoning (7: 171–22, 2: 121; 7: 130, 2: 94). He is also concerned about the growing popularity of skepticism. Skepticism, he tells Bourdin, is "vigorously alive today" (7: 548, 2: 374).⁴ How close, then, is Descartes' skepticism to that of the ancients?

---

³ See below (section II). It is not even obvious what the contrast to "methodological" skepticism could be. Karen Detlefsen has suggested (in conversation) that it might contrast with a more naturally evolving form of skepticism and so translate better as "artificial" skepticism. This suggests a difference in origins although not necessarily a difference in the form of skeptical reasoning. Another possibility is that "methodological" skepticism contrasts with a weaker epistemic attitude, perhaps agnosticism, suggesting that there has been a deliberate effort of will to withhold assent. This involves a difference in the kind of attitude involved, in which case "methodological" characterizes the nature and not simply the scope of skepticism. Ask me whether the number of galaxies is odd or even, and I will say that I do not know, but I do not thereby take myself to be practicing skepticism. I thank Karen Detlefsen for a stimulating exchange on this point.
⁴ Possible sources for Descartes' knowledge of modern skepticism include Pierre Charron's *De la sagesse*, bk. II, chs. 1–2 and Michel de Montaigne's *Apologie*. For the relevant texts from Charron, see Ariew, Cottingham, and Sorrell (1998, ch. 5). For discussion of these connections see Gilson (1925), Rodis-Lewis (1998), and Fine (2000, p. 201).

Descartes' three main skeptical arguments – (1) the argument from illusion, (2) the dreaming argument, and (3) the Demon hypothesis – each has ancient precedents. Arguments from conflicting impressions generated by different senses or circumstances or depending on different states of the perceiver were common among the Pyrrhonists and Academic skeptics. These "tropes" or modes of skeptical reasoning were designed to provoke *epoche* or the suspension of judgment (Inwood and Gerson 1997, pp. 289–92). Examples of illusions or mistaken impressions included those caused by madness, dreaming, sickness, the same object producing contrary impressions on different occasions, or distinct objects (e.g. real and wax pomegranates) producing the same impressions. Cicero reports that the Academics held that no impression is such that one just like it could not have arisen from something with which the impression does not accord (Cicero, *Academica*, II.88).

Even the third skeptical scenario in which all our ideas are produced in us by a deceiving god or demon has two ancient precedents. The first is Plutarch's *De Stoicorum Repugnantiis*, 1057: "Again Chrysippus says, however, that both god and the sage induce false *phantasia*." The second is Cicero's *Academica* II (Lucullus) xv (47), which outlines the following response from the Academics to those Stoics who accepted revelations from the deity:

For, they say, when your school asserts that some presentations are sent by the deity – dreams, for example, and the revelations furnished by oracles, auspices and sacrifices (for they assert that the Stoics against whom they are arguing accept these manifestations) – how, possibly, they ask, can the deity have the power to render false presentations probable and not have the power to render probable those which approximate absolutely [*plane*] most closely to the truth; or else, if he is able to render these also probable, why can he not render probable those which are distinguishable, although only with extreme difficulty, from false presentations, and if these, why not those which do not differ from them at all? (Cicero 1967, p. 527)[5]

Both of these passages concern a rather obscure Stoic doctrine about the workings of providence. The central idea seems to be that providence may sometimes provide impressions (*phantasia*) in order to get someone who is not a sage to act in a certain way. These *phantasia* are such that if the non-sage assented to them in the 'natural' way, he would be deceived. Thus they are deceptive. Plutarch does not hint that these phantasia are

---

[5] For a reply in the *Academica* that this argument is based on a fallacious sorites, see Cicero (1967, p. 531). For discussion, see also Groarke (1984, pp. 286–87).

of a sort which we could not distinguish from *kataleptic* (incontrovertible) *phantasia*. Cicero does consider this possibility but simply rejects it.

That there were precedents for Descartes' skeptical arguments is not, therefore, in dispute. What is in dispute is whether the skeptical tropes carried the same implications for the ancients as they did for Descartes. As far as Descartes is concerned, they do not, but this is because he accepts the stereotype of the Pyrrhonist who is so given not to trust his senses that he cannot live without assistance:

> [W]hen it is a matter of organising life, it would, of course, be foolish not to trust the senses, and the sceptics who neglected human affairs to the point where friends had to stop them falling off precipices deserved to be laughed at. (7: 351, 2: 243)

How then does Descartes think his skeptic is able to avoid such absurdities? In the following passage from the *Replies to the Seventh Set of Objections*, Descartes draws upon a distinction between two kinds of doubts: doubts in practice and (presumably) doubts in theory:

> No skeptic nowadays has any doubt in practice about whether he has a head, or whether two and three make five, and so on. What the skeptics say is that they merely *treat such claims as if they are true*, because they appear to be so; but they do not believe they are certain, because no rational arguments require them to do so. (7: 549, 2: 375)

It is not clear from this what a doubt in practice is but it is clear what it is *not* to have a doubt in practice. Not doubting in practice is *to act as if something is true*, even though one does not have sufficient reason to believe with certainty that it is true. Not doubting in practice p does not, therefore, entail that one believes that p, but it licenses one to act as if p is true. This passage is important because it suggests that it is not the case that practical beliefs are immune to Cartesian skepticism; rather they are seen as not *necessary* for action. I may not know whether the fire exists or whether it is really hot or whether it would be good or bad for me to put my hand in it, but this does not give me a reason to be *indifferent* to where I place my hand. This is what a "methodological" approach to skepticism amounts to and it is arguably not that different from ancient skepticism.

Disputed legends about Pyrrho almost walking off a cliff aside, there is little in the passages considered so far to distinguish Descartes from the ancients. As Gail Fine (2000) argues, there are striking similarities in the kinds of arguments deployed. Skepticism in both cases extends as much to belief as to knowledge, and both ancient and Cartesian skeptics solve the *apraxia* problem by accepting appearances for the sake of action. Although ancient skeptics profess to live "without opinion" (e.g. PH 1.13; 1.24), they too seem to deny that they have doubts in practice:

When we say that skeptics do not hold beliefs, we do not use "belief" in the sense in which some say, quite generally, that belief is acquiescing in something; for skeptics assent to the affections [*pathē*] forced upon them by appearances [*phantasia*]. For example, they would not say, when heated or chilled, "I do not think I am heated (or: chilled)." Rather, we say that they do not hold beliefs in the sense in which some say that belief is assent to some unclear object of investigation in the sciences; for Pyrrhonists do not assent to anything unclear. (Sextus Empiricus 2000, PH 1.13)

This may suggest that, in order to live, the skeptic has to avow beliefs in one context (practical) but not in another (theoretical). Fine argues, however, that we should not read Sextus as here asserting that the skeptics avow beliefs in practical contexts. The skeptic lives "without belief" (*adoxastos*) (PH 1.23–24). Borrowing a distinction from Robert Stalnaker's *Inquiry*, Fine defends the view that the ancient skeptics *accepted* appearances for the sake of action but did not *believe* them to be true.[6] Acceptance and belief are distinct propositional attitudes and acceptance does not entail belief. Accepting that p for the sake of argument or action, reflectively or tacitly, does not entail that one believes that p. Fine takes passages like the following from Sextus to demonstrate the difference between acceptance and belief:

When we investigate whether existing things are such as they appear, we grant that they appear ... For example, it appears to us that honey sweetens (we concede this inasmuch as we are sweetened in a perceptual way). (PH 1.19–20)[7]

---

[6] Stalnaker's (1984, pp. 79–81) definition of acceptance is remarkably Cartesian: "to accept a proposition is to treat it as a true proposition in one way or another – to ignore, for the moment at least, the possibility that it is false" (p. 79). An acceptance is correct, but not necessarily justified, whenever the proposition is true.

[7] See also Diogenes Laertius, *Lives of the Eminent Philosophers* (DL, 9: 104–5): "We only object," [the skeptics] say, "to the non-evident things added onto the phenomena." (As Timon says): "That honey is sweet I do not posit; that it appears so I concede" (Inwood and Gerson 1997, p. 293).

    Plutarch (*On Moral Virtue*, 1122c–d) reports Arcesilaus' distinction between three movements in the soul:

(a) sensation
(b) impulse
(c) assent.

According to Arcesilaus, the skeptic can argue that (a) and (b) are sufficient guides to action; and that (c) is not necessary.

Conceding that honey appears sweet falls short, she claims, of believing that the honey is sweet or indeed of having any beliefs about honey or its properties.

Similarly, Fine reads Descartes' "trusting the senses" in practical affairs to be a matter of accepting without necessarily believing non-doxastic appearances (Fine 2000, p. 215). She further notes the close similarity between the ancient skeptics' reliance on certain practical maxims and the "*morale par provision*" which Descartes develops in the *Discourse on Method*. So that one remains decisive in action while reason requires one to suspend judgment, one must adopt a provisional code of conduct: to obey the laws and customs of the land, to make firm and decisive judgments, to strive to master ourselves and our desires rather than the order of nature, and to review the occupations of others to choose the best life possible (6: 23–27, 1: 122–24). Sextus' "fourfold" way of the skeptical life – to be guided by nature, the necessitation of the affections, customs and laws, and the teachings of kinds of expertise – bears a remarkable resemblance to the *morale par provision* (PH 1.23–24; Fine 2000, pp. 222–23).

Fine is right to draw our attention to these similarities. The ancients' reliance on (what she calls) acceptance rather than belief in practical contexts is much like the Cartesian skeptic's reliance on doubts in practice. But it is a mistake to conclude that both employ exactly the same kind of skepticism. Even the *acceptance* of appearances would, I submit, be too much for a Cartesian skeptic to admit.

III DESCARTES' DEPARTURE FROM THE ANCIENTS

Let us begin by thinking a little more about the nature of acceptance as a propositional attitude. It is "criterial," on Stalnaker's account, that acceptance is correct whenever a proposition is true (1984, pp. 79–80). This presupposes, at the very least, that to accept that p is to accept that p *could* be true, that the acceptance could be correct. Should a Cartesian skeptic grant even this much?[8] Not obviously so. Consider a case of stage

---

[8] Fine may well be correct that the distinction holds for the ancients. It is true that one does not see in ancient skeptical texts doubts about whether the honey *could* be sweet, only whether it is. There is, however, still something odd in Fine's use of the distinction because it suggests that skeptics, ancient or modern, use skepticism to ascertain what they might dogmatically accept. If the enemy is dogmatism, one would expect the skeptic to be opposed to it whether it infiltrates belief or acceptance. Acceptances, according to Stalnaker (1984, pp. 79–81), include propositions unreflectively or tacitly adopted as true, with varying degrees of commitment, which, one would think, should be subjected to skeptical scrutiny as much as one's beliefs.

acting. Do I need, for example, to *accept* that I am Lady Macbeth in order to play the part? Method acting aside, this seems unnecessary, but even if I did manage to get myself into this psychological state, would it count as genuine acceptance on the Stalnaker–Fine account? If there is no possible world in which I could *be* Lady Macbeth, there is no possible world in which this acceptance could be correct. Shouldn't I then be able to act *as if* I were Lady Macbeth without either believing or accepting that I am? It will not do to dismiss this case as one removed from everyday life because, for the skeptic, we are always to some extent acting as if things are a certain way.

I do not deny that Descartes' skeptic ever relies on something like acceptance or even belief in practical contexts, but where she does, the object is always how the mind experiences itself as affected, not corporeal things. Although it could be false that I am seeing a light, hearing a noise, or being warmed by a fire:

Yet I certainly *seem* to see, to hear, and to be warmed. This cannot be false; what is called "having a sensory perception" is strictly just this, and in this restricted sense of the term it is simply thinking. (7: 29, 2: 19)

I can accept that I am experiencing a *seeming-to-be-warmed* without accepting that anything *could* be warm. Understood this way, what Descartes' skeptic accepts does little to support Fine's claim that both ancient and modern skeptics accept appearances in the same way. It is always possible, of course, that acceptance is too strong to capture ancient skepticism as well – the (above) passage at PH 1.13 suggests that the ancient skeptic only accepts their affections. But it is unclear how representative this passage is. Augustine turned the observation that one cannot doubt one's experiences into a weapon against the Academics, suggesting that if the point of accepting affections had been made, its consequences had not been widely grasped.[9] In any event, contrary to ancient skeptical systems, there are distinctive features of Descartes' philosophy that make the acceptance of appearances rationally impossible, and this is something new.

---

[9] Augustine's objection is that restricting oneself to appearances rules out the possibility of deception at least in relation to one's own soul. It is not possible to dissent from 'I know that this looks white to me' just because one doubts that this is white (Augustine, *c. Acad.*, III.11.26). Notable studies of the relationship between Descartes and Augustine are Hatfield (1986), Matthews (1992), and Menn (1998). On the similarity between Descartes and Augustine on the role of self-knowledge and knowledge of God in overcoming skepticism, see Menn (1998, p. 222).

IV CONTENT SKEPTICISM

In his attacks on Academic skepticism, Augustine challenges the skeptic by observing that in doubting the truth of some proposition, the skeptic must at least know what it would be for the proposition to be true, and this constitutes knowledge (e.g. *sol.* II.vi.9; p. 98) It is almost as if Descartes has this challenge in mind while crafting his skeptical arguments, the result of which is a form of skepticism far more radical than that envisaged by the ancients. At its most radical, Cartesian skepticism undermines the first-person authority Augustine takes as incontrovertible – the very assurance each of us has that we at least know what we mean.

Content skepticism arises in two places in the *Meditations*: (1) in the transition between the dreaming and demon arguments, and (2) in the discussion of material falsity. Let us begin with (1).

Descartes begins in the First Meditation by observing that he has *occasionally* been deceived in the past by his senses, from which he reasons that "it is prudent never to trust completely those who have denied us even once" (7: 18, 2: 12). He is dubious, however, about grounding such mistrust on the observation of occasional deception, noting that one would have to be a madman to question *all* the beliefs one has through the senses. This confidence is shattered, however, when he considers the possibility that all his orderly experiences could be part of a perpetual dream: "I see plainly that there are never any sure signs by means of which being awake can be distinguished from being asleep" (7: 19, 2: 13). What began as an observation about isolated instances of deception evolves into global doubt.

The dream argument has an obvious reply. When I dream, he asks, am I not like a painter who, although creating imaginary forms, must fashion them from general kinds or forms of things – eyes, heads, hands, whole bodies, or, at the very least, colors – which are real and exist (7: 19–20, 2: 13–14)? What the painting analogy purportedly establishes is that the scope of doubt can reasonably extend no farther than "composite things" and fails to undermine belief in the "simplest and most general things, regardless of whether they exist in nature or not." These simple things include the subject matter of arithmetic, geometry, and other subjects of this kind, "for whether I am awake or asleep, two and three added together are five, and a square has no more than four sides" (7: 20, 2: 14).[10]

---

[10] Compare the following passage from Augustine (*c. Acad.*, III.11.25):

> For if I am asleep, I may have uttered nothing at all, or if these words did fall from my lips in sleep as sometimes happens, it may be that I did not say them here or to this audience, or while

By this reasoning, mathematical propositions are immune to doubt for "two and three added together make five" is true in every possible world, including those in which I am simply dreaming that an external world composed of bodies and their properties exists.

It is at this point in the narrative that Descartes introduces his most radical form of skeptical argument, the demon hypothesis. He considers two scenarios: (a) that he is the product of chance events or (b) that he is the product of an omnipotent being. If he is the product of a most imperfect cause (a), he is more likely deceived than not. If instead he is the product of an omnipotent being (b), then how can he be certain that the deity has not deceived him about everything he holds most certain, including "the most perfect knowledge," mathematical knowledge of simple propositions (7: 21, 2: 14–15)?

What occurs in the third skeptical argument is not merely a shift from a kind of *property skepticism* (doubts that ordinary objects have the properties they appear to have) to *external world skepticism* (doubts about the existence of a mind-independent world), but the introduction of a kind of doubt that extends to the very contents of our thoughts. External world and property skepticism could co-occur with Augustinian "content dogmatism" – the view that one can always grasp the truth conditions of a proposition even if one doesn't know whether the proposition is, in fact, true. A content skeptic who, because of the uncertainty about the origins of her simple ideas, doubts that *two added to three makes five*, is not someone who can be said to know what *would* make the sentence true. It is natural to suppose that if doubt about our most basic mathematical propositions is possible, it is because we don't know whether or what the terms "two," "three," "five," "add," etc., signify.

The inclusion of mathematical propositions in those subjected to doubt is puzzling for many reasons. First, there is the question of why the truth of these isn't as compelling as the *cogito*.[11] Why should "I think, therefore,

---

sitting so. But the statement itself cannot be false … if the whole human race were snoring away, however, it would still be necessarily true that three times three are nine and this is the square of a number one can comprehend. (Wippel and Wolter 1969, p. 35)

[11] Grene (1999, p. 555) has pointed our attention to the beginning of the Third Meditation where the *cogito* and basic arithmetical propositions are bracketed together as suspect while the demon remains a possibility. She has no explanation for this or for why Descartes thinks it is possible to "leave dangling" logical and mathematical truths other than by appeal to some vague "metaphysical" device that "some God" (not necessarily the demon, she thinks) could be undermining them (p. 569). Broughton (2002, ch. 7), by contrast, isolates what is unique about the *cogito*, namely, that my existence is a *condition* for the very truth of the proposition, *I think, therefore, I exist*.

I am" be any more compelling (as it is in the *Meditations*) than "two added to three makes five"? The signification of "I" was, after all, in dispute. Some thought it synonymous with "human being," others, "rational animal," still others, "the corporeal soul" or "something tenuous, a wind or fire or ether" (7: 25–26, 2: 16–17). None of these meanings are themselves perspicuous, he objects, and only taking the "I" to signify *self-reflexively* the thinking, willing, doubting, affirming, denying, imagining, and sensing thing that each of us is aware of in every thought suffices to resist doubt (7: 25–29, 2: 16–19). Second, there is the question of how our most basic mathematical propositions can fail to have immunity from doubt. It seems as psychologically impossible for me to doubt that two added to three equals five, as it is for me to doubt that I think or exist.

Answering these questions adequately is beyond the scope of this chapter, but I would like to make one or two observations. First, if the *cogito* is known by intuition rather than demonstration, which is admittedly contentious, this may go some way towards accounting for its immunity to doubt. As Descartes points out to Mersenne, the *cogito* belongs not in the class of conclusions the dialecticians call *scientia*, which involves deduction, but is rather a primary notion recognized by the mind in a simple intuition (7: 140, 2: 100).[12] According to the *Rules for the Direction of the Mind*, intuition is "the indubitable conception of a clear and attentive mind which proceeds solely from the light of reason" and includes the *cogito*:

Thus everyone can mentally intuit that he exists, that he is thinking, that a triangle is bounded by just three lines, and a sphere by a single surface and the like. (10: 368, 1: 14)

This does little, however, to justify the privileged place the *cogito* has in Descartes' response to skepticism, for as intuition is there described, simple mathematical ideas are also grasped by intuition.

Another way to account for the discrepancy in the *Meditations* is to see that whereas the *content* of mathematical propositions might be in doubt, even where it appears evident to us, the *cogito* is unique in that what is given in self-awareness is not content per se but *the very thing itself*, the mind, the appearance of which as the content of the thought cannot be accounted for in any other way except by existing. As Descartes asserts to Gassendi, "from the fact that something exists in an idea, I do not infer

---

[12] For the contrary position that the *cogito* must rely on a demonstration because it contains a suppressed premise, see the discussion in Hatfield (2003, pp. 106ff.). I thank Karen Detlefsen for pointing my attention to this.

that it exists in reality, except when we can produce no other cause for the idea but the actual existence of the thing which it represents" (7: 369, 2: 254). The "I" is not an idea like any other. It is an idea that cannot be composed from other ideas, nor, therefore, an idea that could have content and yet refer to nothing. The composite definitions Descartes considers – 'human being', 'rational animal', 'corporeal soul', etc. – may fail to refer. They are, moreover, *general* ideas, which cannot account for the idea *I* have of *myself*. I cannot account for the very appearance of myself in any other way than by my actually being there. Nor can I fail to be present in any of my thoughts – "If I judge that the wax exists from the fact that I touch it, the same result follows, namely that I exist" (7: 33, 2: 22). The demon could only deceive me by not providing me with any awareness at all, but it is too late for that.

The case of mathematical ideas is different. The idea of a triangle may appear to be among the most clear and evident ideas I have, but how can I be sure that the idea is not composite, built up from other terms, constructed within me by the demon to fool me into thinking that I am thinking about something with a true and immutable nature when in fact there is no such thing? Where we have an idea whose content we cannot rule out as being composite, we have no basis for assuming that there is a true and immutable nature that accounts for its content.

We can draw support for this reading by considering those passages in which Descartes distinguishes ideas that are like "mere verbal definitions" from those that denote true and immutable natures. The former include the idea of a chimera, composed from ideas of the parts of animals, and which does not correspond to any true and immutable nature (7: 117–18, 2: 83–84). To this we could add ideas of pseudo-mathematical objects, like the round square, which we can "define" but not (*pace* Meinong) accord any being, actual or potential. What the possibility of the demon generates is doubt about whether *all* our intuitively most evident mathematical ideas are just simple cognitive reflections of verbal definitions.

This is what the atheist geometer cannot rule out (7: 141, 2: 101). Descartes identifies the atheist geometer's skeptical problem with his refusal to grasp the positive being of the infinite. If he could see that *this* idea is really simple, not accountable for by the compositional powers of his own mind, he could secure a ground for mathematical knowledge. The very power to build up ideas of things greater than that we can conceive (such as the idea of numbers greater than we can conceive) presupposes a power greater than ourselves (7: 139, 2: 99–100). Nor is the idea of God in any way like a universal, having being only

in thought, for whereas generic unity adds nothing to the being of sin-
gulars, the idea of God "denotes a certain positive perfection" (7: 140,
2: 100). Were the atheist geometer to see the positive being in the idea
of the infinite, he would be forced to accept God's existence, the only
path back to certainty. The atheist is, however, committed to the idea of
God having been composed from other ideas, and the idea of the greatest number being composed from ideas of finite numbers and negation,
which allows each to equate to vacuous definitions. "His knowledge of
the nature of the infinite – since he regards it as a nonentity and hence
as not having a real nature – must be restricted to what is contained
in the mere verbal definition of the term which he has learned from
others" (7: 141–42, 2: 101).

Part of what is required, then, in sorting the ideas that are immune to
doubt from those which are not is sorting out which cannot be accounted
for by the compositional powers of the human mind. This test works well
for ideas of reason, but applied to sensory ideas this test would yield the
wrong results. For most, if not all, of our sensory ideas strike us as simple
and indefinable. The ideas of particular pains, sounds, colors, etc. resist
analysis into simpler ideas. Yet, Descartes is far from inclined to regard
these as corresponding to true and immutable natures. Indeed, Descartes
is not even prepared to include them in the same category with the idea
of a chimera, which at least represents some being, namely, the parts of
animals represented therein. It is dubious whether sensory ideas represent
anything in nature at all.

V SENSORY IDEAS AND MATERIAL FALSITY

To remove even the slightest reason for doubt, Descartes asserts at the beginning of the Third Meditation that it is necessary first to sort his thoughts
to see which can be said to be bearers of truth and falsity (7: 36–37, 2: 25).
He observes that it is those which are "as it were the images of things" or
"ideas" which are the bearers of truth – not insofar as they are considered
in terms of their "formal reality", that is, as modes of mind, but insofar
as they represent different things on account of their different "objective
reality" (7: 37 and 40, 2: 25 and 27–28). Objective reality comes in degrees
according to the degree of formal reality represented in the content of the
idea. Thus an idea of substance will have more objective reality than an
idea of a mode and the idea of infinite substance the most objective reality
of all. The infinite objective reality in the idea of God can only be (causally) explained by the existence of an infinitely perfect being (7: 44–45, 2:

30–31). With the demon ousted by a non-deceiving God, Descartes can begin rebuilding his house on firm foundations.

The causal argument for God's existence hangs on two related assumptions: (1) that the objective reality of an idea is some being, and (2) that the objective reality of an idea stands in need of a cause. Caterus objected to both, insisting that "objective reality" refers to nothing more than an extrinsic denomination of external objects and, therefore, does not require a cause (7: 93–94, 2: 67). In reply, Descartes is adamant that this is not what "objective reality" means. Although the idea of the sun does not affect the sun *in re*, "to be objectively ... [is] ... to be in the intellect in the way in which objects are accustomed to be in it" and so "the idea of the sun is the sun itself existing in the intellect" (7: 102, 2: 74–75; cf. 7: 41, 2: 28; 7: 161, 2: 113–14). Being is being and always needs a cause.

We saw that the fault in the atheist geometer's reasoning lay in his inability to see the objective being present in the idea of the infinite and that it could not have originated from his own mind. The problem with sensory ideas is subtly different. Here the problem lies with our inability to determine what, if any, objective reality these ideas have and with our tendency to think that they represent real properties of bodies. Preliminary to the causal argument for God's existence in the Third Meditation, Descartes introduces a distinction between two kinds of falsity: *formal*, when a judgment is false, and *material*, when an idea is false. An idea is materially false when it "represents a non-thing as a thing" (7: 43, 2: 29–30). The two are connected in that materially false ideas "deserve to be called false" because they provide material for error in judgment (7: 133–34, 2: 95–96). Of all confused and obscure ideas of sense, including "light and colors, sounds, smells, tastes, heat and cold and other tactile qualities," Descartes denies that he can "know whether they are true or false, that is, whether the ideas I have of them are ideas of real things or of non-things" (7: 43, 2: 29–30).

The paradigm example is the idea of cold:

And since there can be no ideas which are not as if of things [*nisi tanquam rerum*], if it is true that cold is nothing other than a privation of heat, the idea which represents it to me as something real and positive deserves to be called false; and so on for others of this kind. (7: 44, 2: 30)

The idea of cold purports to represent a positive quality of bodies. If there is no such quality, then the idea is materially false.

Given the distinction between two kinds of falsity, we can err in relation to our sensory ideas in two ways: (1) at the level of predication in judgment, or (2) in the ideas themselves, "in the abstract" (5: 152, 3: 337). If I believe that the ice is cold and cold turns out to be a privation, I err not just in believing what cannot be established by the senses, namely, that the ice really is cold, but also in assuming that there really is such a thing as coldness, and hence, that things like ice *could* have that property. If coldness is a privation, it can no more account for the content of my idea than it can be a positive quality of bodies. In Descartes' technical language, since objective being is being, if cold lacks being, it can no more have objective being in the intellect than it can have formal being in the ice.

Now as Arnauld demonstrated in the Fourth Objections, Descartes' stance on material falsity is very difficult to reconcile with his suggestion that ideas are differentiated by the being things have in the intellect (7: 206, 2: 145). To put the problem succinctly, if there is an idea of x which is materially false, for it to be the idea of x, it seems that x must have some positive being (at least, objective being), but for the idea to be materially false, it seems required that x must have non-being, which is contradictory. Descartes also asserts that such ideas "arise from nothing" and are in me "only because of a deficiency and lack of perfection in my nature" (7: 44, 2: 30). Arnauld points to a second difficulty with this assertion: If there can be ideas which appear to denote something positive while arising from nothing, then couldn't the atheist argue that this is precisely what is true of the idea of God (7: 207, 2: 145–46)? Arnauld's advice to Descartes is to abandon the notion of material falsity and accept that all ideas are true and positive.

Descartes' reply to Arnauld maintains his commitment to the potential for material falsity in sensory ideas. Materially false ideas do have objective reality, he asserts, but it is not the objective reality we are accustomed to think is there. The only object present to mind in such cases is the sensory modification of the mind itself, the sensation:

> [I]f cold is only a privation, the idea of cold is not cold itself, as it were objectively in the intellect, but another thing which I take wrongly for that privation; truly, it is the sensation itself which has no being outside the intellect. (7: 233, 2: 163)

The answer to the second objection is that it is not the *idea* of cold which arises from nothing but its *falsity* (7: 234–35, 2: 163–65). The suggestion is that were I more perfect, I would not be misled by my sensory ideas, but my not being more perfect is not something, and so, not a cause either.

How successful Descartes was in his response to Arnauld is not at issue here.[13] The question is rather how this discussion of material falsity bears on the question regarding the nature and scope of Cartesian skepticism. My suggestion is that there remains at the end of the *Meditations* a residual skepticism about the *content* of sensory ideas insofar as they purport to represent real properties of corporeal things. Given this, the Cartesian skeptic must accept that if an idea is materially false, there are no possible conditions under which it could be true. And yet, like his ancient counterparts, Descartes too agrees that sensory ideas are indispensable guides to action. How is it possible for sensory ideas to perform this function for a skeptic who can neither believe nor accept them as true?

VI *APRAXIA* AND TRUST IN THE SENSES

The Sixth Meditation outlines the proper function of sensory ideas. Their role is to preserve the union of mind and body, and, provided we keep that in mind, we will not be led astray: "I know that in matters regarding the well-being of the body, all my senses report the truth much more frequently than not" (7: 89, 2: 61.). In performing its proper function, a materially false idea (e.g. the idea of cold) works as well as a materially true idea (e.g. the idea of heat). Both serve as indicators of the utility/disutility of corporeal things to the mind–body union. If the skeptic treats the appearance of cold in the ice as true, however, then either no proposition is accepted at all (since the proposition that the ice is cold could not possibly be true), or she has accepted the absurd claim that the ice is modified by a sensation, which also could not possibly be true. Clearly, she can act without accepting such an absurdity. The proper path for the Cartesian skeptic would be to withhold both acceptance and belief.[14]

What then does "trust in the senses" constitute for Descartes? We trust that we really are affected in distinct ways by external objects: "I certainly *seem* to see, to hear, and to be warmed. This cannot be false; what is called 'having a sensory perception' is strictly just this, and in this restricted sense of the term it is simply thinking" (7: 29, 2: 19; cf. 8A: 33, 1: 217). But

---

[13] See Brown (2008).

[14] Notice, moreover, that no amount of metaphysical musing can settle the question of what the objective reality of sensory ideas is. Only science can deliver such verdicts based on an investigation of which properties can and cannot be eliminated from a mechanical physics. In the meantime, skepticism is an appropriate reaction to judgments suggested by the senses. Content skepticism should, in other words, outlive the external world and property skepticism of the First Meditation.

we are inclined to combine in thought our sensations with ideas of things external to the soul. Pain, a sensation, cannot literally be in the foot, but the fact that the idea makes it seem as if it is, is useful. Because of the union, I compound (*con*-fuse) the idea of pain with the idea of the foot, which indicates to me that a disturbance in the nerves of the foot is causally responsible for the sensation. This is information I can act upon without adopting any attitude (acceptance or belief) as to what the content of "my foot is in pain" might be.

The model for living with this kind of uncertainty about the external correlates of sensory ideas is provided in Descartes' treatment of the passions. Although they are a species of perception or sensation or emotion, the passions are excluded from the category of materially false ideas because it is of their nature to be "referred" to the soul itself. "As for the will and the emotions, here too one need not worry about falsity; for even if the things which I may desire are wicked or even non-existent, that does not make it any less true that I desire them" (7: 37, 2: 26). If I feel fear, I am primarily aware of my soul as modified in a certain way – it is the soul that is afraid not the menacing stranger – and this cannot be false, even if my situation poses no actual threat to me. The objective reality of a passion is the particular way in which the soul is modified, and although there will be a host of complementary predicates (e.g. "is dangerous"; "is desirable"; "is detestable," etc.) that form in our minds to describe the external causes of our passions, we evaluate bodies according to the way they emotionally affect us and not because of any intrinsic value. This provides us with a model for acting rationally in accordance with our sensations without any epistemic attitude towards what, if any, intrinsic properties of bodies they represent.

The fact that passions wear their content on their sleeves much more so than other kinds of sensory ideas does not mean that they are any better guides to truth. In particular, passions induce us to overestimate the value of external objects. They "almost always cause the goods they represent, as well as the evils, to appear much greater and more important than they are, thus moving us to pursue the former and flee the latter with more ardor and zeal than is appropriate" (11: 431, 1: 377). Because they are produced by disturbances of the blood and spirits, they also have an inertial quality and tend to resist the efforts of reason and will to subdue them (11: 363–66; 1: 345–46). It is, however, only "the very weak and irresolute" that "choose only what passion dictates"; most will use their determinate judgments in regulating their actions (11: 367, 1: 347). The point of having a moral code, even if only "provisional," is thus to have alternative guides to action whenever a passion arises. Ultimately, it is only through their regulation that the passions can contribute productively to the good life.

Even in the case of materially true sensory ideas, therefore, "trust in the senses" is not by any means straightforward. We must use reason and, indirectly, will to gain dominion over the passions. We must also cultivate those passions that are useful aides to the good will, particularly *generosity*, by means of which we esteem things related to our own free wills above those over which we have no control. Other "internal emotions," such as rational love and joy, which originate in the soul through the experience of its own powers, also assist in the regulation of more unruly passions that depend upon a disequilibrium among the spirits (11: 445–48; 440–42, 1: 383–85). We should not, in other words, take passions at their face value in deciding how to act but subject them to as much rational scrutiny as is feasible under the circumstances.

VII CONCLUSION

To return, then, to our original comparison between Cartesian and ancient skepticism, we may conclude that the former represents a significant departure from the latter. For the ancient skeptics, reason is not an independent source of ideas and so cannot be appealed to in adjudicating between courses of action. As Diogenes Laertius reports, the Pyrrhonists held that:

One will not distinguish sensibles by sense perception, since they are all equally apparent to it; nor with one's intellect, for the same reason. But besides these, there is no power of deciding.[15]

Similarly, Sextus observes that when, for example, the honey appears sweet to one person and bitter to another "the intellect basing itself on the senses, is compelled to pronounce differing and conflicting things" (PH 11.63; Inwood and Gerson 1997, p. 344). Lacking an independent account of reason or intellect, the ancient skeptic has no choice but to accept the teachings of nature and "follow the phenomena" in action, however conflicted or contradictory such teachings might, on occasion, be. Descartes' reliance on "the teachings of nature" is a very different affair, one that utilizes all the power of an independent reason and the will to regulate the effects of the senses. The Cartesian sage also relies heavily upon the maturity that comes from long experience. This emphasis on experience

---

[15] DL 9: 92 (Inwood and Gerson 1997, p. 293).

is encoded in the first maxim of the provisional moral code. Of equal importance is possessing a rigorous science of nature, in particular, a theory of matter that enables us to be attuned to what is clearly contained in the content of our sensory ideas, and a theory of human nature that enables us to understand that the proper function of sensory ideas is biological rather than epistemic. In our daily endeavors, vigilance about how the world appears to us in experience is essential. Far from having no place in practical affairs, a residual skepticism is thus pivotal to our avoiding the errors of judgment and associated regrets that are the principal obstacles to our happiness.[16]

---

[16] On the relationship between regret and lack of contentment, see Descartes' letter to Elizabeth, 4 August 1645 (4: 266, 3: 258). See also 4: 284, 3: 263–64, as well as the *Discourse on Method* at 6: 25, 1: 123.

PART II

Substance and cause

CHAPTER 3

Descartes against the materialists: how Descartes' confrontation with materialism shaped his metaphysics

Daniel Garber

It is a historical prejudice that Cartesian dualism was a kind of default position for the seventeenth century, the position that every reader was likely to hold. In actuality, materialism was quite widespread. This is reflected in the *Meditations* and the Objections and Replies to the *Meditations*, where materialism is a frequent issue, a constant undercurrent to the discussion. In this chapter I would like to explore some aspects of Descartes' reactions to materialism. My thesis is that it was at least in part his response to materialism that forced Descartes to make an important move in his thought. I will claim that certain crucial aspects of his doctrine of substance may have come directly out of his confrontation with materialism in the Objections and Replies to the *Meditations*.

I will proceed as follows. I begin not with Descartes, but with the objections that Hobbes made to the doctrine of the real distinction between mind and body in the Third Objections. These objections, I shall argue, turn on a certain feature of the doctrine of substance that Descartes presented in the *Meditations* and in the Appendix to the Second Replies. I shall then show how Descartes' response to those objections resulted in an important shift in his doctrine of substance, one that had profound consequences for his conception of metaphysics.

HOBBES AGAINST DESCARTES: MIND, BODY, AND SUBSTANCE

Among the philosophers that Mersenne invited to comment on the *Meditations* was the Englishman Thomas Hobbes. Hobbes was not particularly young at the time – he was already 52 years old when Mersenne gave him Descartes' text for his comments. But even so, he hadn't yet done much of the work that he was later to be known for. Though he had written an unpublished tract on optics and published the *Elements of Law* in a small edition in London, the *De cive*, the *De corpore*, and the *Leviathan* were still in his future. But he was living in Paris, and was part of Mersenne's circle. His materialistic proclivities must have been well known in the community.[1]

Hobbes' objection to Descartes' proof of the existence of an immaterial soul seems rather puzzling. He ends with the following rather paradoxical reinterpretation of the *cogito*:

The knowledge of the proposition "I exist" thus depends on the knowledge of the proposition "I am thinking"; and knowledge of the latter proposition depends on our inability to separate thought from the matter that is thinking. So it seems that the correct inference is that the thinking thing is material rather than immaterial. (7: 173–74)[2]

How in the world does he reach this conclusion?

Hobbes begins with a critique of what he takes to be Descartes' reasoning in Meditation II:

[F]rom the fact that I am thinking it follows that I exist, since that which thinks is not nothing. But when the author adds "that is, I am a mind, or intelligence, or intellect or reason", a doubt arises. It does not seem to be a valid argument to say "I am thinking, therefore I am thought" or "I am using my intellect, hence I am an intellect." I might just as well say "I am walking, therefore I am a walk." (7: 172)

Hobbes here attributes to Descartes the inference from "I am thinking" to the conclusion that "I am thought." This, he remarks, is obviously nonsense. On his reading, Descartes is not distinguishing properly between a faculty ("*facultas*") or an "*actus*" and the underlying subject in which it exists:

Yet all philosophers make a distinction between a subject and its faculties and *actus*, i.e. between a subject and its properties and its essences. (7: 172–73)[3]

And, Hobbes observes, when we distinguish between the subject and the accidents or faculties that inhere in that subject, then it is at least possible that the accidents or faculties that relate to thought might inhere in a *body* as their subject:

[1] On the exchange between Hobbes and Descartes in the Objections and Replies, see Sorell (1995) and Curley (1995).

[2] References to Descartes are given in the standard form to the canonical edition of Adam and Tannery. Translations are taken from CSM, though I have felt free to alter them from time to time.

[3] I am leaving the scholastic term of art "*actus*" in the Latin. The "*actus*" here is meant to contrast with potentialities; the "*actus*" are the accidents a thing actually has, while the potentialities are those accidents that it may acquire.

Hence it may be that the thing that thinks is the subject to which mind, reason or intellect belong; and this subject may thus be something corporeal. The contrary is assumed, not proved. Yet this inference is the basis of the conclusion which M. Descartes seems to want to establish. (7: 173)

Once we recognize that there is a distinction between the accidents and faculties on the one hand, and their underlying subject, then we must ask the question: what is the nature of the subject? When we do, Hobbes claims, the door is open to materialism, the idea that it is *body* that is the ultimate subject for thought.

But it is more than a possibility for Hobbes. Hobbes goes on to argue that the underlying subject *is* body. He writes:

It seems to follow from this that a thinking thing is something corporeal. For it seems that the subject of any *actus* can be understood only in terms of something corporeal or in terms of matter. (7: 173)

Where does this come from? Hobbes attributes this conclusion to Descartes himself ("as the author himself shows later on in his example of the wax"). While this is a clever bit of rhetoric, it isn't at all clear what Hobbes has in mind here. Descartes very quickly rejects the attribution of this conclusion to his discussion of the wax at the end of Meditation II. But a path to that conclusion can easily be found in other writings of Hobbes. In chapter 3 of the *Leviathan* he writes:

[B]ecause whatsoever (as I said before) we conceive has been perceived first by sense, either all at once or by parts, a man can have no thought representing anything not subject to sense. No man therefore can conceive anything, but he must conceive it in some place, and endued with some determinate magnitude, and which may be divided into parts; nor that anything is all in this place, and all in another place at the same time; nor that two or more things can be in one and the same place at once; for none of these things ever have, or can be, incident to sense, but are absurd speeches, taken upon credit (without any signification at all) from deceived philosophers, and deceived or deceiving schoolmen.[4]

While the text itself derives from a decade after he wrote the objections to the *Meditations*, there is every reason to believe that it expresses the view that he had then as well. The argument here is that since all of our thoughts derive from the senses, we have no conception of anything that is not extended and thus body. If we can have no conception of anything but body, it follows, Hobbes holds, that the subject of accidents of thought could not be anything but body. And hence the conclusion:

---

4 Hobbes ([1651] 1994), p. 15.

The knowledge of the proposition "I exist" thus depends on the knowledge of the proposition "I am thinking"; and knowledge of the latter proposition depends on our inability to separate thought from the matter that is thinking. So it seems that the correct inference is that the thinking thing is material rather than immaterial. (7: 173–74)

Cogito ergo corpus sum: I think therefore I am a body.

It should be noted that this argument depends crucially on the premise that substances are to be thought of as accidents and faculties that inhere in an underlying subject. (This is what I will call the *ultimate subject conception of substance*.) It is because substance is so construed that Hobbes' argument can get a foothold. We have direct access only to the accidents and faculties of mind; that is evident. But the underlying subject is quite something else. For Hobbes, general theoretical considerations about what is intelligible and what is not determine what that ultimate underlying subject must be like.

In the passage that I have been discussing, Hobbes' target is the treatment of mind in Meditation II, the claim that I am a thinking thing on the basis of the *cogito* argument. Interestingly enough, Hobbes never addresses directly the real distinction argument in Meditation VI. But in his answer to Hobbes, Descartes alludes to the argument in an interesting way, as we shall later see.[5]

DESCARTES ON SUBSTANCE: THE *MEDITATIONS* AND THE SECOND REPLIES

We all now think of Descartes' treatment of substance in terms of the canonical discussion he offers in the *Principia philosophiae*, where he characterizes substance in terms of the capacity for independent existence and distinguishes between substance, attribute, and mode. But things aren't quite that organized in the *Meditations*.[6]

---

[5] I should also note that there is another arguably materialist critique of the *Meditations*, that of Gassendi in his Fifth Objections. These objections are fascinating, very similar to Hobbes' in some ways, though different in others. But there is the complication that they were written by Gassendi after the transformation in Descartes' conception of substance that I shall be documenting further on in the chapter, but presumably without any knowledge of Descartes' answers to Hobbes or to Arnauld in the Fourth Replies. Furthermore, one might argue that Gassendi didn't mean actually to assert a materialist position, unlike Hobbes, but only intended to show the weakness of Descartes' case for dualism, though this is not at all clear. On this see LoLordo (2007), ch. 10. Nevertheless, I will bring Gassendi into the discussion on a few occasions below.

[6] For a careful account of the development of Descartes' account of substance from his early writings to his late, see Beyssade (1996). Beyssade's main interest is somewhat different from mine. He is mainly interested in determining whether the conception of substance that applies to finite beings is the same as that which applies to God.

The term "substance" first appears in Meditation III, in the course of his argument for the existence of God. There Descartes is surveying the ideas he has of various things, in order to determine whether they could derive from himself or whether they require an external source.

With regard to the clear and distinct elements in my ideas of corporeal things, it appears that I could have borrowed some of these from my idea of myself, namely substance, duration, number and anything else of this kind. For example, I think that a stone is a substance, or is a thing capable of existing independently, and I also think that I am a substance. (7: 44)

Substance here is conceived of as that which is capable of existing independently. Though the full development of the idea will have to await later Meditations, Descartes here recognizes different kinds of substances, extended and thinking:

Admittedly I conceive of myself as a thing that thinks and is not extended, whereas I conceive of the stone as a thing that is extended and does not think, so that the two conceptions differ enormously; but they seem to agree by falling under the common concept [*ratio*] of "substance". (7: 44)

The last phrase is interesting here: "*in ratione tamen substantiae videntur convenire.*" Though distinct, mind and body still have something in common insofar as they are substances, a common *ratio*. A few paragraphs later Descartes takes up the question of God, also a substance, but an infinite substance. There he writes:

It is true that I have the idea of substance in me in virtue of the fact that I am a substance; but this would not account for my having the idea of an infinite substance, when I am finite, unless this idea proceeded from some substance which really was infinite. (7: 45)

This, of course, leads directly to the conclusion that God, the infinite substance, exists as the cause of my idea of infinite substance. But I am interested in the first part of that sentence: "I have the idea of substance in me in virtue of the fact that I am a substance." That is, Descartes is acknowledging that there is a common idea of substance that applies to both thinking and extended substances, and that I have by virtue of the fact that I am a substance myself.

The notion of substance is raised again in Meditation VI, immediately after the proof for the real distinction between mind and body (to which we will later return). Descartes writes:

Besides this, I find in myself faculties for certain special ways of thinking, namely imagination and sensory perception. Now I can clearly and distinctly understand myself as a whole without these faculties; but I cannot, conversely, understand these faculties without me, that is, without an intellectual substance [*substantia intelligens*] to inhere in. This is because there is some intellection included in their formal concept; and hence I perceive that the distinction between them and myself corresponds to the distinction between the modes of a thing and the thing itself. (7: 78)

Descartes goes on to discuss extended substance in parallel terms:

Of course I also recognize that there are other faculties (like those of changing position, of taking on various shapes, and so on) which, like sensory perception and imagination, cannot be understood apart from some substance for them to inhere in, and hence cannot exist without it. But it is clear that these other faculties, if they exist, must be in a corporeal or extended substance and not an intellectual one; for the clear and distinct conception of them includes extension, but does not include any intellection whatsoever. (7: 78–79)

In these passages Descartes suggests that there are two kinds of substances, thinking substances and extended substances, which support two kinds of faculties, "faculties for certain special ways of thinking" and faculties that involve changing position, taking on various shapes, etc. (It is interesting here that what is at issue are *not* the individual ideas in a mind or the individual shapes, motions, etc. in a body, as they will be in later texts, but two *faculties*; we are still some distance from his final position.) These faculties require something in which they inhere, namely one of the two kinds of substances that he recognizes. Furthermore, these faculties inhere in substance as "the modes of a thing." But Descartes doesn't give us an account of the two basic kinds of substances, thinking and extended. How are these to be understood? Later, in the *Principia philosophiae* these will be understood in terms of the notion of principal attribute, as we shall see. But here they are just taken for granted.[7]

In the *Meditations* the treatment of the notion of substance is relatively informal. While we can discern the basic outline of his mature account of substance, there are no formal definitions and no clear account of what substance is and how exactly it is related to its accidents. The first formal definitions are found in the Geometrical Appendix to the Second Replies.[8] Descartes had been asked to set out his arguments *more geometrico*, in

---

[7] Commentators often assume that in the *Meditations* Descartes has the full metaphysical apparatus later developed in the *Principia philosophiae*. On this see, for example, Rozemond (1998), pp. 9, 26–27. For reasons that will be obvious as this chapter progresses, I think that this assumption is unwarranted.

[8] For some background on the history of the Geometrical Appendix to the Second Replies, see Garber (1995).

the style of the geometers. In doing so, he offers the following formal definitions:

V. *Substance.* This term applies to every thing in which whatever we perceive immediately resides, as in a subject, or to every thing by means of which whatever we perceive exists. By "whatever we perceive" is meant any property, quality or attribute of which we have a real idea. The only idea we have of a substance itself, in the strict sense, is that it is the thing in which whatever we perceive (or whatever has objective being in one of our ideas) exists, either formally or eminently. For we know by the natural light that a real attribute cannot belong to nothing.

VI. The substance in which thought immediately inheres is called *mind.* I use the term "mind" rather than "soul" since the word "soul" is ambiguous and is often applied to something corporeal.

VII. The substance which is the immediate subject of local extension and of the accidents which presuppose extension, such as shape, position, local motion and so on, is called *body.* Whether what we call mind and body are one and the same substance, or two different substances, is a question which will have to be dealt with later on. (7: 161–62)

This is the whole discussion of substance and related notions: there are no definitions of 'mode' or 'attribute'. What is interesting here is that Descartes doesn't define substance as he seemed to have done so in Meditation III, in terms of the capacity of independent existence. Not that he ignores that feature of substantiality. The following is the last definition in the series:

X. Two substances are said to be *really distinct* when each of them can exist apart from the other. (7: 162)

This is a definition of what it means for two substances to be really distinct, but it isn't a definition of what it is to be a substance. Substance is presented as the *subject* to which we attribute "any property, quality or attribute" and in which they exist. Mind or thinking substance is a substance in which thought immediately inheres, and body or extended substance is the substance in which extension immediately inheres. The Geometrical Appendix ends with the real distinction proof: "There is a real distinction between the mind and the body" (7: 169). Needless to say, the proof makes no mention of attributes or modes.

It is clear that there are a number of strands in Descartes' conception of substance in the *Meditations* and the Second Replies, the texts that precede his confrontation with Hobbes in the Third Objections and Replies. Descartes clearly has the idea of substance as a thing capable of independent existence and the idea of modes as things that depend on substance for their existence. But when asked to define the term 'substance' explicitly, he clearly defines it as the subject of accidents. In this way, as Descartes explicitly acknowledges in his treatment of substance in Meditation III, there is a common notion of substance that is shared by both thinking substance and extended substance. What distinguishes the one from the other, thinking substance from extended substance, is just what accidents inhere in that ultimate underlying subject, whether it be thought or extension.

In this way, in the texts that precede Hobbes' objection, Descartes seems to hold what I have called the ultimate subject conception of substance, the very conception of substance that will generate the objections to Cartesian dualism that Hobbes advances (and that Gassendi will advance later in the Fifth Objections).

DESCARTES ON SUBSTANCE: THE REPLY TO HOBBES

Descartes' reply to the portion of Hobbes' objections that relate to Meditation II are rather too long to discuss in their entirety; he goes into great detail, addressing all of the main points that Hobbes had made. But let me move directly to the central issue from our point of view, his treatment of the notion of substance. He begins as follows:

> If I may briefly explain the point at issue: it is certain that a thought cannot exist without a thing that is thinking; and in general no *actus* or accident can exist without a substance for it to belong to. But we do not come to know a substance immediately, through being aware of the substance itself; we come to know it only through its being the subject of certain *actus*. Hence it is perfectly reasonable, and indeed sanctioned by usage, for us to use different names for substances which we recognize as being the subjects of quite different acts or accidents. And it is reasonable for us to leave until later the examination of whether these different names signify different things or one and the same thing. (7: 175–76)

It seems clear that the concept of substance at issue here is the ultimate subject conception of substance. Substance, on this view, is the ultimate underlying subject in which the accidents and the *actus* are supposed to inhere. It is particularly striking how he conceives of mind and body: they are the different *names* of the different subjects that underlie the different collections of accidents, those that are different varieties of thought, and those that are different varieties of extension. We can distinguish the two substances (subjects) by the different kinds of accidents that they contain, and leave until later the question as to whether the ultimate underlying subjects of the two kinds of accidents are the same or different.

Descartes goes on to examine the different kinds of accidents (*actus*) that pertain to finite substances. He divides them into two different kinds: those that have the common concept (*ratio communis*) of extension, and those that have the common concept of thought:

For *actus* of thought have nothing in common with corporeal *actus*, and thought, which is the common concept [*ratio communis*] under which they fall, is different in kind from extension, which is the common concept of corporeal acts. (7: 176)

So far so good. But this just distinguishes accidents into two classes; it doesn't seem to penetrate to the ultimate underlying subject in which those different kinds of accidents inhere. This is what Descartes takes himself to be addressing in the final sentence of the answer:

Once we have formed two distinct concepts of these two substances, it is easy, on the basis of what is said in the Sixth Meditation, to establish whether they are one and the same or different. (7: 176)

But does this really address the problem?

At this point let us look briefly at the real distinction argument in Meditation VI (7: 78). The argument to which Descartes is alluding here goes something like this. Descartes begins with a premise about God: "everything which I clearly and distinctly understand is capable of being created by God so as to correspond exactly with my understanding of it." From this he concludes: "Hence the fact that I can clearly and distinctly understand one thing apart from another is enough to make me certain that the two things are distinct, since they are capable of being separated, at least by God." He then observes that his ideas of himself and body satisfy this condition: "on the one hand I have a clear and distinct idea of myself, in so far as I am simply a thinking, non-extended thing; and on the other hand I have a distinct idea of body, in so far as this is simply an extended, non-thinking thing." And so, he concludes: "it is certain that I am really distinct from my body, and can exist without it."

At the end of his answer to Hobbes, Descartes claims that this argument is sufficient to establish that mind and body are really distinct substances. Interestingly enough, this is *not* exactly the conclusion that Descartes presents in Meditation VI; there the issue is not whether mind and body are distinct *substances*, but only whether they can exist apart from each other. But *does* the argument support the stronger conclusion that they are distinct substances? I'm not at all sure. If substance is the underlying subject of properties, as both Hobbes and Descartes seem to hold at this moment, then the real distinction argument construed as an argument for a distinction between two kinds of substance faces some serious challenges.

Suppose first that we really have a clear and distinct idea of the two apart, the mind without a body, and the body without a mind. God can thus create them apart, Descartes claims. But even so, this doesn't necessarily show that they are distinct *substances* in a sense. Remember this passage from the definition Descartes offers of substance in the Geometrical Appendix to the Second Replies:

The only idea we have of a substance itself, in the strict sense, is that it is the thing in which whatever we perceive (or whatever has objective being in one of our ideas) exists, either formally or eminently. (7: 161)

If this is so, then the separate existence of mind and body would seem to be fully consistent with the claim that they share a common underlying *substance*. Though the mental qualities can exist in something that lacks material qualities, and vice versa, both might have a common substratum, the same underlying subject.[9] Though it may be convenient to give the two substances different *names*, as Descartes notes earlier in his reply, there is nothing in the argument that establishes that there are different underlying *subjects*, that is, that the two aren't at root the same *substance*.

This may not be so bad; after all, even if there may be a common subject, it still looks as if Descartes can hold that mind and body can exist apart from each other, and thus that there can be a non-extended mental substance that is distinct from an extended material substance, even if they share the underlying substantial ground.

But it gets worse. If we adopt the ultimate subject conception of substance, can we even say that we have a clear and distinct idea of the two apart from each other? We certainly *think* that we can conceive mind and body apart from each other, but can we really do so, and can we do so clearly and distinctly? Again, let us think about the underlying subject on the conception of substance that Descartes and Hobbes share at this moment. Hobbes argues that the only conception that we have of this underlying subject is as a body, and offers an argument to that effect. If he is right, then, of course, Descartes' real distinction argument fails, since we *couldn't* then conceive clearly and distinctly of mind apart from body. Descartes, of course, rejects Hobbes' argument. He argues, instead, that we have only a relatively thin idea of the underlying substance as the

---

[9] This is a point that Gassendi, and after him Locke, will later make. See Gassendi (7: 275–77) and Locke ([1690] 1979), 4.3.6.

subject of its properties. But if so, how can we be said to *know* whether or not it is extended? If we don't know what the underlying subject is really like, how could we exclude the possibility that contrary to what may *seem* evident to us, the nature of the underlying subject prevents mental properties from being present unless there are also physical properties as well? This, in a way, is what Descartes worried about in Meditation II when he wrote the following passage:

And yet may it not perhaps be the case that these very things which I am supposing to be nothing, because they are unknown to me, are in reality identical with the "I" of which I am aware? (7: 27)

Gassendi, who pressed Descartes at length on this question and argued that the underlying substance, the underlying subject of properties, remains unknown to Descartes even at the end of the *Meditations*, was asking for just such an argument when he urged Descartes to undertake what seems like a very odd program:

You should carefully scrutinize yourself and conduct a kind of chemical investigation of yourself, if you are to succeed in uncovering and explaining to us your internal substance. (7: 277)

This is how Descartes responded to this request:

You want us, you say, to conduct "a kind of chemical investigation" of the mind, as we would of wine. This is indeed worthy of you, O Flesh, and of all those who have only a very confused conception of everything, and so do not know the proper questions to ask about each thing. But as for me, I have never thought that anything more is required to reveal a substance than its various attributes; thus the more attributes of a given substance we know, the more perfectly we understand its nature. Now we can distinguish many different attributes in the wax: one, that it is white; two, that it is hard; three, that it can be melted; and so on. And there are correspondingly many attributes in the mind: one, that it has the power of knowing the whiteness of the wax; two, that it has the power of knowing its hardness; three, that it has the power of knowing that it can lose its hardness (i.e. melt), and so on. (7: 359–60)[10]

From this reply it is clear that Descartes didn't have the foggiest idea what Gassendi had in mind. But it seems clear enough to me. If substance is the real underlying subject, then if one is going to assert a doctrine as strong as substance dualism, you have to know something about the nature of the underlying subject. Otherwise one can never be sure that

---

[10] It is obvious here that "attribute" is not being used in the technical sense of the principal attribute, as we will see it used in the *Principia philosophiae*.

the claim that the one can be conceived without the other may, for all we know, simply rest on illusion. In that way, the ultimate subject view of substance that Descartes held at that moment would seem to call the Meditation VI argument and at least one of its premises into doubt.

As long as we maintain the ultimate subject notion of substance, Hobbes' materialist's objections cannot be answered. If we think of substance as the subject in which the accidents of which we are directly aware inhere, then the ultimate nature of this underlying subject will remain open to the materialist's position, even after the real distinction argument of Meditation VI.

DESCARTES ON SUBSTANCE: THE REPLY TO ARNAULD AND BEYOND

This is where things stand after Descartes' reply to Hobbes. But they don't end there.

At the end of his response to Hobbes on mind and body, it seems that Descartes doesn't really understand the predicament that he is in: the conception of substance that he shares with Hobbes undermines his Meditation VI argument for the real distinction between mind and body. But the very next set of objections, Antoine Arnauld's Fourth Objections, gives him another opportunity to address the problem.

Arnauld is very much in tune with the kind of problems that I have been pressing. Arnauld prefaces his objections by recalling to Descartes what he himself had written in Meditation II, as I quoted earlier:

And yet may it not perhaps be the case that these very things which I am supposing to be nothing, because they are unknown to me, are in reality identical with the "I" of which I am aware? (7: 27, quoted 7: 198)

He then goes on to call into question the assumption that we do have a clear and distinct conception of mind apart from body and vice versa. He writes:

But someone may ... maintain that the conception you have of yourself when you conceive of yourself as a thinking, non-extended thing is an inadequate one; and the same may be true of your conception of yourself as an extended, non-thinking thing ... It therefore remains to be proved that the mind can be completely and adequately understood apart from the body. (7: 200–1)

Arnauld goes on to illustrate his point by appeal to a geometrical example: one may know that a given triangle is a right triangle, but at the same time not know that the sum of the squares on the sides equals the square

on the hypotenuse. In the same way, one might know that the mind is a
thinking thing but be ignorant of the fact that it is also a body, even when
it really is.

Descartes' reply to Arnauld involves an interesting elaboration of his
notion of substance, indeed, important changes over what he had written
in earlier texts. For one, there is a change in the very definition of substance. As I pointed out earlier, there is a gap in the real distinction argument of Meditation VI. While he may (at best) be able to show that mind
and body can exist apart from each other, he doesn't show that mind and
body are distinct *substances*. Nor does the explicit definition of substance
in the Appendix to the Second Replies help here:

The only idea we have of a substance itself, in the strict sense, is that it is the
thing in which whatever we perceive (or whatever has objective being in one of
our ideas) exists, either formally or eminently. (7: 161)

Understood in this way, the real distinction argument of Meditation VI
would seem not to address the question of distinct substances at all. For
this reason, Descartes advances an alternative definition of substance in
his reply to Arnauld. He writes:

But now I must explain how the mere fact that I can clearly and distinctly understand one substance apart from another is enough to make me certain that one
excludes the other. The answer is that the notion of a substance is just this – that
it can exist by itself, that is without the aid of any other substance. (7: 225–26)

This, of course, is not entirely new; it harkens back to the definition of
substance suggested in Meditation III. But it is a change over what he
had offered as a definition of substance in the Appendix to the Second
Replies.

More significant still is another new element he introduces here
in the Fourth Replies. On the question of whether we really can conceive of mind and body apart from each other in a clear and distinct
way, Descartes offers a detailed consideration of Arnauld's geometrical
example. In the course of his reply, Descartes picks up where he left off in
the answer he gave Hobbes, but he makes a very significant revision of his
view. Returning to the discussion in the Third Objections and Replies,
Descartes reminds Arnauld: "We do not have immediate knowledge of
substances, as I have noted elsewhere" (7: 222). He continues:

We know them only by perceiving certain forms or attributes which must inhere
in something if they are to exist; and we call the thing in which they inhere a
"substance". But if we subsequently wanted to strip the substance of the attributes

through which we know it, we would be destroying our entire knowledge of it. We might be able to apply various words to it, but we could not have a clear and distinct perception of what we meant by these words. (7: 222; cf. Descartes to Gibieuf, 19 January 1642, 3: 474ff.)

This is a very significant change over what he had written in earlier texts, including the *Meditations*, the Second Replies, and the Third Objections and Replies.

In those earlier texts, substance was understood as the ultimate underlying subject in which accidents inhere. As such, the notion of substance could be understood independently of thinking substance and extended substance, for Descartes at least: it is the element that they have in common. (For Hobbes, of course, it is a bit different, insofar as the underlying subject has to be body.) But this text seems to be radically different. Here he seems to deny that thinking substance is substance plus thought, the underlying subject to which we have added the accident of thought, or that body is the underlying subject to which we have added the accident of extension. Rather, the underlying substratum is substantialized thought, or substantialized extension. And to talk of the underlying subject in the two cases is not to talk of the metaphysical foundation of the thing, but to abstract from what is really there: the thinking thing and the extended thing.

And this, then, becomes Descartes' new doctrine of substance, the view that gets set out in its most rigorous form in Part I of the *Principia philosophiae*, which Descartes was drafting at the same time as he was composing the replies to the objections he had solicited to his *Meditations*.[11]

In the *Principia philosophiae*, Descartes now sets out as his canonical definition of substance the one that he had offered in his reply to Arnauld:

By *substance* we can understand nothing other than a thing which exists in such a way as to depend on no other thing for its existence. (*Princ.* 1.51)

As in the earlier writings, a substance is known not directly but through its accidents:

However, we cannot initially become aware of a substance merely through its being an existing thing, since this alone does not of itself have any effect on us. We can, however, easily come to know a substance by one of its attributes, in

---

[11] For a general discussion of Descartes' doctrine of substance as developed in the *Principia philosophiae*, with particular attention to its roots in Suárez and scholastic thought, see Marion (1996). Marion, though, does not emphasize the importance of the inseparability of the principal attribute and the substance.

virtue of the common notion that nothingness possesses no attributes, that is to say, no properties or qualities. Thus, if we perceive the presence of some attribute, we can infer that there must also be present an existing thing or substance to which it may be attributed. (*Princ.* 1.52)

However, in his discussion of the accidents by which we become aware of a substance, Descartes now draws a distinction between the modes of substance, and what he now, for the first time, calls the principal attribute of a substance:

A substance may indeed be known through any attribute at all; but each substance has one principal property which constitutes its nature and essence, and to which all its other properties are referred. Thus extension in length, breadth and depth constitutes the nature of corporeal substance; and thought constitutes the nature of thinking substance. Everything else which can be attributed to body presupposes extension, and is merely a mode of an extended thing; and similarly, whatever we find in the mind is simply one of the various modes of thinking. (*Princ.* 1.53)

And so, for example, extension is basic in body insofar as all of the accidents of body presuppose extension: that is what Descartes means when he says that all the other properties "are referred" to the principal properties.

But what is most important in the account of substance in the *Principia philosophiae* is what he has to say about the relation between attributes and substances. Now, for any given mode, a substance can have that mode or not. But the substance cannot lack its principal attribute. And so you can have a body that is not round or not square, but you cannot have a body that is not in some way extended. The situation is similar for thought and its different varieties. But what is particularly interesting here is the relation between the principal attribute and the substance.[12] What Descartes claims is that there is only a *distinction of reason* (*distinctio rationis*) between a substance and its principal attribute:[13]

Finally, a *distinction of reason* is a distinction between a substance and some attribute of that substance without which the substance is unintelligible ... Such

---

[12] One must be a little careful here. Even in the *Principia*, Descartes uses "attribute" and "mode" as synonyms. See e.g. *Princ.* 1.57. What came to be called the "attribute" of a substance in later Cartesian literature is, for Descartes, the principal attribute in the *Principia*.

[13] A fair number of studies take special note of this central feature of Descartes' conception of substance. Though this view of Descartes is widely recognized, what isn't recognized is that this seems to be something new in the Fourth Replies and in the *Principia*, and how exactly Descartes came to hold the view. See e.g. Marignac (1980), Nolan (1997), Rozemond (1998), ch. 1, Dutton (2003), Secada (2005), Normore (2008), and Rodriguez-Pereyra (2008).

a distinction is recognized by our inability to form a clear and distinct idea of the substance if we exclude from it the attribute in question. (*Princ.* 1.62)

What he then says about thinking and extended substance is this:

Thought and extension can be regarded as constituting the natures of intelligent substance and corporeal substance; they must then be considered as nothing else but thinking substance itself and extended substance itself – that is, as mind and body. In this way we will have a very clear and distinct understanding of them. Indeed, it is much easier for us to have an understanding of extended substance or thinking substance than it is for us to understand substance on its own, leaving out the fact that it thinks or is extended. For we have some difficulty in abstracting the notion of substance from the notions of thought and extension, since the distinction between these notions and the notion of substance itself is merely a distinction of reason. (*Princ.* 1.63)

We must be rather careful here. Descartes certainly continues to maintain that substance is the underlying subject of modes, the seat of shape, size, and motion for bodies, or thoughts and volitions for minds. But what he does seem to deny here is that this underlying subject is to be understood as a bare substratum to which we add the notions of thought or extension. That is to say, what is basic are the notions of *thinking* substance and *extended* substance, substantialized thought and substantialized extension: the notion of a bare substance, neither mind nor body but the ultimate subject of thought and extension itself, is an abstraction from the notions of mind and body, and *not* something more basic and foundational, as it is on what I have called the ultimate subject view of substance. In a later section, dealing now with extended substance, Descartes is more explicit, and perhaps even more radical still:

9. *If corporeal substance is distinguished from its quantity, it is conceived in a confused manner as something incorporeal.*
    Others may disagree, but I do not think they have any alternative perception of the matter. When they make a distinction between substance and extension or quantity, either they do not understand anything by the term "substance", or else they simply have a confused idea of incorporeal substance, which they falsely attribute to corporeal substance and leave for extension (which they call an accident) the true idea of corporeal substance. And so with their words they express something different from what they grasp with their minds. (*Princ.* II.9)

This last quotation is a bit awkward. But what Descartes means is this. Consider the ultimate subject view of substance that Descartes himself earlier held. On that view we distinguish between the ultimate underlying subject and the extension that is supposed to inhere in it. When we do so, Descartes claims, we are making a big mistake. When, on that view, we talk about the ultimate underlying subject/substance, we are dealing not with a clear and distinct idea, but only the ghost of a conception – a "confused idea of incorporeal substance." And when we are talking about the accident of extension that is supposed to inhere in the ultimate underlying subject, we are, in reality, talking about corporeal substance itself, the substance of body, improperly construed as an accident. And so, Descartes concludes, the ultimate subject view of substance results in deep confusion. In the end, he wants to say, what there is is extended substance, and *not* substance with extension, considered as two distinct constituents.

With this the ultimate subject conception of substance is dead. There is no longer a gap between extension or thought and the ultimate underlying subject in which the accidents inhere. The subject in which they inhere is no longer a bare subject plus extension, or bare subject plus thought, but a unitary extended substance or thinking substance. With this, the gap that the materialists' arguments exploited in Descartes' proof for the real distinction between mind and body no longer exists. On Descartes' new conception of substance, in grasping the substantial ground of thought and the substantial ground of extension, we are grasping the natures of the substances as such. If Descartes is right, there is nothing more to say about them, and nothing more to ask.

In this way, the doctrine of substance in the *Principia philosophiae* is a significant advance over the treatment of substance in the *Meditations* and in the definitions of the Second Replies. But even so, puzzles remain.

An explicit consequence of the doctrine presented in the *Principia philosophiae* is that there is, strictly speaking, no idea of substance as such, or, at least no clear and distinct idea: among the finite substances, leaving God aside, all we have are ideas of thinking substance and extended substance. If that is so, what then becomes of the argument for the existence of God in Meditation III? If there is no idea of substance as such, then it would seem no longer true to say that I could get the idea of the stone as a finite substance from the idea that I have of myself as a substance, as he would seem to argue there. This, it seems, would undermine the strategy that Descartes uses in Meditation III for proving the existence of God as the only idea that I couldn't get from the idea of myself.[14] It may be significant that in Meditation III, the implicit definition Descartes offers of substance is not in terms of an ultimate underlying subject, but

---

[14] In a very closely related way, it would seem to undermine what Jean-Luc Marion has called "la déduction égologique de la substance," the way in which the very idea of substance is supposed to derive from a reflection on myself. See Marion (1986), pp. 161–80.

in terms of the capacity for independent existence: "For example, I think that a stone is a substance, or is a thing capable of existing independently, and I also think that I am a substance" (7: 44). This, of course, is what Descartes will adopt in the *Principia philosophiae* as his official definition of substance. But this just raises another puzzle.

Descartes holds that the notion of substance abstracted from the notions of thought and extension fails to be clear and distinct; indeed, he claims in the reply to Arnauld that "if we ... wanted to strip the substance of the attributes through which we know it, we would be destroying our entire knowledge of it" (7: 222). But if this is the case, then what possible sense could be made of the official definition he offers of the notion of substance in *Princ.* 1.51? If substance as such is incapable of a clear and distinct idea, then what status does the definition have? Indeed, the problem is not just with the particular definition that he offers in the *Principia philosophiae*: *any* attempt to give a definition of what it is that thinking and extended substances have in common as substances would seem to be doomed in exactly the same way.[15] As clear as the doctrine of substance seems to be by the time of the *Principia philosophiae*, it is still not fully formed.

CONCLUDING REMARKS

With this my main argument is over. I have tried to show how, in reaction to the danger of materialism, Descartes radically revised his view of the nature of substance. In reaction to the claim that his arguments did not penetrate to the nature of substance, Descartes rejected the ultimate subject conception of substance that he had held while writing the *Meditations* and adopted a very different conception of substance. In particular, he adopted the notion of the principal attribute, and a conception of substance on which there is no real distinction at all between the subject of the modes and the principal attribute by which we know it.

But while this move allows Descartes to fortify his philosophy against the attacks of the materialists, it comes at something of a cost. On the new view of substance that Descartes adopts in response to the materialist

---

[15] Rodriguez-Pereyra (2008), pp. 78, 81–82, 85, offers an argument to the effect that the conception of substance in accordance with which there is only a distinction of reason between a substance and its principal attribute is a direct consequence of the definition of substance as a thing that has the capacity for independent existence. Given the fact that the intimate relation between substance and principal attribute would seem to undermine that definition, this could not be correct.

attacks against his view of mind and body, he rejects the idea that there is a substratum below the accidents of mind and body that we directly perceive: the thoughts we have and the shapes we see in bodies reveal the true inner nature of the substance in which they inhere. But on this view, there is no longer anything that mind and body have in common as substances: there is thinking substance, and there is extended substance, but, in a way, there is no such thing as substance itself, the bare substratum that underlies both, the being, the *ens*. Now, scholastic metaphysics generally distinguishes between general and special metaphysics. General metaphysics is the science of being *qua* being, while special metaphysics treats detached immaterial substances, such as the human soul and God. Descartes might be said to have a special metaphysics insofar as he does have a doctrine of God and the human soul, as he sometimes seems to acknowledge.[16] But if we consider metaphysics in the general sense as the science of being as such, there can be no Cartesian metaphysics.[17]

---

[16] See e.g. the introduction to the French version of the *Principes de la philosophie* (9b: 10), where he calls God and the soul "les choses immaterielles ou Metaphysiques."

[17] This is the conclusion argued for in Marignac (1980), pp. 302–3, 306, 307–8, 312. Though Marignac offers a very sophisticated argument for this position, he does not seem to appreciate the path by which Descartes arrived at this conclusion. Jean-Luc Marion also argues for the conclusion that Descartes has no metaphysics, though from different premises. Instead he prefers to see Descartes' project grounded in a *philosophia prima*. See Marion (1986), ch. 1.

CHAPTER 4

Thinking: the nature of Descartes' mental substance

Martha Brandt Bolton

The signature doctrine of Cartesian metaphysics, the real distinction between mind and body, is a theory of substance. A mind is a substance whose nature is to think; body is a substance the nature of which is to be extended; as a consequence, a mind and its body can be separated one from the other. In the Aristotelian tradition, a substance is, at least initially, defined as a being that other things inhere in or depend on, which does not inhere in or depend on anything else. For Descartes, God is the only such being. A created substance is defined by its relative independence: its existence depends on nothing but the concurrence of God; it inheres in nothing, and other things inhere in it.[1] Minds and bodies have this intermediate metaphysical status. Most important, a mind does not depend for its existence on a body nor does a body depend on a mind. As for things that exist only if they do belong to something – which are variously called "accidents," "affections," "qualities," "attributes," "acts," or "modes" – Descartes maintains that the nature of a substance determines the range of modes, as I will say, that can belong to it.[2] It does this with such stringency that no mode of a given substance could possibly inhere in a thing with a different nature. A mind is capable of having thoughts, volitions, sense perceptions, and the like; by contrast, its body is the subject of motion, rest, figures, and various configurations of parts. But that bodies should have thoughts, or minds have shapes, is impossible.[3]

I am grateful to the NY–NJ Research Group and Yale Early Modern Philosophy Colloquium for helpful discussion of material in this chapter, especially Ken Winkler and my commentator, Elliot Paul. I also want to thank Martin Lin for helpful comments on a draft of this chapter.

[1] See 7: 44, 2: 30; 7: 161, 2: 114; 7: 222, 2: 156; *Princ.* 1.51.
[2] *Principles* fixes on "mode" to signify the things that inhere in substances. *Meditations* and Replies are less regimented in the use of terms, but "modes" tends to be used when Descartes strives for precision, e.g. 7: 78, 2: 54.
[3] "[A]ll the attributes which belong to a body can be denied of [the mind]. For it is of the nature of substances that they should mutually exclude each other" (7: 227, 2: 359).

Mind–body substance dualism comes in for a good deal of critical scrutiny in the Objections to the *Meditations*. Issues surrounding dualism can distract attention from the more basic account of the constitution of a substance, as such, but this is the ground on which dualism is built, and it attracts some attention from several acute contemporaries of Descartes. In the seventeenth century, non-Aristotelian theories of substance proliferate, and they bear an explanatory burden. The science of metaphysics is far less prominent in the period than in the heyday of scholasticism, but theories of substance come under this head. A substance theory, broadly speaking, maintains that everything we have reason to say there is fits in one of two categories, substances and accidents. The success of such a theory is judged largely by the adequacy of its account of how a substance is constituted. What elements and relations make up the substance itself? What is the inherence relation between substance and modes? An account of these matters should explain properties of a substance such as: the unity of the modes that belong to one substance and that in virtue of which a substance endures as its modes change. The present chapter examines Descartes' non-Aristotelian account of the constitution of substance in light of criticisms on the part of some of his prominent contemporaries.

The basic constituents of a Cartesian substance are: (i) a nature which serves to determine the range of modes that can belong to the substance; (ii) the several modes that do, in fact, belong to it; and (iii) the inherence relation between the nature and the modes. To anticipate a central concern, noted by Arnauld among others, we can begin to see that the notion of the nature of a mind is less than obvious. Thinking is the nature of a mind; passing acts of thought are modes; but if thinking *qua* nature is not successive acts of thinking, what is it? No familiar notion provides a suitable answer, which might lead to the speculation that the notion of thinking nature is merely formal, a primitive relation among modes. By contrast, however, the nature of a corporeal substance seems much less conceptually austere. Extension considered without regard for motion and figure can be intelligibly described; it is everywhere divisible, impenetrable, three dimensional. Yet Descartes offers a single model of substantial constitution that pertains to both mind and body alike. So it seems that we should press for an intelligible account of thinking nature.

I

For information about Descartes' notion of thinking nature, we can look to the process of discovery implemented in *Meditations*, which culminates in the demonstration of the real distinction in Meditation 6. The final argument depends on nothing but two claims about the respective natures of mental and corporeal substance. They are so logically powerful that the demonstration is strictly valid and only the truth of the premises can be questioned. We are not primarily concerned with the probative force of the proofs of the premises; nevertheless, they are of interest to us for what they reveal about Descartes' understanding of what thinking and extension, regarded as natures, are.

The *Meditations* deploys a general method of inquiry about substances which is briefly described in several Replies:

> We do not have immediate knowledge of substances, as I have noted elsewhere. We know them only by perceiving certain forms or attributes which must inhere in something if they are to exist; and we call the thing in which they inhere a "substance". But if we subsequently wanted to strip the substance of the attributes, through which we know it, we should be destroying our entire knowledge of it. (7: 222, 2: 156)[4]

Brief as this is, it would be familiar to Descartes' contemporaries. He adapts an epistemic principle of the scholastics: that because substances, as such, do not affect our senses, we know them only by knowing their accidents, which do affect our senses.[5] In the version we have in view, however, substances are known by use of a non-Aristotelian faculty of intellect. We might put it this way: in perceiving an accident (mode), one achieves intellectual grasp of a fact (such-and-such mode exists) which evidently points to a substance to which the mode belongs. More than this, it points to the nature of the substance: "it is by means of the accidents that the nature of the substance is revealed" (7: 216, 2: 277).

Notice that although substance and nature are grasped by acts of intellect, this is an a posteriori mode of inquiry which begins with data collected from experience of particular things.[6] Yet the nature of a substance, which is thereby known, determines *all possible* accidents of the substance. How is it, according to Descartes, that facts about a relatively few modes of a substance prove a general truth with this modal force? The evidence derives from nothing but operations of the Cartesian faculty of intellect.

The method is at work in the *res cogitans* argument at the beginning of Meditation 2. The method prescribes the following sequence of steps:

---

[4] Also 7: 175–76, 2: 124; *Princ.* 1.52, 8a: 25, 1: 210.

[5] "Accidents are known before substances. The reason is: because accidents are the things most open to the senses; substances are concealed, not per se sensible, and thus not very quickly nor easily known" (Sancto Paulo 1648; my translation).

[6] It is also a posteriori in the original sense, of arguing from known effects to their causes.

(A) immediate perception that a certain mode exists; (B) direct intellectual grasp that this mode belongs to a substance; (C) careful attention to the question of the nature of this substance confirmed by discovering other particular modes that belong to it; (D) knowledge of the nature of this substance provided the previous steps are properly done.

The method is applied as follows. (i) The meditator immediately perceives that he doubts that bodies exist.[7] (ii) Directly he (supposedly) grasps that there is a substance to which the doubt belongs. First-person pronouns are used to refer to it. (The mode of inquiry underwrites the generalization: necessarily if I doubt x, then I exist.) (iii) The meditator considers *what* he is, that is, what he can be certain that he is. At this stage: (a) he reviews all the bodily things he formerly supposed himself to be and dismisses them because their existence is presently in doubt; (b) he then fixes on the modes which he is certain belong to him, that is, his particular thoughts, and thereby (allegedly) discovers with certainty that he is a thinking thing. "Thinking alone is [known to be] inseparable from me"; (c) this is followed by inquiry into what a thinking thing is, which is said to reveal that it engages in several activities: doubting, understanding, affirming, denying, willing, being unwilling, imagining, and perceiving by sense; (d) this prompts the meditator to collect further perceptual data and apply the first three steps of the method to them. (a′) He immediately perceives with certainty that he presently doubts many things, understands some things, affirms some things, denies others, desires to know more, is unwilling to be deceived, etc.; (b′) he (supposedly) grasps by intellect that each of these modes belongs to the same substance, namely, himself; (c′) in this light, he considers again what the nature of this substance is, and (purportedly) grasps that each act points to the same nature, thinking. (iv) These results are said to show that his nature is thinking, which can take the form of any of the activities just mentioned.

Our interest lies in what this shows about the relevant notion of a substantial nature, but it may help to clear the air to consider the basis on which the method licenses the inferences and generalizations announced in steps (ii) and (iii). According to Descartes, no act (mode) can be perceived unless it is conceived as an act, and no act can be conceived without a subject to which it belongs; moreover, no act of thought can be conceived apart from a substance that thinks.[8] The theory behind the method posits a tightly organized array of ideas (concepts) already present

---

[7] In subsequent Meditations, this intellectual grasp is called "clear and distinct perception."

[8] "[W]e cannot conceive an act without its subject. We cannot conceive of thought without a thinking thing, since that which thinks is not nothing" (7: 175, 2: 123).

in our minds which represent a mode as having a certain relation to a substance with such-and-such nature. Perceiving a mode activates ideas which predetermine intellectual acts that reveal the mode–substance–nature connection.

It is well known that at this stage Descartes does not claim that his nature is only to think, but rather claims his knowledge of himself depends on nothing but his having thoughts.[9] The text explicitly acknowledges: "I do not know [whether I am something presently unknown to me], and for the moment I shall not argue the point, since I can make judgments only about things which are known to me" (7: 27, 2: 18). At this stage, the existence of body is uncertain. Descartes' nature is left open here, and finally decided by the demonstration in Meditation 6.

Nonetheless the evidence with regard to the nature of his mind and the nature of body is on the table in Meditation 2.[10] In the second part of this meditation, the method we have in view is used, allegedly, to discover the nature of a body from data collected by examining a piece of wax. The procedure proves that it is the nature of a body to be "something extended, flexible and changeable" in indefinitely many ways (7: 30–31, 2: 20). But although Descartes explains in his Reply to Arnauld that the proof is effectively complete at this point, the explicit presentation of the argument for the real distinction is postponed. This is in order that all possible doubt about what is clearly and distinctly perceived might be discharged.[11] Validation of a criterion of truth is extrinsic to the proof of the natures of mental and corporeal substance from which the real distinction logically follows.

The reply to Arnauld also identifies the operative methodological canon: "the order in which things are mutually related in our perception of them corresponds to the order in which they are related in actual reality" (7: 226, 2: 159). In other words, A is metaphysically dependent on B if, but also only if, attentive perception of A shows its dependence on B. If this canon is reliable, then if thinking (extension) were an accident that inheres in some other nature, we would, in the course of carefully using the method, perceive thinking (extension) to depend on this other nature, just as we perceive our present thoughts to depend on a substance which thinks. Descartes explains that in order to know the nature of a mind, it

---

[9] See 7: 8, 2: 7; 7: 215, 2: 285.
[10] See 7: 220–39 and 226, 2: 155–61 and 159; 7: 357, 2: 247; 7: 8, 2: 7; 7: 13, 2: 9.
[11] See 7: 226, 2: 159.

is not necessary to have a complete enumeration of the modes that belong to a mind. Instead, it is enough to show that a substance that thinks is complete in the sense that it has "all the forms or attributes which enable me to recognize that it is a substance"; it needs nothing but God's concurrence (Fourth Replies, 7: 221, 2: 156). The argument is that perception of acts of thought includes knowledge of thinking nature, which does not include knowledge of anything else, so thinking nature depends on nothing else, save the concurrence of God. The method is grounded on epistemic and metaphysical doctrines to the effect that the ideas we use to judge that there is an accident of such-and-such a sort are entirely accurate and complete representations of the dependence relations comprised in a substance. To put it differently, immediate perception of accidents provides data for a method of discovery very different from the inductive inferences typical of empiricist methods of inquiry.

What, then, can we say about thinking *qua* nature? In fact, it is plausible that we cannot conceive an act of thought without a thing that thinks, not just a thing that has this particular thought, but a thing that also has the ability to think. This is at least part of Descartes' notion of thinking nature.[12]

Several authors of Objections take thinking nature to be the faculty, or power, of thinking. They do not object to this. But Hobbes complains about what it is supposed to show, that "I am a mind, or intelligence, or intellect or reason."

It does not seem to be a valid argument to say "I am thinking, therefore I am thought" or "I am using my intellect, hence I am an intellect." I might just as well say "I am walking, therefore I am a walk." M. Descartes is identifying the thing which understands with intellection, which is an act of that which understands. Or at least he is identifying the thing which understands with the intellect, which is a power of that which understands. Yet all philosophers make a distinction between a subject and its faculties and acts. (7: 172–73, 2: 122)

Accepting that thinking is a faculty, Descartes resists the charge that he conflates the faculty and the subject endowed with it. Unlike the word "walk," "'thought' is sometimes taken to refer to the act, sometimes to the faculty, and sometimes to the thing which possesses the faculty" (7: 174, 2: 123). Whereas Hobbes holds that a faculty inheres in another entity, a substance, Descartes maintains that a substance and a faculty are, in this

---

[12] This terminology is used at 7: 53f., 56, 57, 58, 73, and 79. "Faculty" is used frequently to refer to the essence of a mind in *Comments on a Certain Broadsheet*.

case, the same; he uses "faculty of thinking" and "thinking substance" to refer to one and the same existing entity.[13] So far, we can say that a thinking nature is the faculty manifested by acts of thinking (affirming, willing, etc.); the faculty is identical to the thinking substance; the existence of the faculty depends on nothing else, except for God. Moreover, particular thoughts cannot be conceived without a thinking nature. *Mutatis mutandis*, for extension *qua* nature of body.

II

In 1648, Arnauld, writing anonymously to conceal his location, sent the first of two letters to Descartes in which, among other things, he challenges his correspondent's doctrine that thinking is the nature of a mind: "Nor indeed does it seem necessary that the mind be always thinking, even if it is a thinking substance, for it is enough that the power of thinking be always in it, just as corporeal substance is always divisible, even if it is not always actually divided" (Arnauld 1990, p. 186). The line of inquiry we traced in Meditation 2 may plausibly be regarded as proving that the meditator's nature is the ability to think, yet failing to prove that it consists in actual thinking. Actual thoughts are required for Descartes' knowledge that he exists, but nothing in the argument seems to show them to be necessary for his existence. Descartes defends his position: "It seems necessary that the mind always actually think, because thought constitutes its essence, just as extension constitutes the essence of body, and must not be conceived as an attribute which can be present or absent in the way that division of parts or motion is conceived in a body" (Arnauld 1990, p. 189). This hardly seems relevant. Arnauld is fully aware that thinking is supposed to be the essence of a mind and what this implies; his point is that the power of thinking is better suited to play this role than actual thinking.

Perhaps Descartes thinks it adequate to respond with elementary points of logic, but this is difficult to believe in view of the general tenor of his letter. More likely, the response reaches more deeply into metaphysical issues about faculties. The mere power to think is not sufficient for the essence of a substance, because just as divisibility can be manifested or not in a substance, the mere power to think might be exerted or not. The distinction between a power, on one hand, and its exertions, on the

---

[13] There is a "conceptual distinction" between a substance and its essence (see *Princ.* 1.60; letter to ***, 1645 or 1646, 4: 348, 3: 279–81; cf. Nolan 1997).

other, raises at least two questions: (i) how is the power, by contrast with its manifestations, present in the mind, or what is it in virtue of which the mind has the power? (ii) given that the mind has the power, what is required to exercise it? Descartes passes over the first question, but implicitly gives this answer to the second: there is nothing in a mind – an immaterial substance which can evidently exist apart from anything corporeal – to prevent its manifesting its power to think.[14] That is, a substance that has the complete power thereby satisfies conditions sufficient for it to exert the power. Still, a created mind does not fully exert its power, since it can, at a given time, think of things about which it has not had a thought so far and, indeed, things of which it may never actually have thoughts. Evidently something prevents the mind exerting its power to think of many things in particular, and this inhibiting factor may have implications for the make-up of thinking substance.

In his second letter, Arnauld accepts that it is a necessary truth that a mind always thinks. He objects that Descartes' theory doesn't explain it. The second letter articulates several reasons why thinking cannot be the essence of a mind.[15] (1) "Since our thoughts are constantly changing, it would seem that the essence of our mind is constantly changing" (Arnauld 1990, p. 191). We alluded to this problem above – thoughts are acts; thinking is a succession of acts. Neither notion suits the essence of a mind. (2) Reasoning that he is the source of his present thoughts, Arnauld contends that if thinking were his essence, then he could be the author of his essence and, likewise, conserve his own existence. To this, Arnauld surmises, Descartes is likely to say that we owe to God that we think, and to ourselves that we think of this or that. "But it can scarcely be understood how thought in general can be separated from this or that thought, except by an abstraction of the understanding." Thought in general is the kind to which all, and only, particular thoughts belong. Apparently, Arnauld is a conceptualist about universals; on this view, thought in general is nothing but an abstract conception that we use to represent many particular thoughts. A mental abstraction cannot be part of an actual mind. Furthermore, according to Arnauld, even if thinking in general could be a constituent of a mind, it would not do everything it is required to do.

This is because Descartes identifies thinking as his essence, in particular. (3) "Furthermore, a singular thing with a determinate essence must be

---

[14] "But why should [the soul] not always think, since it is a thinking substance?" (7: 356, 2: 247).
[15] The letter raises some objections not discussed here.

singular and determinate, and therefore if thought is the essence of mind, its essence must be constituted not only by thought in general, but by this or that thought. However, that cannot be said" (Arnauld 1990, pp. 191–92). A singular thing (nature) is an individual by contrast with a general thing, or kind.[16] The essence of an individual thing must be determined to that individual rather than any other. By Arnauld's lights, thinking is determined by the object(s) of thought; that is, thinking of this or that. Yet it is simply not the case that the essence of an individual mind is to think of a certain object that is unique to it, an object about which no other mind thinks; or, so says the passage just quoted.

The final objection (4) focuses the problem of individual essence on the fact that thinking cannot undergo change:

> It is not the same with a body, for although its extension can seem to vary, yet it always retains the same quantity, and the entire variation consists in this, that if something decreases in length it increases in breadth or depth, unless indeed it can be said that the thought in our mind is always the same, while it is directed now to this object and now to that, which I very much doubt. (Arnauld 1990, p. 192)

In effect, the essence of a substance serves as a substrate for its changing modes. The extension of corporeal substance neatly fulfills this role. By contrast, thinking as Arnauld understands it apparently offers nothing to serve as the enduring subject of changing thoughts.[17] Descartes is on the spot to say how thinking can be unique to him, as an individual, and how it can endure in the change of particular thoughts.

Difficult problems, but Arnauld finishes with a tentative suggestion. With the problem of change in view, he takes a second look at the possibility that the essence of a mind might be continual thought of some object unique to that mind. The stability of such a determinate thought now seems a candidate for the enduring constituent of a mind. His subsequent treatise *Les idées vraies et fausses* proposes just such a theory of the essence of a singular mind.[18] But it is a theory of his devising.

---

[16] See Arnauld and Nicole (1970), pp. 86f.

[17] See 7: 14, 2: 10.

[18] "Perhaps we could speculate that there is in me some thought which does not change and which can be taken as the essence of my soul. I can find only two thoughts that might be considered to be like this: the thought of a universal Being and that of my own soul. Both of these are to be found in all other thoughts: that of the universal Being, because it contains the idea of being in its entirety, whereas our soul only knows something under the notion of possible or existent being; and the thought that our soul has of itself because, whatever it is that I know, I know that I know by an implicit reflection that accompanies all my thoughts" (Arnauld 1990, pp. 53–54).

Descartes' response can seem uninformative. To clarify the difference between thought *qua* essence and thought *qua* mode, he refers to two entries in the *Principles of Philosophy* (1.63 and 64). To my mind, they are unhelpful. Still, this response is important because it explicitly confirms that the essence of a mind is not thinking in general; it is not "something universal which includes [*comprehenden*] all modes of thinking, but rather a particular nature which receives all those modes, just as extension is a nature which receives shapes" (5: 221; Arnauld 1990, p. 194) Descartes agrees that universals are mental abstractions, which cannot be constituents of actual beings.[19] This important point is often overlooked.[20] Present-day readers are likely to assume that the essence of a mind is the activity of thinking in general. There can be no doubt that this is not Descartes' view.

Descartes does not deny that all and only modes of a mind belong to a kind. The point is that the relation between the nature of a mind and its modes is not the relation that thinking in general has to either sorts of thinking or instances of thinking. The remark that thinking in general includes, or comprehends, all modes of thinking may refer either to relations of subsumption among concepts or the relation among members in a concept's extension. Entirely different from either of these, a thinking nature "receives" modes, apparently as effects of efficient causes.[21] This may seem to do little to clarify the conception of thinking nature and its relation to modes, but Arnauld is apparently satisfied, aside from the problem of accounting for the singularity and endurance of particular minds, which he solves for himself. He defends the Cartesian account of the essence of a mind in *Les idées vraies et fausses*, his all-out attack on certain theories urged by Malebranche.

III

Malebranche has his own complaint about those who say that the soul needs nothing more than the God-given faculty of thinking. According to Malebranche, a created mind is causally inefficacious; events in created minds are only occasions for God to cause thoughts in these minds. The following argument is in the service of his contention that it is inconceivable that finite minds have causal powers at all:

---

[19] See especially *Princ.* 1.58–59. [20] See also Glouberman (1978), pp. 320–43.
[21] This is implied by the Latin verb; also see Deferrari and Barry (1948).

I am amazed that the Cartesian gentlemen who so rightly reject the general terms *nature* and *faculty* should so willingly employ them on this occasion. They criticize those who say that fire burns by its *nature*, or that it changes certain bodies into glass by a natural *faculty*, and yet some of them do not hesitate to say that the human mind produces in itself the ideas of all things by its *nature*, because it has the *faculty* of thinking. But, with all due respect, these terms are no more meaningful in their mouths than in the mouth of the Peripatetics. (*Elluc.* 11; Malebranche 1980b, p. 622)

This assumes that Descartes conceives the essence of a mind to be part of the cause of its ideas or thoughts, a readiness to cause them when conditions are right. Because Descartes' explicit statements about the nature of a mind explain neither the basis nor operation of the cause, Malebranche charges him with an error moderns allege against the scholastics. That is defining a power in terms of nothing but its observed effects and then explaining its effects by reference to the power – a famously vacuous mode of explanation. Moreover, those who commit this error are unable to specify the range of possible manifestations of the power except by naming the very effects from which its existence was inferred. Yet, Descartes claims that the essence of a mind precludes the possibility of the mind's having any modes of the sort that inhere in bodies. On Malebranche's interpretation, his account of the essence of mental substance is defective on several crucial counts.

A functional-causal view of the nature of substance is proposed by other seventeenth-century philosophers, such as Locke. Malebranche is not alone in ascribing the model to Descartes.[22] A few texts may lend some credence to this interpretation.[23] Moreover, there are hints that a mind contains incipient causes of thoughts, since it contains innate ideas in the guise of tendencies, or proclivities, for forming thoughts of the objects of the ideas. It is in virtue of these native tendencies that a mind contains within itself apparatus sufficient for it to engage in thinking.

---

[22] Rozemond (1998), p. 9. See also Beck (1965) which notes a tension but suggests a distinction between essence and nature with the latter having the role of cause: nature is the "essence as known, in relation to its actualization in the spatio-temporal series, and therefore not, strictly speaking, as it is in itself" (Beck, 1965, 118–22).

[23] See 7: 160, 2: 113; 7: 8, 2: 7; *Comment on a Certain Broadsheet*, 8b: 358, 1: 302. Consider the following text: "the rational soul *in solâ cogitatione, sive cogitandi facultate, ac interno principio (supple ad cogitandum) consistere*" (8b: 347). It is often translated in causal terms: the rational soul is "the inward source (sc. of thinking)" (Haldane and Ross 1979, 1.34), or "the internal principle by means of which we think' (CSM 1.296). But on a more literal translation: the rational soul "consists only in the faculty of thinking, or the internal principle (add: of thinking)," where the parenthetical remark is an instruction to the reader. (I am indebted to Ken Winkler for help with this translation.)

Still, if Descartes envisages an operational mechanism from which particular thoughts result, it is nowhere in view in passages on the nature, or essence, of a thinking substance. Malebranche isolates a strain in Descartes' theory of mind which, even though present, is not part of his basic account of the nature of mental substance. That account is intended to explain metaphysical properties of the substance such as its independence, individuality, its possible modes, and endurance in change.

IV

Taking stock, the nature of a substance delimits its possible accidents; it is a structure on which the existence of modes depends; it excludes all modes of other substances from existing in it.[24] We are also told that it has more reality than its modes.[25] An informative account that satisfies these demands is difficult to find in the texts. Familiar passages such as the following state necessary truths:[26] the faculties of imagination and sense perception cannot be understood "without ... an intellectual substance to inhere in" (7: 78, 2: 54). Again, "Size, figure, motion ... cannot be thought of apart from local extension" (7: 176, 2: 124). They say nothing about the metaphysical arrangements in virtue of which they are true.[27]

Some texts place the substance–essence–mode connection in a familiar problem space: why is it that several things form one thing?

Notice that if we have different ideas of two things, there are two ways in which they can be taken to be one and the same thing: either in virtue of the unity or identity of their nature, or else merely in respect of unity of composition. For example, the ideas we have of shape and of motion are not the same, nor are our ideas of understanding and volition, nor are those of bones and flesh, nor are those of thought, and of an extended thing. (7: 423, 2: 286)

Flesh and bones, if found in the same animal, are "one and the same" because of a unity of composition; so are a thinking thing and an extended thing if found in the same human being. Such compositional unities are not just wholes composed of parts, but also functional unities, which comprise a causal apparatus. But unity of nature is of an entirely different kind.

---

[24] See 7: 227, 2: 159; 7: 78, 2: 54.

[25] See 7: 41–44, 2: 28–29, 30–31; 7: 165, 2: 117.

[26] They reiterate *Princ.* 1.60–62, which cites as the criterion for distinguishing modes from principle attributes and substances, that the former cannot be conceived without the latter, whereas the latter can be conceived without the former.

[27] Also Secada (2000), pp. 195 and 209, on the theory of distinctions in *Princ.* 1.53.

Things with unity of nature have a mutual affinity:

[I]t cannot be supposed that one substance is the subject of shape, and another substance is the subject of local motion etc., since all these acts come together beneath a common account pertaining to extension [*conveniunt sub unâ communi ratione extensionis*], as understanding, willing, and so on agree under a common account belonging to a thinking thing [*ratione communi cogitationis*] … [but] acts of thought have no affinity with corporeal acts, and thought, which is their common account is different in kind from extension, which is the common account of the others. (7: 176, 2: 125; translation altered)

Although *communi ratione* is often translated "common concept," I have used "common account" instead. A *ratio* might be any intelligible basis of unity, including a plan, theory, order, rule, and so on.[28] In connection with a classical instance of the unity question, the problem of universals, Descartes is a conceptualist. Along similar lines, we might ask whether he has a realist or conceptualist view of what unifies the modes of the same substance.

A realist account might be modeled on the doctrine of determinable and determinate characteristics. As Jorge Secada points out, the relation between a determinable and its determinates fits many things Descartes says about the inherence relation.[29] To be more precise, the essence of a substance can be regarded as a highest-order determinable and the modes of the substance, as either lower-order determinables, for example, faculties of judging, imagining, willing, or its determinates, particular acts of judging, imagining, etc. This model provides neat explanations of the metaphysical properties of a substance, according to Descartes. For instance, following W. E. Johnson's analysis of change, we might say that the essence of a substance is a determinable character which the substance continually manifests by its determinates.[30] Two determinates of the same determinable cannot characterize the same subject at the same time. It is true that an act of thought is simultaneously determinate with regard to intentional object and attitude (imagining, willing, etc.); in the same way, a body has at once a determinate size and figure. This is because a determinable may have several dimensions which are determined independently of each other but cannot be separated;[31] the intentional object and attitude that determine an act of thought are, then, dimensions of the one

---

[28] The term is *raison commune* in the French version.
[29] Secada (2000), pp. 184–96. Secada mentions no specific version of the distinction, but Johnson (1921) is the classic source.
[30] Johnson (1921), 3: 84–86.
[31] Johnson (1921), 1: 182 cites hue, saturation, and brightness as dimensions of color.

determinable, thought. Because two determinates of the same determinable cannot characterize a subject at once, a substance which manifests two or more determinates of its essential determinable undergoes change. The substance and determinable character endure as its determinates arise and perish. Furthermore, the model can explain the basis on which a substantial essence limits the modes of a substance and excludes the modes of any other substance; the possible modes of a given substance are all and only determinate values of the determinable nature of the substance. With regard to the particular and determinate nature of a mind, it is suggested that an individual mind is characterized by a determinable unique to it; so, for example, no mode of Descartes' mind could possibly be a mode of the mind of Arnauld. Finally, a determinable does not collect determinates in the manner in which a universal unites its species or its instances. A determinable is not a general feature F which can be ascribed to all its determinates; nor can its determinates be defined in terms of a genus and difference.[32] In this way, the suggestion that a substantial essence is a determinable serves to distance the mode–essence relation from the instance–kind relation. But although the twentieth-century logical-metaphysical theory is in some ways suited for the explanatory role required of a theory of substance, it is not available to a seventeenth-century philosopher. Descartes is not interested in the logical issues addressed by the doctrine of determinables; he does not propose to replace the view that predicate adjectives are ordered by genera and species with the view that they are related as determinables and determinates. He does not deny that modes of thought belong to the kind, thoughts, but only denies that modes are related to the nature, thought, as instances to kinds. At best, one might say that Descartes' theory in some ways anticipates the later doctrine.

This much is plainly true, the essence of a Cartesian substance is, broadly speaking, undetermined in respects in which its modes determine it. We should seek to model this on exemplars of relatively more and less determined entities which are accessible in the seventeenth century. Along these lines, Glouberman argues that a substantial essence is a universal in context of Descartes' conceptualist theory of universals.[33]

Although some texts on the relation between modes and a substance argue from a perceived mode to a substantial nature, which then seems to unify many modes, Glouberman observes that other passages stress the enumeration of the modes of a substance, for example step (iii) in the *res cogitans*

---

[32] Johnson (1921), 1: 172–85 intends the doctrine of determinables to replace the theory of genus and species for purposes of logic and metaphysics.

[33] Glouberman (1978).

reasoning.[34] He contends that the mode–nature connection is not funda-mental. Texts that review modes of a substance address the question what it is for two or more modes to come together in one substance. Glouberman urges that the latter have more theoretical importance than mode–essence passages. As he sees it, the fundamental substance-constituting relation is a uni-level relation which holds among all and only modes comprised in the same substance. He thinks of this as a relation expressed by an iterative rule that can be applied to one particular mode to derive another, and so on for all modes of the same substance. The result is a "modal totality," which, he suggests, should be identified with a Cartesian substance. The substance is nothing but its modes, taken together. We might, then, naturally take the nature of a substance to be the general rule. As such, it is a universal even though it is "tied down" to a particular series by application to one of its concrete segments. But Descartes rates universals as mental abstractions. "The relevant implication is that Cartesian principal attributes (sc. substan-tial essences or natures) are partially abstract vis-à-vis the modal features which, in their totality constitute a substance."[35] Descartes is said to tolerate this element of abstraction in arguing for the real distinction to compensate for the fact that human knowledge of the modes that belong to any par-ticular body or mind is inevitably inadequate.[36] Nevertheless, no abstrac-tion is metaphysically basic according to Descartes. In concrete reality, a substance is a modal totality.

Elegant as this is, it is difficult to square with two closely related doc-trines of Descartes: (i) the modes of a substance depend on the substance and its nature, and the latter do not depend on its modes;[37] (ii) the sub-stance has more reality than its modes. Contrary to (i), the totality of modes (here taken to be the substance) depends on each of the modes it comprises, since the whole does not exist unless its parts exist. Doctrine (ii) mentions a property of special importance because reference to it is indispensable in the proof of the existence of God in Meditation 3.[38] The *Meditations* and Replies suggest that the reality of a thing is a measure of its metaphysical independence: apparently A is more real than B just in case fewer beings are necessary for the existence of A than for B.[39] In view

---

[34] Also 7: 360, 2: 247.   [35] Glouberman (1978), p. 342.

[36] See 7: 221–22, 2: 156.

[37] "In the case of created things, some are of such a nature that they cannot exist without other things, while some need only the ordinary concurrence of God in order to exist. We make this distinction by calling the latter 'substances' and the former 'qualities' or 'attributes' of those substances" (*Princ.* 1.51; French translation, 9B: 47, 1: 210).

[38] See 7: 166, 2: 117.

[39] See 7: 160–68, 2: 113–18; 7: 185, 2: 130.

of (ii), if the present interpretation is right, then it should turn out that the number of things necessary for the existence of a modal totality is fewer than that required for the existence of one of its modes. Yet each of its members is necessary for the existence of the totality; the sum of modes requires as many beings as it has modes. As for its modes, granted that the rule that connects all modes of the same mind assures that all previous thoughts of a mind are necessary for each of its successive thoughts, it would seem to follow that the number of entities required for the existence of the totality is equal to or greater than the number required for each of its modes. It seems, then, that a substance is not more real than any of its modes. The interpretation faces a further problem explaining what there is in a mind that undergoes change. If a mode is added to a totality, the result is a numerically different totality.

We have said that thinking *qua* nature of a substance is undetermined in some respect in which its modes determine the substance and, further, the nature is more metaphysically independent than the modes. To us, nowadays, it may seem difficult to satisfy these two demands. The set of actual modes is an asymmetrical supervenience base for the set of actual natures, a fact which inclines us to say that modes are metaphysically more basic than natures. The discrepancy between present-day views and those of Descartes can be explained by a Neoplatonist doctrine still current in the seventeenth century. It accords metaphysical primacy (and perfection) to an intrinsically unlimited being which grounds the possibility of limited beings. This ground is conceptual, as well as causal; that is, the concept of the infinite does not include the finite, but the concept of the finite includes the infinite.[40] This asymmetric relation can be adapted to finite beings. A subject with an essence undetermined in some respect is then considered to be replete with the possibility of states that determine it in this respect. This is the model on which to understand Descartes' theory of the relation between a substantial essence and its modes, as I suggest.

Because the nature of a mind is undetermined with regard to intentional objects of thought and attitude toward them, the mind is capable of having a variety of particular thoughts determined in these respects. The existence of the nature grounds the possibility of the mind's having any one of a vast number of determinate thoughts. That is, the existence of the thinking nature is a conceptually and causally necessary condition

---

[40] On the infinity of God, see letter to Clerselier (5: 356, 3: 377). Also see Malebranche (1980b), Dialogue VIII.

of the existence of the mind's particular thoughts, but the nature does not determine which possible thoughts the mind actually has. This comports with the *res cogitans* argument, which claims to show that the meditator's particular thoughts cannot be conceived without his thinking nature, and the latter can be conceived without any thought in particular. This is important because the nature has more reality than its modes, according to Descartes. If the nature of a mind, taken alone, comprised the actual modes of the mind, and the nature could not be conceived without these very modes, then the existence of the modes would be, trivially, a necessary condition for the existence of the nature; then the reality of nature and mode would be on a par.[41] The Cartesian doctrine of degrees of reality points to a metaphysical dependence relation hardly familiar nowadays, on which a thing is dependent on a conceptually and causally necessary condition of its existence which makes it possible.

Descartes characterizes the essence of a mind in two ways, as the faculty of thinking and as thinking undetermined in respect of intentional object, etc. They are two ways of describing the same ground of possibility. Manifestations of the faculty are acts of the mind determined with regard to intentional objects, etc. Because something in addition to the nature is needed for the existence of the modes, the doctrine that the nature has more reality than its modes is repected. Yet Descartes maintains that the essence of a mind consists in thinking. Evidently he supposes that the existence of a mind, whose nature is to think, is sufficient for its having actual thoughts, as we argued in section 3. Descartes walks a thin line, as I understand it. A thinking substance and its nature depend on God's concurrence alone; its modes need in addition an efficient cause which is not entirely comprised in the nature. The substantial nature establishes just that the substance can receive a range of possible modes; its actual modes are due to efficient causes at least partly extrinsic to this nature considered in itself. The need for an efficient cause not only preserves the doctrine of reality, but also promises to explain why a substance, which cannot be prevented from exerting its thinking nature, still does not form all the thoughts it is capable of having. Yet, to return to the central point, the nature of a created mind, strictly taken, does not include the full causal mechanism that produces its modes. I can only conclude that Descartes is committed to saying that a finite thinking substance encompasses a causal apparatus in addition to the three elements we mentioned at the

---

[41] The reality of God is greater than that of creatures, but I would not want to say, similarly, that the existence of the essence of God is not sufficient for the creatures God causes and sustains, according to Descartes. Why there should be this difference between God and creatures needs more attention than I can give it here.

start: a nature, several modes, and the inherence relation. Apparently he holds that nothing more than these three elements is relevant to a theory intended to explain the distinctively metaphysical properties of a finite substance.

If we are right, then "unity of nature" can be explicated as follows: a substantial essence is (an) F which is undetermined in certain respects; F corresponds to a range of things which are determined in these respects. All, and only, things in that range have a unity of nature in relation to F. For example, if undetermined thinking is intellectual representation, it is undetermined with regard to objects represented. All fully determinate acts, or modes, of a thinking substance are unified by being determined in regard to the object they represent. No mode which is not determined in this regard can be party to this unity; in particular, no modes determined in respect of figure, motion, and magnitude.

This suffices for the real distinction, but as mentioned above, this works for Descartes only if the essence of a particular mind is a partially undetermined faculty of thinking unique to it. Because the essence of a substance excludes modes that can belong to other substances, the essence of Descartes excludes thoughts that do, or could, belong to Arnauld. The great difficulty of specifying a partially undetermined faculty of thinking unique to an individual substance was noted by Arnauld, and also by Leibniz: "I admit that there is one principal attribute of every substance which expresses its essence, but if we mean an individual substance, I doubt whether this can be explained in words and especially in a few words" ("Critical thoughts on the General Part of the Principles of Descartes," Pt. 1, Art. 52; G 4.354–92; L. 390).[42]

In conclusion, let me return to an issue mentioned at the start, that we seem to have no notion of thinking insofar as it is supposed to be the essence of a mind. I have suggested that thinking *qua* nature is undetermined in respects which collect all and only the possible determinate acts of the substance; it is a faculty (capacity) to have thoughts, a ground of their possibility which is necessary, but not sufficient, for their existence; it is not the full cause of particular thoughts. Although this is not a familiar notion of thinking nowadays, and even Arnauld doesn't understand it at once, it is intelligible in the context of technical notions adapted from Neoplatonist thought.

---

[42] Leibniz [1875–90] (1965), 4.354–92; Loemker (1989), p. 390. For Leibniz, such an account has the form of a rule or the law of a series; see e.g. marginal notes in Loemker (1989), p. 155.

CHAPTER 5

Causation and causal axioms

Tad M. Schmaltz

The authors of the Second Objections [→ audience] end their critical remarks on the *Meditations* by requesting that Descartes set out the arguments in his text "in geometrical order" (*more geometrico*), starting with definitions, postulates, and axioms, so that they could be comprehended "as it were at a single glance" (7: 128, 2: 92). In his Second Replies, Descartes protests that this manner of presentation is not suitable for metaphysical subjects, but nonetheless obliges his critics by offering a "short exposition" in this style of arguments for selected conclusions in the *Meditations* (7: 159, 2: 113). Included in this exposition is a list of "axioms or common notions," three of which directly concern the nature of causation. The first of these axioms states that one can always seek the "cause or reason" of the existence of a thing, the second that the same sort of cause is required for conserving an object in existence as would be required to create that object anew, and the third that an effect must be contained "formally or eminently" in its "efficient and total" cause (7: 164–65, 2: 116).

This chapter is devoted to a consideration of the role that these axioms play in the *Meditations*. I also explore the ways in which the axioms are indebted to, but also deviate from, early modern scholastic discussions of causation, emphasizing in particular the discussion in the *Metaphysical Disputations* of the early modern Jesuit Francisco Suárez. This text, which was known to Descartes,[1] includes what is perhaps the most comprehensive treatment of causation in the early modern period.[2] Though Descartes' rhetoric may encourage the view that the axioms derive simply from his unaided natural reason, it is clear that his use of the axioms

---

[1] Descartes refers to Suárez's discussion of material falsity in the *Metaphysical Disputations* in the Fourth Replies, at 7: 235, 2: 164.

[2] The discussion of causation, which spans Disputations XII through XXVII, covers a total of 590 pages in the Vivès edition of the *Metaphysical Disputations* (reprinted in Suárez 1965), about a third of the total work.

involves a grappling with the understanding of causation dominant in the schools. → Purpose sentence 3

I take up Descartes' axioms in reverse order. The third axiom, which I call the Causal Containment Axiom (CCA), is the most prominent of the three axioms in the *Meditations*. The axiom itself is borrowed from scholastic discussions of causation, which appeal to the need for the "formal or eminent containment" of the entire "perfection" of an effect in its "total" cause. However, I argue that Descartes' actual use of this axiom in the Third and Sixth Meditations reveals an understanding of both formal and eminent containment that not only differs from scholastic views such as that found in Suárez, but also is in some tension with his own definitions in the Second Replies of these kinds of containment.

The second axiom – the Conservation-Is-Creation Axiom (C-I-CA) – is important for one of Descartes' arguments for the existence of God in the Third Meditation, according to which he depends on God at each moment for his own existence. It is not uncommon for commentators to take this argument to assume a "cinematic" view of conservation, according to which God conserves the world by constantly re-creating it anew at each moment. However, I claim that in this case Descartes hewed to the line in Suárez that divine conservation consists in the mere continuation of the efficient causality involved in God's initial act of creation *ex nihilo*.

→ They say

→ I say

The first axiom – the Universal Causation Axiom (UCA) – is linked to controversies over the implication in the Third Meditation that God is *causa sui*, a being that derives its existence from itself. I show how Descartes attempts to respond to scholastic objections to this implication of the axiom by denying that it requires that God is an efficient cause of his own existence. In contrast to the case of the first two axioms, this axiom is meant to expand the notion of causation beyond the paradigmatic case of efficient causality.

→ purpose / in order to sentence 3

I CAUSAL CONTAINMENT AXIOM (CCA)

In the Second Replies, Descartes takes as axiomatic that "whatever is of reality or perfection in some thing is formally or eminently in the first and adequate cause of it" (*quidquid est realitatis sive perfectionis in aliqua re, est formaliter vel eminenter in prima & acaequanta ejus causa*) (7: 165, 2: 116). This axiom plays a crucial role in the *Meditations*. For instance, it is central to the two arguments in the Third Meditation for the existence of God, both of which require that the cause of our idea of God formally contain everything that is contained objectively in this idea (7: 40–47,

human beings can only create the ideas of material things and not material things—Descartes. The anonymous writer says then humans can create the world → Descartes says lets keep it to a rule about ideas—eminent containment.

2: 28–32; and 7: 48–51, 2: 33–35).[3] But there also is the argument for the material world in the Sixth Meditation, which has as its conclusion that the cause of the objective reality of our sensory ideas is not something "more noble than body" that contains this reality only eminently, but rather a body that formally contains the reality (7: 79–80, 2: 55).

In the Third Meditation, Descartes suggests that his knowledge of the axiom that a cause contains its reality formally or eminently – that is, CCA – derives simply from his own "natural light," since this light reveals that "there must be at least as much in the efficient and total cause as in the effect of that cause" (7: 40, 2: 28). However, in this case it is clear that Descartes' views were conditioned by his scholastic upbringing. For instance, in his *Metaphysical Disputations* Suárez offers the following explication of a causal principle that one finds in other scholastic texts:

[A]n effect cannot exceed in perfection all of its causes taken together. It is proved that nothing of perfection is in the effect that it does not have from its cause; therefore the effect can have nothing of perfection that does not pre-exist in any of its causes, either formally or eminently, because causes cannot give what they in no way contain. (*MD* XXVI.1.2, 1: 916)[4]

Descartes' insistence that all of the effect be contained in the total cause is reflected in Suárez's claim that the perfection of the effect is contained in "all of its causes taken together." And though Suárez does not explicitly restrict his principle to efficient causes, he makes clear that such causes best satisfy his stipulation that "a cause is a *per se* principle from which being flows into another [*influens esse in aliud*]" (*MD* XII.2.4, 1: 384). This view that efficient causes are most properly said to inflow being into another clears the way for Descartes' claim in the Third Meditation that the requirement of CCA that a cause contain its effect applies specifically not only to total but also to efficient causes.[5]

What requires explanation at this point, however, is what it means to say that the total and efficient cause contains its effect "formally or eminently." Descartes offers technical definitions of the notions of formal and eminent containment when he says in the Second Replies that things "are said to be *formally* in the objects of ideas, when they are such as we perceive them [*talia sunt in ipsis qualia illa percipimus*], and *eminently*, when

---

[3] For the difference between the two arguments, see the remarks at the beginning of section 2 of this chapter.

[4] *MD* = Suárez 1965; cited by disputation, section, and paragraph, and volume and page.

[5] For documentation of Suárez's position that among the four Aristotelian causes, the notion of cause applies best to the case of efficient causes, see Schmaltz (2008), section 1.2.2. For more on Descartes' restriction of CCA to efficient and total causes, see Schmaltz (2008), section 2.1.2.

they are not such [as we perceive], but so great that they can take the place of such things [that are such as we perceive] [*quando non quidem talia sunt, sed tanta, ut talium vicem supplere possint*]" (7: 161, 2: 114). I want to claim, however, that the actual examples of formal and eminent containment that Descartes offers in the *Meditations* reveal that these definitions are in varying degrees problematic.

(i) *Formal containment.* In the Third Meditation, Descartes illustrates CCA by noting that heat cannot be induced in a subject "unless from a cause of at least the same order of perfection as heat" (7: 41, 2: 28). Similarly, Suárez earlier used the case of "fire when generating fire" as an example of a "univocal cause," that is, one which "effects an effect of the same kind" (*efficit effectum ejusdem rationis*) (*MD* XVII.2.21, 1: 591). Yet the specific accounts that Suárez and Descartes offer of the sort of containment present in this particular case differ. Whereas Suárez held that the heat of both the generating and generated fire is a real accident that is a *res* distinct from the fire itself, Descartes rejects the containment of any such *res* in a purely material being. In Descartes' view, the physical heat (as opposed to the sensation of heat) that the body contains and produces can be only a certain kind of local motion of its parts.[6]

However, this disagreement concerns only what is formally contained in particular cases, and not the very notion of formal containment. In order to understand the relation of Descartes' notion to what we find in the work of the scholastics, it is helpful to start with the definition that he offers in the Second Replies. A distinctive feature of this definition is its mentalist cast, as reflected in its reference not only to what is in the "objects of ideas," but also to features of objects that are "such as we perceive them." This connection between our perceptions or ideas and their objects is further mediated by the objective reality of an idea, which Descartes defines in the Second Replies – just prior to defining formal and eminent containment – as "the entity of the thing represented by the idea [*entitatem rei repraesentatae per ideam*], insofar as it is in the idea ... For whatever we perceive as in the objects of ideas, they are in the ideas themselves objectively" (7: 161, 2: 113). For Descartes, then, the paradigmatic case of formal containment is one in which the entity as it exists outside of our idea is "such as" the reality insofar as it is represented by our idea.

Although the notion of objective reality, along with the notions of formal and eminent containment, may seem to be fairly scholastic in

---

[6] See, for instance, Descartes' account of heat in his early work *The World*, at 11: 7–10, 1: 83–84.

nature, there was in fact some scholastic resistance to Descartes' view that objective reality is a kind of "entity" in ideas. Thus, in the First Objections, the Dutch scholastic Johan de Kater, or Caterus, objects to Descartes that "objective being" is "the act of intellect itself terminating through a mode of the object," and thus is merely "an extrinsic denomination, and nothing real" (7: 92, 2: 66–67). The denomination of the act of intellect as possessing objective being is merely "extrinsic" since the being belongs to the object toward which the act is directed, rather than to the act itself.[7]

Caterus' understanding admittedly reflects a more Thomistic view; Scotists were inclined to posit an "objective concept" as a *tertium quid* between the act of intellect and the cognized object. But on this particular point Suárez sided with the Thomists, holding that the reality that exists in an idea (or, as he put it, in an objective concept) is nothing other than the reality of the object itself.

Even given these differences on points of technical detail, though, it seems that Suárez could agree with Descartes on the basic point that an object formally contains all that which is "such as we perceive it." At least in the case of clear and distinct perceptions, there is a fairly straightforward sense for Descartes in which objects are such as we perceive them to be. After all, he emphasizes in the Sixth Meditation that everything is in bodies "that I clearly and distinctly understand, that is, all that, viewed generally, are comprehended in the object of pure mathematics" (7: 80, 2: 55). Here we do appear to have a case in which the objects of our ideas are such as we perceive them.

Nonetheless, Descartes does not restrict CCA to clear and distinct ideas. Indeed, his Sixth Meditation argument for the material world invokes the axiom specifically in the case of the causation of our confused and obscure sensory ideas. In that text, the axiom underlies the argument that bodies must exist as causes that formally contain the reality that is present objectively in our sensory ideas. As far as the Sixth Meditation is concerned, then, CCA applies primarily to the case of the causation of the objective reality of our sensory ideas.

 However, it is just in the case of sense perception that Descartes' own definition of formal containment seems to be most problematic. For one thing, there is scholarly disagreement over whether Descartes even allowed

---

[7] By the same token, 'being known' is an extrinsic denomination of the object known since it is known simply in virtue of a feature of the intellect, and not in virtue of anything in itself.

that bodily features are present objectively in sensory ideas.[8] I myself take the Sixth Meditation argument to indicate clearly enough that he did intend to allow for such containment. Without the assumption that sensory ideas have an objective reality that requires a cause, this argument could not even get off the ground. Nonetheless, it must be admitted that Descartes' claim in the Second Replies that features that exist formally in objects are "such as we perceive them" seems at least initially to fail in the case of sensory ideas. For just before claiming that bodies have everything that we clearly and distinctly perceive to be in the object of pure mathematics, Descartes warns that bodies may not exist "in a way that is entirely such as [*talia omnino ... qualia*] the senses comprehend them, insofar as the comprehension of the senses is in many cases very obscure and confused" (7: 80, 2: 55). I have mentioned Descartes' view that heat as it exists in bodies is nothing more than a certain motion of their parts, and thus something that does not resemble our sensation of the heat. Given this view, it seems very difficult for him to say without considerable qualification that we sense heat such as it is in the object.

One possible response is that Descartes claims in the Second Replies not, as in the Sixth Meditation, that objects are "entirely such as" we perceive them, but merely that they are not "such as" we perceive them. So perhaps there is no formal contradiction here.[9] Even so, it still seems that the Second Replies definition is best suited to the case of clear and distinct perceptions of objects, and that for Descartes, though not for the scholastic, an object can be "such as" we sense it only in a very attenuated sense.[10]

(ii) *Eminent containment.* I have noted the obscurity of Descartes' claim in the Second Replies that objects eminently contain what "indeed is not such [as we perceive], but so great that it is able to take the place of such things [that are such as we perceive]" (7: 161, 2: 114). Eminent containment is supposed to accommodate cases in which the cause differs in nature from its effect, and so cannot contain this effect "such as we perceive it." However, contemporary critics such as Daisie Radner have objected that Descartes in fact has no coherent conception of eminent containment, and thus has no clear explanation of a case in which a cause

---

[8] The disagreement is most evident in the massive literature on Descartes' account in the Third Meditation of "material falsity." For a review of this literature, see Kaufman (2000).

[9] For an emphasis on this point, see Carriero and Hoffman (1990), pp. 101–2.

[10] In Schmaltz (2008), pp. 66–67, I appeal to Descartes' suggestion that sensory ideas direct the mind to qualities in virtue of their regular causal connections to those qualities in support of the proposal that bodies formally contain what is in our sensory ideas in the sense that they have the qualities to which those ideas direct the mind.

produces an effect that differs in nature from it (1985b, pp. 232, 233–34).
This objection is behind the charge in Radner and others that Descartes'
CCA precludes the causal interaction of objects with different natures. In
particular, it precludes the interaction of mind and body given that, for
Descartes, the mind as a thinking thing differs in nature from the body
as an extended thing.[11]

In order to address this charge, we need to start with Descartes' technical definition of eminent containment, which will indeed turn out to
be problematic in certain respects. One striking feature of this definition is that it seems to fit in a fairly straightforward manner a scholastic understanding of eminent containment. At one point, for instance,
Suárez notes that a heavy body (unum grave) that moves another heavy
body to a particular place contains that place "virtually or eminently, but
not formally" since that place is contained only in the "active principle"
that brings about the downward motion (MD XVIII.9.10, I: 671). When
the heavy body is in that place, the place can be said to be in the body
"such as we perceive it," and so, in Descartes' view, be contained there
formally. In the case where the body is not in the place "as we perceive it,"
it can nonetheless be said to be there eminently insofar as the body has
an active principle that is "so great" that it can stand in for the place by
possessing it "virtually."

But if Descartes' definition of eminent containment fits Suárez's
example fairly well, the same cannot be said for his own example of eminent containment in the Sixth Meditation. There Descartes considers the
containment of the objective reality of our sensory ideas either in God
or in something "more noble than body," namely, some finite thinking
thing.[12] With respect to this example, it is not the case that what is eminently contained in the object of our idea is something so great that it can
take the place of what we perceive in the object. For one thing, the objects
that contain the reality of our sensory ideas are neither God nor things
more noble than body, but rather bodies themselves. Bodily qualities are
supposed to be eminently contained in some object that differs from the
objects of our sensory ideas insofar as the former object has features that
are "so great" that they can "take the place of" such qualities.

---

[11] See Radner (1985a). Cf. Gorham (2003). For the apologetic rejoinder that Descartes' view of
causation allows for the causal interaction of dissimilar objects, and thus for genuine mind–
body interaction, see Loeb (1981), pp. 134–56; Richardson (1982); Loeb (1985); Richardson (1985);
and O'Neill (1987).

[12] See, for instance, Descartes' claim to Elizabeth that our soul "is much more noble [beaucoup plus
noble] than body" (4: 292, 3: 266).

My own sense is that if we are to capture Descartes' understanding of eminent containment, we are better off following his example of such containment in the Sixth Meditation and not the rather scholastic definition of it in the Second Replies. An initially puzzling feature of the example is that the suggestion that finite minds are more noble than body does not seem to be reflected in the ontological hierarchy that Descartes sometimes links to CCA. The statement of this axiom in the Second Replies refers to the "reality or perfection" of the effect, and in another axiom he explicates this feature of the effect in terms of the fact that "substance has more reality than an accident or a mode, and infinite substance more than finite substance" (7: 165, 2: 117). According to this ontological hierarchy, finite mental substance is on the same level of reality as finite bodily substance.

This hierarchy suffices for the purposes of the use of CCA in the Third Meditation, which after all focuses on the existence of God as infinite substance, and thus does not need to consider differences among finite substances. However, Descartes emphasizes in the Sixth Meditation that "there is a great difference between mind and body, inasmuch as body is by its very nature divisible, whereas mind is utterly indivisible" (7: 85–86, 2: 59). This difference indicates the greater nobility of mind given the principle in the Second Replies that "it is known *per se* that it is a greater perfection to be undivided than to be divided" (7: 138, 2: 99). These remarks suggest an "enhanced" ontological hierarchy in which God as infinite substance remains at the top and modes of finite substances at the bottom, but in which minds as indivisible finite substances have more reality, or are more noble, than bodies as divisible finite substances.

In emphasizing that bodily qualities are eminently contained in something more noble than bodies, Descartes suggests that the eminent containment of a feature requires that the containing object be higher in the (enhanced) ontological hierarchy than what contains this feature formally. This suggestion is captured by the analysis of eminent containment that Eileen O'Neill has offered on Descartes' behalf. On this analysis, it is a necessary condition of a property ø being eminently contained in an object X that (i) "ø is not formally contained in X," and (ii) "X is an entity displaying a greater degree of relative independence than any possible Y which could contain ø formally (i.e., higher up in the ontological hierarchy than any such Y)" (1987, p. 235).[13] Thus, God or minds can

---

[13] But cf. the alternative analyses of eminent containment in Clatterbaugh (1980) and Gorham (2003).

eminently contain sensory qualities in bodies since they do not formally contain those qualities, and since they are higher in the (enhanced) onto-logical hierarchy than the bodies that do formally contain the qualities.

However, this analysis would not satisfy critics of Descartes' notion of eminent containment, since they are looking for an account of precisely how features are so contained. In terms of the definition in the Second Replies, the challenge is to explain what it is in God or finite minds that is so great that it can take the place of bodies and their modifications. One obvious proposal is that even though God and finite minds cannot formally contain features of the material world, they do have the power to represent such features in thought. An account of eminent containment in terms of this power could provide an initial response to the objection that CCA cannot allow for the interaction of objects with different natures insofar as it is restricted to formal containment.

There is further textual evidence for attributing such an account to Descartes in one of the rare texts outside of the *Meditations* in which he explicitly discusses eminent containment. This text is from a 1641 exchange with his pseudonymous critic "Hyperaspistes." This critic objected that in Descartes' view, "since a corporeal thing is not more noble than the idea that the mind has of it, and mind contains bodies eminently, it follows that all bodies, and thus the whole of this visible world, can be produced by the human mind" (AT 3: 404). Such an implication is said to be prob-lematic insofar as it undermines our confidence that God alone created the visible world. In response, Descartes does not dispute that our mind emi-nently contains the visible world, but only protests that we can produce "not, as objected, the whole of this visible world, but the idea of the whole of things that are in this visible world" (3: 428, 3: 193). The suggestion here is that the whole visible world is eminently contained in our mind in the sense that we have the power to produce the idea of this world. In apply-ing this suggestion to the example in the Sixth Meditation, we have the view that minds can eminently contain bodily qualities in virtue of the fact that they have the power to produce the reality present objectively in our sensory ideas of those qualities.

The exchange with Hyperaspistes also reveals the need to modify the third condition for eminent containment that O'Neill takes to be neces-sary (and with the other two conditions indicated previously, sufficient) for eminent containment. This condition is that (iii) "X has the power to bring about the existence of ø" (1987, p. 235). In defense of this condition, she appeals to Suárez's claim that "what is said to contain eminently has a perfection of such a superior nature that it contains by means of power [*virtute*] whatever is in the inferior perfection," where this power is said to be the power that "can produce [*potest … efficere*]" the inferior perfection (*MD* xxx.i.io, 2: 63, cited in O'Neill [1987], p. 239). But though Descartes obviously was influenced by the scholastic view that the effect must be contained formally or eminently in its total and efficient cause, his remarks to Hyperaspistes indicate that he did not adopt Suárez's particular account of eminent containment. According to these remarks, eminent containment requires the power to produce not ø itself, but only the idea of ø, or more specifically, the objective reality of this idea.[14]

This alteration of O'Neill's account may seem to be minor, but in fact I think it serves to highlight an important difference between the accounts of eminent containment in Suárez and Descartes. Suárez had no difficulty applying the notion of eminent containment to the case of bodily causes, as in his previously noted discussion of the containment of the future place of a heavy body in that body itself. Though this discussion seems to be in line with the definition of eminent containment in the Second Replies, Descartes' discussion of this same example reflects a different understanding of this sort of containment. In the Sixth Replies, Descartes cites the misguided thought he had in his youth that "heaviness [*gravitas*] carried bodies toward the center of the earth, as if it contained in itself some cognition of this" (7: 442, 2: 298). What is interesting is that Descartes apparently assumes that a future effect not actually present in the object can be contained in that object only by means of cognition. Implicit in this assumption is the rejection of the view in Suárez that there can be qualities or powers in bodies "more noble than" bodily effects that eminently contain those effects. Descartes' own examples of eminent containment suggest that all alterable features of body have the same kind of reality as modes of extension, and that only an infinite mind or finite minds can have the sort of nobility that allows for the eminent containment of bodies and their modifications. For Descartes, then, the bodily principle that Suárez posited as eminently containing its effect could be conceived only on the model of a mind that acts in accord with

---

[14] Whereas Suárez invoked God's eminent containment of an object in order to explain the fact that he can create such an object, the emphasis in the *Meditations* is on God's production of the *objective reality* of our ideas (that is, in the Third Meditation, of our idea of God, and in the Sixth Meditation, of our sensory ideas). Descartes' considered view seems to be that though eminent containment of the world is a *necessary* condition for God's production of it, it is not *sufficient* for this production. A further consideration is that the production of the world involves the production of substance *ex nihilo*, which is something that Descartes thinks only God can bring about (as indicated in his remarks in the First Replies, at 7: 111). Thanks to Karen Detlefsen for drawing my attention to this issue.

its cognition of an end. In the case of all other total and efficient bodily causes, only formal containment can be at issue.

2 CONSERVATION-IS-CREATION AXIOM (C-I-CA)

I have noted that there are two arguments for the existence of God in the Third Meditation. Both arguments rely on CCA, and both conclude that the total and efficient cause of the objective reality of our idea of God must formally contain everything that is present objectively in that idea. These similarities explain why Descartes says in the First Replies that his second argument is not so much a new argument as "a more thorough examination" of the original argument (7: 106, 2: 77). Nonetheless, there is an element of the second argument that serves to distinguish it from the first. This element is introduced after the first portion of the argument, in which Descartes claims that he cannot have derived his existence from himself since in that case he would have produced in himself all of the perfections he desires but in fact lacks. He then considers the objection that he may not need any cause of his existence now given the assumption that he has always existed. Descartes responds:

[S]ince the whole time of life can be divided into innumerable parts, each single one of which depends in no way on the remaining, from the fact that I was shortly before, it does not follow that I must be now, unless some cause as it were creates me anew at this moment [*me quasi rursus creet ad hoc momentum*], that is conserves me. For it is perspicuous to those attending to the nature of time that entirely the same force and action [*eadem ... vi et actione*] plainly is needed to conserve a thing at each single moment during which it endures, as would be needed to create it anew, if it did not yet exist; to the extent that conservation differing solely by reason from creation is also one of those things that is manifest by the natural light. (7: 49, 2: 33) –page 96 – Descartes

The claim here that "the same force and action is needed to conserve a thing ... as would be needed to create it anew" is reflected in the axiom in the Second Replies – which I have labeled C-I-CA – that "no less a cause is required to conserve a thing than to produce it at first" (7: 165, 2: 116). In the Third Meditation, C-I-CA is said to be perspicuous to those who consider "the nature of time," and is said to yield the result that conservation differs "solely by reason" from creation. The author of the Fifth Objections, Pierre Gassendi, challenges the assumption of C-I-CA in the Third Meditation by claiming that Descartes could have a power to conserve himself that is not a power to create himself anew, but rather a power "that suffices to guarantee that you are preserved unless a corrupting cause intervenes" (7: 302, 2: 210). The suggestion here is that the presence of such a power is revealed by the fact that continuation in existence is the default condition. What requires an external cause is not this continuation, but only the initiation and cessation of existence.

In his response to Gassendi in the Fifth Replies, Descartes insists that the claim that conservation requires the "continual action of the original cause" is "something that all Metaphysicians affirm as manifest." Drawing on remarks from the *Summa Theologiae* of Thomas Aquinas, Descartes appeals to the distinction between "causes of becoming" (*causae secundum fieri*) and "causes of being" (*causae secundum esse*).[15] Descartes also follows Thomas in illustrating the distinction between these two kinds of causes by noting the difference between the builder as the cause *secundum fieri* of the house and the sun as the cause *secundum esse* of the light. Since the builder merely works on pre-existing material, the action of the builder is not required for the house to remain in existence. But since the sun is the cause of the very being of the light, and since God is the cause of the being of the things he creates *ex nihilo*, both must continue to act in order for what they produce to remain in existence (7: 369, 2: 254–55).

Suárez uses the Thomistic analogy to the sun to support Thomas' own conclusion that God conserves creatures by means of the very same act by which he created them. Suárez claims that there is no more justification for saying that God conserves by means of an act distinct from the initial creation *ex nihilo* than there is for saying that the sun continues to propagate light by means of an act distinct from that by which it first produced the light (*MD* xxi.2, 1: 791). In the case of the sun, the difference between production and propagation is merely that the term for the former connotes the prior absence of that light, whereas the term for the latter connotes the prior presence of light. The difference here is only a difference in the manner in which one and the same act is described, and so is a mere "distinction of reason" (*distinctio rationis*), and not any distinction in reality. Likewise, in the case of God the difference between creation and conservation consists in the fact that the term for the former connotes the prior absence of a particular *esse*, whereas the term for the latter connotes the prior presence of that *esse*. Here again, the difference is in the words used to describe the action rather than in the action itself.

Descartes states as an axiom in the Second Replies that "no less a cause is required to conserve something than is required to create it in

---

[15] Aquinas (1964–81), 1a, qu. 104, art. 1, ad 4.

the first place" (7: 165, 2: 116). This axiom may seem to at least allow that the acts of initial creation and subsequent conservation are not token identical, but merely of the same type. Moreover, his claim in the Third Meditation that the whole of his life can be divided into distinct parts, and that he would not exist at a moment "unless some cause as it were creates [him] anew" at that moment, may seem to suggest that a cause must conserve him in existence over time by means of a series of distinct creative acts. Indeed, there is the view that Descartes deviates from scholastic orthodoxy in holding that God must "re-create" an object anew at each moment that it exists. Thus, Alan Gabbey has endorsed the claim in the earlier work of Étienne Gilson that

Descartes and Aquinas differ in their respective interpretations of God's conservation of the world: for Aquinas, conservation is a simple continuation of the creative act, whereas for Descartes it is a re-creation at each (independent) instant. (Gabbey 1980, p. 302n. 40, citing Gilson [1925], pp. 340–42)

The (non-Thomistic and non-Suárezian) position attributed here to Descartes has been described as a "cinematic view" of divine conservation, according to which God conserves an object by creating separately each distinct "frame" of its existence.[16]

However, the evidence from the Third Meditation does not clearly indicate that Descartes is committed to a cinematic view. After all, he says in the Third Meditation not that a cause must create him anew at each moment of his existence, but only that such a cause must "as it were" (*quasi*) so create him. Moreover, he continues by noting that a cause conserves an object with the same force and action that it *would need* to create that object anew *if it did not yet exist*. Again, the language here does not require that an object needs to be revived at each of the various moments of its existence by something that creates it anew at those moments. Finally, in light of the Suárezian context, it is significant that Descartes claims in this text that it is "manifest by the light of nature" that conservation differs from creation "solely by reason" (*sola ratione*) (7: 49, 2: 33). Descartes inherited from Suárez the view that in the case of a distinction of reason there are only different ways of considering one and the same *res*. If Descartes held that there is only a distinction

res -thing

---

[16] For the *locus classicus* of the cinematic interpretation of Descartes, see Gueroult (1953), vol. 1, pp. 272–85.

[17] For Descartes' official account of a distinction of reason, see *Princ.* 1.62 (8a: 30, 1: 214–15). On the relation of his theory of distinctions to the theory we find in Suárez, see Schmaltz (2008), pp. 27–28.

of reason between the initial act of creating an object *ex nihilo* and the subsequent act of conserving that object in existence, he would have to conclude, with Suárez, that there is in this case merely the continuation of the initial act.

Admittedly, Descartes does not indicate explicitly in the relevant Third Meditation passage that the act of conservation is distinct in reason from an initial act of creation *ex nihilo*. However, we do have his endorsement in the *Discourse on the Method* of "an opinion commonly received among the Theologians" that "the action by which [God] now conserves [the world] is entirely the same as [*toute la mesme que*] that by which he has created it" (6: 45, 1: 133). This same theological opinion, which is found in both Thomas and Suárez, is central to Descartes' later claim in the *Principles of Philosophy* that "the world now continues to be conserved by the same action [*eadem actione*] as created it then" (*Princ.* II.42; 8A: 66, 1: 243). Though commentators continue to claim that Descartes identified conservation with "continual re-creation,"[18] it seems clear enough that he accepted rather the view in scholastic "theologians" such as Thomas and Suárez that divine conservation involves merely the continuation of God's initial act of creation *ex nihilo*.

I have noted that Descartes appeals to CCA in the Third Meditation to get from the claim that *some cause* must *quasi* create him anew at each moment to the conclusion that *God* must so create him. However, in the First Replies Descartes indicates a route to that conclusion that bypasses CCA. He writes in that text, "what I have not written before," that when we search for the ultimate cause of our existence, "we arrive in no way at any secondary cause, but altogether at that in which there is such great power that it conserves a thing external to itself, it so much the more has the power to conserve itself, and thus is *a se*" (7: 111, 2: 80). The assumption here seems to be that only something that has the power to conserve itself, and thus exists *a se*, can conserve an object external to itself.[19] There is the suggestion in Descartes – which would have been unobjectionable to a scholastic such as Suárez – that God conserves an object external to himself merely by continuing his act of creating that object *ex nihilo*. As we will see, however, what is objectionable from a scholastic perspective is

---

[18] See e.g. the references to Descartes' "causal re-creationism" at several points in Machamer and McGuire (2009).

[19] There is a version of this "short" argument from conservation to the existence of God in *Princ.* I.21 (8a: 13, 1: 200).

Descartes' further claim that God exists *a se* in the sense that he conserves himself in existence.

3 UNIVERSAL CAUSATION AXIOM (UCA)

Both CCA and C-I-CA concern efficient causes. The former is restricted explicitly to the "efficient and total cause," and though the restriction of C-I-CA to efficient causes is perhaps not as evident, it is significant that Suárez held that conservation is simply a species of efficient causation.[20] Moreover, Descartes himself makes clear that when we consider God's activity in the world, including his conservation of creatures, we must "consider him as the efficient cause of all things" (*Princ.* 1.28, 8A: 15–16, 1: 202).

Indeed, it is tempting to think that Descartes held that efficient causality is the only genuine species of causal activity. Certainly Vincent Carraud suggests as much when he concludes that for Descartes "the expression 'cause efficiente' is henceforth redundant" (2002, p. 179). However, Carraud also draws attention to the notion in early modern philosophers of a "cause or reason" (*causa sive ratio*), and it turns out that Descartes' use of this notion compromises his purported view that only an efficient cause can be causally efficacious.

The notion of a cause or reason emerges from the first of Descartes' causal axioms in the Second Replies. In this text, the axiom is stipulated as follows: "No thing exists of which it cannot be asked what is the cause why it exists [*Nulla res existit de qua non posit quæri quænam sit causa cur existat*]." Descartes anticipates the objection, which we will consider presently, that there can be no cause of existence in the case of God. Thus, he adds the following addendum: "This can be asked even of God himself, not because he needs any cause in order to exist, but because the immensity of his nature itself is the cause or reason [*causa sive ratio*] why he needs no cause to exist" (7: 164–65, 2: 116).

Despite this addendum, the claim that God needs no cause to exist seems to be in some tension with the suggestion in the Third Meditation that God in fact is the efficient cause of his own existence. Thus, in the second argument in that text for the existence of God, there is the claim that God derives his existence from himself. In the course of that argument, Descartes notes that he cannot possess everything contained in his

---

[20] Thus, Disputation XXI, on conservation, is included in a set of disputations devoted to efficient causality (namely, Disputations XVII–XXII).

idea of God since he does not have the power to derive his existence from himself (7: 48, 2: 33). Given the stress on efficient causes in the Third Meditation, it would be natural to take Descartes to say that a being who possesses everything contained in his idea of God must be the efficient cause of its own existence.

In any event, Caterus reads Descartes in just this way, and objects that God can derive his existence from himself only in a negative sense – that is, not from another – and not in a positive sense – that is, from a cause. He adds that this negative sense is the manner "in which everyone takes the phrase" in the case of God (7: 95, 2: 68). Indeed, the view that God has no cause is something of a scholastic commonplace. Thus, Suárez insists that "not all beings comprehended under the object of this science [of metaphysics] have a true and proper cause, for God has no cause" (*MD* XII, 1: 372). This exception in the case of God explains his conclusion later in this text that although "what is said to be *ex se* or *a se* seems to be positive, it adds only a negation, for being cannot be *a se* by a positive origin or emanation" (*MD* XXVIII.1.7, 2: 2).

In light of Descartes' reference to a "cause or reason" in his discussion of UCA, it is noteworthy that Suárez allows that there are certain reasons (*rationes*) for truths concerning God that "are conceived by us as if they are causes of the others" (*concipiuntur a nobis ac si essent causæ aliarum*) (*MD* XII, 1: 372–73). Even so, the claim here is not that the reasons are a kind of cause, but rather that they are merely conceived "as if" they are causes. Thus, Suárez does not anticipate the point in Descartes that the immensity of God's nature is a special kind of cause of his existence.

In any event, Descartes answers Caterus in the First Replies by claiming that it is legitimate to assume that each thing requires an efficient cause of its existence, and so to inquire into its cause. Descartes continues by noting that even though the fact that God has "great and inexhaustible power" reveals that he does not require an external efficient cause for his existence, still since "it is he himself who conserves himself, it does not seem too improper for him to be called *sui causa*" (7: 109, 2: 79). Given that God can be called a *causa sui*, "we are permitted to think that in some manner [*quodammodo*] he stands in the same with respect to himself as an efficient cause stands with respect to its effect, and thus is positively from himself" (7: 111, 2: 80).

Dissatisfied with this explanation, the author of the Fourth Objections, Antoine Arnauld, counters that we must reject the conclusion that God's existence has an efficient cause given that his existence is identical to his essence. Arnauld adds that since nothing can stand in the same relation to itself as an efficient cause does to its effect, God cannot stand in this relation to himself (7: 213–14, 2: 149–50).

Though Descartes protests in the Fourth Replies that Arnauld's complaint "seems to me to the least of all his objections" (7: 235, 2: 164), he responds to it there at some length. He begins by insisting that he had never said that God is an efficient cause of his own existence, but only that God "in some manner" (*quodammodo*) stands in the same relation to his existence as an efficient cause does to its effect. In order to explain more precisely the sense in which God can be said to be the cause of his existence, Descartes appeals to the claim in Aristotle that the essence of a thing can be considered as a "formal cause" of certain features of that thing (7: 242, 2: 169). He concedes to Arnauld that the fact that God's existence is identical to his essence reveals that he does not require an efficient cause, but he claims that God's essence provides a kind of formal cause of his existence that "has a great analogy to the efficient [cause], and thus can be called an efficient cause as it were [*quasi causa efficiens*]" (7: 243, 2: 169).

One has the sense that at this point Descartes was not entirely on top of his game. For instance, it is understandable that Arnauld read the remarks in the First Replies as an attempt to apply the notion of efficient causality to the case of God's existence. After all, Descartes counters Caterus' suggestion that God can derive existence from himself only in a negative sense by claiming that he never denied that something can be the efficient cause of itself (7: 108, 2: 78). Moreover, we have seen that Descartes gives Caterus permission to think that God stands to himself as an efficient cause stands to its effect.

Nonetheless, it is perhaps clear enough that Descartes does not take God literally to be the efficient cause of his own existence, and that when he speaks as if God's existence has such a cause, it was only, as he told Arnauld, "on account of the imperfection of the human intellect" (7: 235, 2: 165). Whereas in the case of all other beings, the reason for existence is provided by an efficient cause, in the case of God the "cause or reason" for existence is merely the rational ground for the truth that his existence requires no efficient cause, which ground is provided by the immensity of his own power or essence. In the end, therefore, Descartes could consistently reject the view that God is the efficient cause of his own existence.

UCA thus requires that there be a reason for the existence of everything, including God, even though in the case of God alone the reason is provided by his power or essence rather than by an efficient cause. However, his claim to Arnauld that we must conceive of the reason for

God's existence as analogous to an efficient cause indicates the imperfection of our grasp of this reason. Descartes notes in the Fourth Replies that we are to understand this reason by extending our conception of an efficient cause to a case where the essence serves as a formal cause of existence. He compares this sort of extension to the extension in geometry of the concept of a rectilinear polygon to the concept of a circle (7: 239–40, 2: 167). Even though the geometrical concepts are not commensurate, our grasp of the nature of polygons can lead us to recognize certain truths concerning circles. In a similar manner, Descartes suggests, the differences between efficient and formal causes do not prevent our understanding that the existence of finite beings must be grounded in efficient causes from yielding a recognition of the fact that a formal cause is required as the reason for God's existence.

But why do we need the comparison to efficient causes in the first place? Why can we not just see directly that God's nature provides a special kind of reason for his existence that does not involve true efficient causality? Descartes did not address this question directly, but it is significant that he appeals in the First and Fourth Replies alike to "great and inexhaustible power" (*tanta et inexhausta potentia*) as the "reason or cause" of God's existence (cf. 7: 110, 2: 79; 7: 236, 2: 165). Even more telling is his claim in the First Replies that this grounding power is "immense and incomprehensible" (*immensam et incomprehensibilem*) (7: 110, 2: 79). This reference to divine incomprehensibility is significant given the prominence of this property in Descartes' discussion of his famous (or infamous) doctrine of the creation of eternal truths. Thus, in the 1630 correspondence with Mersenne that introduces the doctrine, Descartes claims that though "one can know that God is infinite and all-powerful," still it is the case that

our soul being finite [God] can be neither comprehended nor conceived; in the same way that we can touch a mountain with our hands, but one cannot embrace it as we could a tree or some other thing that is not too large for our arms. (1: 152, 3: 25)

Admittedly, this passage directly concerns not the dependence of God's existence on his essence, but rather the dependence of the eternal truths on his free will. Whereas Descartes is emphatic in his remarks to Arnauld that God is not the efficient cause of his existence, moreover, he is equally emphatic in this letter to Mersenne that "God disposed the eternal truths … as the efficient and total cause" (1: 151–52, 3: 25). Nevertheless, it seems that just as we cannot comprehend the power on which the eternal truths depend, so we cannot comprehend the power on which God's existence depends. It is for this reason that we cannot directly comprehend the unique case of the derivation of existence from the divine essence, and so must conceive of the derivation in terms of the production of an effect by its efficient cause.[21]

It is instructive to compare Descartes' view of our knowledge of the "cause or reason" for God's existence with what we find later in Spinoza. In his *Ethics*, Spinoza argues that God is the cause of himself insofar as his essence includes existence, and indicates explicitly that the sort of causality involved here is efficient causality.[22] In some ways, Descartes' UCA anticipates the guiding principle in Spinoza that there must be a reason for the existence of any being, including (and even especially) God. However, what is missing from Spinoza is Descartes' scholastic reluctance to apply the notion of efficient causality in a straightforward way to the case of divine existence. In offering an explication of the nature of God as *causa sui*, Spinoza is able to appeal to an efficient cause where Descartes could invoke only a formal cause.

---

[21] One paradox lurking here is that Descartes sometimes suggests that the scope of his doctrine of the creation of the eternal truths is universal, including even truths concerning God's nature. If the scope were universal in this way, then God would have to be the efficient cause of the truth that he exists. I discuss this paradox further in Schmaltz (2011).

[22] See the claim in *Ethics* Ip25s that "God must be called the cause of all things in the same sense in which he is the cause of himself," and the claim in Ip26D that in the case of any cause that has been determined to act in a particular way, "God, from the necessity of his nature, is the efficient cause both of its essence and of its existence" (in Spinoza [1925], vol. II, pp. 67–68).

PART III

Sensations

CHAPTER 6

Sensation and knowledge of body in Descartes' Meditations

John Carriero

Descartes is often thought to embrace some form of "indirect realism" in the *Meditations*, at least when it comes to sensory cognition. Broadly, there are two main grounds for attributing such a position to him. First, in the *Meditations*, Descartes presents an argument for the existence of bodies. But what else could the purpose of this argument be, if not to get us from an inner world of our sensory ideas to an outer world of bodies? (Kant, for one, seems to have understood Descartes as having set some such problem for himself.) Second, Descartes denies in the *Meditations* that sensory ideas resemble things in bodies. This, on its face, would seem to make for a gap between our sensory cognition of features of bodies and the features themselves.

Although for many years I read the *Meditations* in this way, I have come to think better of it. In the Third Meditation, Descartes sketches a "pre-critical" conception of sensory cognition, that is, the conception of the senses that he takes the meditator to have entered the *Meditations* with. This conception has affinities with an Aristotelian "realist" account of sensation. In the Sixth Meditation he presents his own theory of the senses. While there are important differences between the earlier position and the later one, I have come to think that it is easy to exaggerate the differences and that the new position is better seen as a modification of the Aristotelian "realist" picture than its abandonment.

Portions of this chapter overlap with the first part of chapter 3 of my *Between Two Worlds: A Reading of Descartes's "Meditations"* (2009). I am grateful to Princeton University Press for permission to use that material here.

Earlier versions of this chapter were presented at conferences in Helsinki, London, Los Angeles, Santa Clara, Texas A&M, Rio de Janeiro, and at a philosophy department colloquium at the University of California at Riverside. I am grateful to those audiences for their questions and comments. Karen Detlefsen's perceptive suggestions were particularly helpful for getting this chapter into its final form.

I PRE-CRITICAL AND POST-CRITICAL
CONCEPTIONS OF SENSATION

Pre-critical view of sensation

Let's begin by considering the picture of sensation that Descartes takes the meditator to start out with. Near the beginning of the Third Meditation, Descartes says this about his previous views:

But there was something else which I used to assert, and which through habitual belief I thought I perceived clearly, although I did not in fact do so. This was that there were things outside me from which these ideas proceeded [*a quibus ideae istae procedebant*] and which resembled them in all respects. Here was my mistake; or at any rate, if I judged truly [*verum judicabam*], it was not thanks to the force [*vi*] of my perception. (¶3; 7: 35, 2: 25)[1]

There seem to be three main components to the view described here: sensory ideas are (1) caused by bodies, which bodies (2) exist and (3) resemble those ideas.

Let's consider these components more carefully, beginning with the last one, resemblance. The thought that sensory ideas resemble things located outside of me falls out of an Aristotelian picture of cognition. Aristotelians take cognition to involve a sort of assimilation of the known by the knower: as Aristotle says, "the soul becomes all things." This assimilation results from the cognizer's acquiring a form of the thing cognized. The new form is an image or replica – a "resemblance" – of the original form: through his possession of the form, a cognizer comes to be "formally identical" with the thing cognized. Although the acquired form has the same nature as the form in the thing cognized, it has a special "spiritual" manner of being in the cognizer, different from its "material" manner of being in the thing cognized.[2] So, for example, when I sense the red of a soccer referee's red card, the form red comes to exist in me "spiritually," and I become "in a way" identical with the red.

One thing to be careful about here is the following. When the sensible species comes to exist in me, I do not need to inspect it with some set of interior eyes in order for my sensory cognition of red – my seeing of the red – to

---

[1] In addition to the usual references to the Adam and Tannery edition of Descartes' works and the Cottingham, Stoothoff, and Murdoch translation, I often provide references to the individual paragraphs of the *Meditations*, so that, for example, III.¶3 is the third paragraph of the Third Meditation.

[2] As Alison Simmons has emphasized in correspondence, forms existing in various media, e.g. in light or in a mirror, also were supposed to have a spiritual manner of being.

occur.[3] There is nothing more to my seeing red than my power of sensation being "actualized" by the species. For the card's red to exist in me (or for me to be formally identical with the card) is what it *is* for me to sense the red. We might think, then, of my seeing red as a matter of my having my sensory cognition "shaped up" or "formed" in a certain way by the redness of the card.

Descartes presents the belief in resemblance as a naïve commitment rather than a technical philosophical one, so it is worth doing what we can to make it recognizable and familiar. Naïvely, we think of the senses as providing us with information about the world, and we often think of this as happening through the senses making aspects (colors, sounds, and so forth) of the world present to us in more or less the way those aspects are. We take there to be a qualitative match between our sensory cognition and the thing sensed. We don't, to be sure, expect the match to be perfect; perhaps when the referee holds up his red card, because of the sun's glare I find myself presented with something orange. We might put it thus: I see the card's color as orange. (We wouldn't say, of course, that my sensory cognition got "formed" or structured orange-wise, but, all the same, I'm not sure that we would find that mode of expression unintelligible.) When I see the red as orange, there is still some match or similarity – still some resemblance – between my sensation or experience and the card's color, even if there is also some failure of match, some dissimilarity. And, it seems, there are boundaries to how much dissimilarity – how much lack of resemblance – our ordinary picture of sensation will tolerate. If, for example, the referee blows his whistle and I wind up seeing red, it is hard to think of this transaction as the sensing, even the very poor sensing, of the sound of the whistle. Something rather different seems to have happened.

There are two other components in the account of sensation that the meditator starts with. She supposes that these resemblances (sensible species, sensory ideas, sensory experience, sensory cognition, etc.) are (1) caused by bodies that (2) exist. Descartes puts this idea variously: he says that sensory ideas "proceed [*procedere*]" from bodies, and later, in the Sixth Meditation, he speaks of bodies as "emitting [*emittere*: to send out]" ideas or "immitting [*immittere*: to place in]" ideas. The basic thought here seems familiar enough. When the referee holds up the red card, we think of the card as somehow producing my sensory cognition of it. The card

---

[3] Aquinas makes the analogous point about intellectual cognition in a well-known article in the *Summa Theologiae* (1, q.85, a.2), where he argues that the intelligible species is not what is (in the first instance) known, but rather that by which something external to the soul is known. In the course of his argument, though, he makes it clear that he thinks that the same thing holds of the sensible species, i.e. the sensible species red is not what I see, but rather that by which I see some red thing in the world.

or something in the card determines my cognition (so that my cognition becomes similar in some respect to the card). Because information about the card seems to flow from the card to me, we might put it that the card is the "source" of my cognition (in the sense of a "source" of information). Of course, the card gets a lot of help from the media and my physiology, but we tend to think of these other factors as helping along the flow of information and not as the cognition's source. Descartes describes this source as something from which my sensory ideas "proceed," or as something that sends out or "emits" sensory ideas or places sensory ideas in me.

The way we think about sensing the red card differs from the way we think about imagining the red card. When I imagine a red card, we don't think of the card as the source of what I imagine: either I myself am the source, or (perhaps better) there is no source in the relevant sense, i.e. my imaginative ideas do not "proceed from" anything (which is not to deny that my imaginative ideas may be the result of creatively working with ideas that did proceed from something). Also, when I see the card, because of the way in which the card is the source of my sensory cognition, it has to exist while I see it.[4] Here we might contrast seeing the card with visually recalling it: in the case of visually recalling it, the card may be the source of the memory – the ideas that make up the remembered experience may originate with the card and proceed from it – but not in such a way that the card need (now) exist.[5]

Criticism of pre-critical view; sketch of new position

So much for an account of the meditator's starting point on sensation. Descartes, of course, criticizes our initial conception of perception, and we might expect that our final conception will be very different. (After all, he terms his initial view his "chief mistake.")

Descartes' main critical discussion of the initial view comes at the beginning of Meditation Three, in ¶¶8 through 12. Although he is especially concerned about resemblance, it seems clear that the entire view is under consideration, as his rather harsh-sounding conclusion indicates:

All these considerations are enough to establish that it is not reliable judgement [ex certo judicio] but merely some blind impulse [caeco aliquo impulsu] that has made me believe up till now that there exist things distinct from myself which

---

[4] Modern sophistication about the speed of light calls for modification of this naïve commitment: e.g. sometimes the source of what I see – the distant star – no longer exists, even if the light that it threw off does.

[5] For discussion of the difference between the view described in the text and contemporary naïve realism, see Carriero (2009), p. 140. Sometimes VI.¶6 (7: 75, 2: 52) is thought to show that the meditator enters the *Meditations* with indirect realist commitments. I explain why it does not on pp. 140–42.

transmit [*immittent*] ideas or images of themselves through the sense organs or in some other way. (¶12; 7: 39–40, 2: 27)

Does this assessment signal a radical departure from our initial view of sensation? Well, possibly. But let's keep in mind that in the Third Meditation, Descartes is not arguing that this familiar picture of perception is false, just that he cannot (at least yet) find any reason to embrace it. So, in ¶8, Descartes asks after his reasons for his initial, pre-critical beliefs about the senses. He finds he is able to muster two sets of considerations. The first is simply that (1) nature seems to teach him these things. Perhaps this means that, when I look at the referee's red card, I find it natural to think that the card exists, is the source of my experience, and is more or less as I experience it to be. The second argument is a little more complex. (2a) Sensory ideas (or experience) come to me independently of my will. If I look at the red card, I see it whether I want to or not. This suggests that sensory ideas come to me from things distinct from me. (2b) But – and notice the thinness of the argument at this point – if this is so, "the most obvious judgement for me to make is that the thing in question sends in [*immittere*] to me its own likeness rather than something else" (7: 38, 2: 26).

In the next three paragraphs, Descartes examines the first argument and each of the two steps of the second. The fact that we find ourselves naturally inclined to believe various things about the senses does not show that what we are thus inclined to think is true. The fact that sensory ideas come to us against our will does not show that they come from external things. And, even if they do, that doesn't show that the ideas resemble the things that produce them.

Now, while Descartes is critical of the meditator's grounds for holding the initial view, it is striking that each of them, suitably reshaped, finds its way into the final view.

To see this, recall the argument that Descartes eventually offers for the existence of body in VI.¶10. It has two stages. In the first, he establishes that there's an active power for producing sensory ideas, corresponding to my passive ability to receive sensory ideas, and that this active power is in a substance that is distinct from me. At this point, it is left open what that power might be. We have it, on general metaphysical principles, that the power has at least as much reality as the ideas contain objectively, but this requirement is compatible with the hypothesis that God or an angel should place the ideas in me. In the second stage, Descartes eliminates this hypothesis by appealing to my "great propensity to believe" that the source of my sensory ideas has the same reality as is found objectively in the ideas.

Notice, then, the following similarities between my initial and final beliefs about the senses:

(1) Initially, I thought nature taught me what the senses do. This is explicated as follows: "When I say 'Nature taught me to think this,' all I mean is that a spontaneous impulse leads me to believe it." A teaching of nature is something we simply find ourselves naturally inclined to believe or do – for example, when we are thirsty, we find ourselves inclined to seek drink and to think that drink would be good for us. Now, in the Sixth Meditation argument for the existence of body, in order to eliminate the possibility that my sensory ideas are sent to me by God or an angel, Descartes appeals to the great propensity I have to "believe that [sensory ideas] are emitted [*emitti*] by corporeal things" (7: 80, 2: 55). And so my final theory of what the senses do rests on, as I had originally thought, what I find myself naturally inclined to believe about them.

(2a) In both my initial and final view the fact that sensory ideas come to me willy-nilly is part of an argument for their proceeding from something distinct from me.

(2b) Although Descartes rejects the resemblance thesis, he makes another assumption about the relationship between what sensory ideas represent and their source, namely, that their source contains in the same form (i.e. "formally" rather than "eminently") whatever reality is found objectively in the ideas. Because it is cloaked in scholastic jargon, "reality," "found objectively," and "contains formally," it is hard to know exactly what to make of this shift.

This gives us a working picture of how the meditator's thinking about what the senses do develops over the course of the *Meditations*. In the remainder of this chapter I want to look more closely, first, at the suggestion that our beliefs about what the senses do is somehow rooted in our natural inclinations or propensities, and second, at what's involved in Descartes' rejection of the resemblance thesis and his replacement of it with a view about formal and objective reality. Does either of these developments indicate a move toward "indirect realism"?

II NATURAL INCLINATIONS AND GREAT PROPENSITIES

Often the fact that Descartes presents an argument for the existence of body in the *Meditations* is taken to show that he thinks we directly sense only our own mental states and must make an inference to get from those mental states to the bodies that cause them. The goal of the Sixth Meditation argument, it is thought, is to provide the basis for such an inference: it is supposed to build a bridge from our sensory ideas to bodies. Kant seems to have read Descartes this way. In his "Refutation of Idealism," he classifies Descartes as an idealist and explains idealism as the position "that the only immediate experience is inner experience, and that from it we can only *infer* outer things."[6] To assess this reading, we need to have a better view of the natural tendency (i.e. the "great propensity") that, in a certain sense, lies at the bottom of the Sixth Meditation argument for the existence of body.

Both my initial and final beliefs about what happens when I sense depend on my natural tendencies: In the Third Meditation, I take my beliefs about the senses to be teachings of nature; in the Sixth Meditation, my belief that sensory ideas proceed from bodies rests on my "great propensity to believe that [sensory ideas] are emitted by corporeal things." Descartes thinks, then, that my beliefs about the senses and the external world have a different character from my beliefs about my mind, God, or geometry. I believe that this difference in character is something of a discovery that I am supposed to make, and that this discovery is integral to my coming to realize that I don't yet have (in the Third Meditation) a successful argument for the existence of body. The pivotal text here perhaps is ¶9, where I examine what I mean by nature's teaching me something:

When I say "Nature taught me to think this," all I mean is that a spontaneous impulse leads me to believe it, not that it has been shown to be true by some natural light. There is a big difference here. Whatever is revealed to me by the natural light—for example from the fact that I am doubting it follows that I exist, and so on—cannot in any way be open to doubt. This is because there cannot be another faculty both as trustworthy as the natural light and also capable of showing me that such things are not true. But as for my natural impulses, I have often judged in the past that they were pushing me in the wrong direction when it was a question of choosing the good, and I do not see why I should place any greater confidence in them than in other matters (¶9; 7: 38–39, 2: 27)

---

[6] Kant's emphasis, Kant (1965), B276; see Wilson, "Descartes on Sense and 'Resemblance'," reprinted in Wilson (1999), p. 17:

I do not see how there can be any legitimate question that in the *Meditations* Descartes treats knowledge of physical existence as secondary to, and inferentially derivative from, knowledge of mental ideas ... These familiar considerations, it seems to me, establish a clear sense in which Descartes does hold a veil-of-ideas theory with respect to the perception of bodies – i.e. our knowledge that we actually perceive any bodies is dependent upon, and derived from, the epistemologically prior affirmation that we have in our minds ideas "of them".

My suggestion is that matters are not quite so clear when one thinks about the nature of the "inference" in question. I should mention that, even though I have come to disagree with Wilson's article, I've found it extremely helpful for thinking about this topic.

This is an intriguing passage. At the risk of overstructuring, let me lean on the idea of truth being revealed to me in the one case and not the other, and mark the contrast that Descartes draws here as the difference between what I believe because I *can see that it is so* (according to Descartes: from the fact that I am doubting, it follows that I exist, God exists, and two and three added together make five) and what I find myself spontaneously inclined to believe without *seeing that it is so* (according to Descartes: that sensory ideas come from bodies, that I have a body that has various needs). Understood thus, the natural light works through insight or understanding, and teachings of nature or natural inclinations don't. When I recognize that I cannot doubt unless I exist, I see why this is so. By way of contrast, when I am thirsty and form a desire to drink water (or find myself with an inclination to think that water would be good for me), I do not thereby see why water would be good for me; my thirst may point me in the right direction, but it does not give me any insight into the matter.

Now, Descartes also says in this passage that what's revealed to me by the natural light is not open to doubt, whereas teachings of nature are. But not being open or being open to doubt does not seem foundational here: rather this difference seems to point to a more basic difference between the two kinds of cognition. When I perceive something through the natural light, I see why it has to be the case and *that's* why I cannot doubt it. Consider the *cogito* argument: as I work through it I see that if I doubt, I must exist, and it is this seeing that makes it impossible for me to hold back, to doubt. It is this insight or understanding into the truth that determines my judgment. The case of natural inclination is different. When I am thirsty I find myself desiring water or thinking that water would be good for me without a sense of why water would be good. I do not "see" a connection between thirst and water's being good. This makes it possible for me even when very thirsty to wonder whether water would be in fact good.

Now, one of these natural tendencies – namely, my "great propensity" to believe that sensory ideas are produced by something with the same reality as is found in those ideas – plays a crucial role in the argument for the existence of body that Descartes presents in the Sixth Meditation. Yet, in the Third Meditation our natural tendencies were not to be trusted: they were regarded as mere "blind impulses." Why the difference in attitude?

Well, in the Third Meditation I did not know that the author of my nature was God, and so I did not know where natural tendencies ultimately came from. In the Sixth Meditation, I know that they come from God, and that tells me that they (generally) point me in the right direction. By placing my natural inclinations and impulses within the larger structure that has been developed over the intervening part of the *Meditations*, I am able to achieve an understanding of my position that I previously lacked. What I acquire in the *Meditations*, then, is a reason to go along with a constellation of natural tendencies and cues that I was previously unsure just what to make of. In particular, my natural inclination to believe that when I sense, the source of my sensory ideas is (existing) bodies, receives both explanation and endorsement: this inclination comes from God, who will have set things up so that, *ceteris paribus*, I will be led to the true and the good.

Let's return to our main question, does Descartes' argument for the existence of body indicate that he takes our cognitive position to be one where we start out behind a wall of sensory ideas? The answer to this question is sensitive to what Descartes takes to be the content of our natural views about what the senses do. On an indirect realist reading of my great propensity, I would need to have a natural inclination to take sensory ideas that terminate in my mind to be caused by external bodies. On a direct realist reading, I would need to have instead a natural inclination to think that sensory ideas that I took to be (immediately) of bodies to be also caused by those bodies.

The indirect realist understanding encounters difficult problems about (1) how the meditator is supposed to be brought to the view that her sensory ideas terminate in the mind, and (2) why, having arrived at this position, she continues to find herself inclined to think that these purely mental items are caused by bodies (that is, having arrived at such a position she finds herself naturally inclined toward corporeal realism rather than Berkeleyan idealism). Let me explain.

To begin with (2), we would have to think that the great propensity works along these lines: I find myself in a situation where I have somehow learned that what I immediately perceive are my ideas, and yet I still feel some urge to hypothesize or postulate a realm of bodies which cause these ideas. If we were to come to think that we immediately perceive only ideas (and not tables and chairs), it is unclear to me that we would have a natural tendency to believe anything about their origin. It is, it must be admitted, a pretty disorienting place to find oneself in, and positing a natural inclination to get us mind-independent bodies back seems rather desperate. It is hard to recognize ourselves in such an account of what we are supposed to find it natural to believe.

Turning to (1), it is difficult to see where, in the *Meditations*, the meditator is supposed to have learned that sensory ideas terminate in her mind. It might be suggested that a major function of the dreaming doubt is to cut back the content of sensory experience to that which we would be certain of under the assumption of a dreaming skepticism, so whatever else (if anything) is in the picture turns out to be, strictly speaking, extrinsic to our sensory cognition itself.[7] There is much to argue about here, but notice that a big problem with this suggestion is that it assumes that the dreaming doubt commits one to a certain theory of sensory cognition. Here, it is important to separate, as I believe Descartes is careful to do, questions about what the senses actually do from questions about what one believes or judges that they do. It is easy to see how one might come out of the dreaming doubt (indeed ought to come out of the dreaming doubt) unsure about what the senses do, about what they actually accomplish. Maybe sensory ideas proceed from bodies in such a way as to make them immediately present to my mind; maybe they don't. It is much harder to see, however, how the doubt might be supposed to settle this question.

A direct realist understanding of the natural inclination encounters no such problems. It is much easier to recognize ourselves in a story where we have a natural inclination to think that sensory ideas, which are (immediately) of bodies, are caused by the bodies which they are of. Such an account seems a fair description of our naïve and pre-theoretical sense of such matters.

Now, if we go with this second understanding of the content of the inclination, it seems to me that Kant's overall picture of what Descartes is doing is misleading. To be sure, it is true, as Kant says, that Descartes holds that my knowledge of my mind is prior to my knowledge of body: Descartes' argument for the existence of body runs through my prior knowledge that I exist, come from a supremely perfect being, and find myself with various instinctual beliefs about what to make of the senses. But, it seems to me, the beliefs that are endorsed through the divine guarantee concern what the senses *do*, that is, how the senses *function*. And so we might look at the progress I make between the Third and Sixth Meditations in this way: there is this thing that I do that I call "seeing a red card," and I'm trying to work out for myself what this activity is. Of course, I find myself with strong views about what's going on when I sense – I am naturally inclined to think that when I see a red card, or when I have a sensory idea of a red card, the redness in the red card is informing or shaping my thought, and so is noninferentially present to ("exists

---

[7] The end of II.¶9 (7: 29, 2: 19) is sometimes read as cutting back the content of sensory experience to something mental. I argue against such a reading in Carriero (2009), pp. 100–5.

objectively in") my mind. Eventually, in the Sixth Meditation, I come to see why what I'm inclined to believe in this regard has to be so (otherwise God would be a deceiver). Since Descartes' argument works this way, I don't think it implies that he holds that my "only immediate experience" is of sensory ideas and that I get to bodies and their qualities only subsequently through inference. Rather, I believe he holds that what the senses do (and have been doing all along) is to make the redness in the red card "immediately" present to the mind. In other words, Descartes' position has the overall effect of God's instructing me, through my nature, that the portal to the world that I naïvely take the senses to afford me is in fact there; it is not as if the world's scenery has been painted on the wall of the mind or beamed into me by God or an angel. God is telling me through my nature that there is no veil of ideas.

III SAMENESS OF REALITY AS OPPOSED TO RESEMBLANCE

The view of the senses that the meditator ends up with in the *Meditations* is not the same as the view that she entered with. Descartes highlights an important mistake he finds in a common-sense conception of sensation, namely, the view that sensory ideas resemble features of bodies. It might be thought – I certainly used to think this – that Descartes' denial of resemblance was tantamount to the endorsement of some form of indirect realism. Let me explain why.

One common and historically situated way to give content to the (admittedly slippery) contrast between direct and indirect realism draws on the Aristotelian conception of sensation sketched near the beginning of this chapter.[8] On an Aristotelian conception, when I cognize something I become in a way identical with the thing that I cognize. This identity makes the relation between the knower and the known immediate in at least one sense of immediate. In particular, the form (or "species") in the soul which brings about this "in a way" identity does not function as an epistemic intermediary: for my soul to possess the sensible species which makes it identical with some quality in an outward body *is* what it is for my soul to sense that quality. My cognition of the species is

---

[8] While this general way of looking at things is fairly common, I mention that it is not uncontroversial. Paul Hoffman, for example, has argued – in "Direct Realism, Intentionality, and the Objective Being of Ideas," reprinted in Hoffman (2009a); see especially section 2 (pp. 166–69) – against this approach, that Aquinas' commitment to cognitive species makes him a "representationalist" (which Hoffman opposes to direct realism); and certain contemporary "naïve realists" would view any commitment to forms, species, or ideas with suspicion (see note 5 above).

not prior to my cognition of things in the world, and I do not make an outward inference from the species in the soul to things in the world.[9] In a reasonably intuitive way, an Aristotelian account of cognition falls on the "direct realist" side of the divide.

For purposes of contrast, what might count as an "indirect realist" view of sensory cognition? Well, to keep matters simple, let's consider the following view. Suppose we take the primary relationship that sensory ideas have to the things they are of (i.e. to their "objects") to be causal covariance, so that the same sorts of causes in bodies bring about the same sorts of effects in the mind. For example, let's imagine that what connects sensory ideas of hot in my mind to hot things in the world (say, things whose internal parts are moving rapidly) is simply the fact that this kind of sensory idea is (typically) caused by hot things, and what connects sensory ideas of cold to cold things (say, things whose parts are moving slowly) is simply the fact that that kind of sensory idea is (typically) caused by cold things. Evidently, on this model, we are no longer thinking of sensory ideas as essentially defined by the world's structure: as being fundamentally the spiritual or mental existence of (some of) the world's structure. Rather we are thinking in terms of a mental order of ideas which is systematically causally correlated with an independent physical order of corporeal features.[10] This makes it more natural to think of such a view as indirect realism. We directly cognize an order of mental items and indirectly cognize, via a systematic causal correlation, an independent order of physical items.

This way of drawing the contrast between direct and indirect realism is rough,[11] but it will serve our purposes. Now, for purposes of gauging Descartes' attitude toward the Aristotelian conception, it would appear that his remarks about *resemblance* take on special significance. For, typically on that view, the *sensible species* which brings about identity between the knower and the known is supposed to be *resemblance of* some sensible form in the known thing. And so it is easy to take the following passage from the Sixth Meditation to mark a rejection of an Aristotelian, direct realist account of sensation:

And from the fact that I perceive by my senses [*sentiam*] a great variety of colours, sounds, smells and tastes, as well as differences in heat, hardness and the

---

[9] See note 3 above.

[10] Indeed, had those correlations been set up differently, the same ideas (mental items) could have been of other things (different qualities in bodies).

[11] I think Locke, for example, may hold a view that combines elements of both. See Carriero (2003), p. 33.

like, I correctly conclude that there is in bodies from which these various perceptions of the senses come [*perceptiones sensuum adveniunt*] a variety corresponding [*respondentes*] to, though perhaps not resembling [*similes*], them. (7: 81, 2: 56)

Not only is it easy to understand this remark as signaling Descartes'
rejection of the Aristotelian direct realist conception, but it would appear
that he is simultaneously taking a step toward a causal covariance (indirect realist) conception, inasmuch as it would seem that *respondentes* (corresponding) would come down to causal covariance and nothing more.[12]

Although I used to read the Sixth Meditation passage in this way, here
are some reasons to think that Descartes' response to the Aristotelian picture is rather more measured.[13]

At a textual level, the reservations about resemblance that Descartes
expresses in the *Meditations* are qualified in two ways. First, he never
denies the resemblance doctrine outright, but argues only that we do not
have enough reason to affirm it.[14] Second, he sometimes puts his point in
terms of whether we have reason to believe that bodies are completely or
wholly – *omnino* – as we perceive them, apparently leaving room for the
thought that they do resemble, just not *omnino*, completely or wholly.[15]
(One might, of course, take the point of the *omnino* to be that there *is*
resemblance when it comes to shape or size, but there is no resemblance at
all when it comes to color or sound, but this involves reading something
into the text that is not obviously there.)

---

[12] There is no sign of such a departure at the level of intellectual (or distinct) cognition: Descartes
does not deny that we are in a position to conclude that our distinct ideas resemble their objects.
So, often, Descartes is taken to have in effect a hybrid theory of cognition, according to which
intellectual (and distinct) cognition works in a more or less Aristotelian way, involving something like formal identity, and so belongs to the "direct realist" side of the ledger, whereas
obscure sensory cognition works in some other way, perhaps mainly through causal covariance,
and so belongs to the "indirect realist" side of the ledger. Such a position seems awkward.

[13] In rethinking my views on this topic, I have profited from extensive discussion with Joseph
Hwang and from his unpublished dissertation (2008). See especially ch. 3, "Sensing, Perceiving,
Ideas," where Hwang defends the proposal that perceiving a sensory idea for Descartes occupies
roughly the same ground as receiving a sensible species does for Aristotelian scholastics.

[14] Marleen Rozemond and Janet Broughton have offered different explanations of why all Descartes
intends to and needs to argue is that we shouldn't affirm the resemblance doctrine, not that we
ought to deny it. See Rozemond (1998), pp. 66–75, and Broughton (2002), pp. 49–61, especially
pp. 53 and 57. See also helpful discussion of Rozemond in Sarah Patterson, "Nature and Habit:
The Case for Mechanism in Descartes' *Meditations*" (unpublished). Even so, I find Descartes
surprisingly circumspect about the doctrine, and have come think that at least some of that
circumspection is to be accounted for by the fact that his positive views are not as far from an
Aristotelian picture of cognition as might be supposed.

[15] See 7: 35, 2: 25 and 7: 80, 2: 55; note also the *plane similes* in 7: 82, 2: 56. I've been helped by
Patterson's careful discussion in "Nature and Habit."

At a more philosophical level, it is difficult to find a reason for Descartes to abandon the Aristotelian picture. To be sure, his scientific views call for some sort of revision of the picture when it comes to things like our sensory cognition of *hot* and *red*, but, as I explain below, I think the primary revision he has in mind – namely, whether and in what sense *hot* and *red* count as "realities" – can be accommodated within an Aristotelian framework, according to which sensory cognition of the world is a matter of identity.[16] Remaining at a philosophical level, Descartes does not work through the problems associated with an alternative conception of sensory cognition. For example, he does not explain what makes my white sensory idea be of the (distal) white on the page rather than of the (proximal) jiggling in my optic nerve, both of which, after all, causally co-vary with the idea.[17]

In view of these prima facie problems, I think it is worth considering whether Descartes' remarks surrounding resemblance mark anything quite so dramatic as the abandonment of the Aristotelian "formal identity" picture of sensory cognition. Perhaps Descartes was still operating with this conception rather than erecting a new framework, *ab initio*, based on causal covariance.[18]

With this in mind, let's consider how Descartes describes sensory cognition in the Sixth Meditation:

But since God is not a deceiver, it is quite clear that he does not put the ideas in me [*immittere*] either immediately [*immediate*] from himself, nor by some mediating creature [*mediante aliqua creatura*], in which their objective reality

---

[16] I've argued above that Descartes' dreaming does not give us a reason to think this.

[17] To be sure, Descartes does explain in the Sixth Meditation why God sets things up so that I receive an idea of foot pain (rather than, say, an idea of some other goings on in my nervous system involved in the transmission of the idea), but he does not explain what makes the idea be an idea of foot pain (*dolor tanquam in pede*) as opposed to motion in a nerve (for more on this point, see note 22 below).

[18] Des Chene (2010) offers the following proposal in response to my claim that Descartes is still thinking of sensory cognition as a matter of identity, in a quasi-Aristotelian way: "Without denying Carriero's account altogether I would like to suggest that Descartes is, so to speak, on the verge of a quite different conception ... According to this conception, sensory ideas, like words, *signify* without resembling, that is, their relation to their objects is *arbitrary*" (p. 10).

Descartes does compare sensory ideas to words (9: 3–4, 1: 81); and he indicates in the Sixth Meditation that God had some leeway in how he put together the nature of man. What I find hard to determine here is whether, as I am inclined to think, Descartes makes these remarks from within an "identity" framework, according to which corporeal structure is imported to the mind via the senses, and indicating that, even so, that structure can be present only obscurely and confusedly, or whether, as Des Chene suggests, these remarks signal the replacement of the "identity" framework with "a quite different conception." The fact that Descartes does not seem to develop the different conception in very much detail leads me to think that Descartes continues to draw in a substantial way on the general picture of sensation he inherited from scholastic Aristotelianism.

is contained not formally but only eminently. For, since God has given me no faculty at all for recognizing this, but rather on the contrary has given me a great propensity to believe that they are emitted from corporeal things [*a rebus corporeas emitti*], I do not see on what grounds [*qua ratione*] he could be understood not to be a deceiver, if they were emitted otherwise than from corporeal things [*a rebus corporeas emitterentur*]. (VI.¶10; 7: 79–80, 2: 55)

When Descartes claims that the immitting/emitting causes of my sensory ideas contain formally the reality that those ideas contain objectively (namely, corporeal reality, since sensory ideas present bodies to me), he is in effect claiming that those ideas are immitted/emitted by corporeal things.[19] Descartes is thinking of sensation as a matter of the transfer of corporeal reality or structure from a corporeal source to the mind. So, he holds, as in the scholastic view, that structure that starts out in the world makes its way into the mind. Let's call the assumption that Descartes thinks we are naturally inclined to make, the sameness-of-reality assumption. We have a great propensity to believe that the structure or reality found in our sensory ideas is the same as that originally found in their causes, and so a sensory idea is a way for that structure to be transmitted from the cause (body) to the mind.

This is in keeping with how ideas in general function for Descartes, namely, as vehicles that make real structure available to the mind. That is, all ideas – whether purely intellectual (such as my idea of myself or of God) or imaginative (such as my idea of a chimera or my visualization of a triangle) or sensory (such as my idea of greenness) – exhibit or present reality to the mind: the reality contained in the thing that is being thought of exists objectively in the idea. (In the First Replies [7: 102–3, 2: 75], Descartes puts the point this way: the idea *is* that structure existing objectively.[20]) What seems distinctive about sensory ideas is that in their case the structure comes to us (via some process of emission/immission) from their objects (their "sources").[21]

What is important here is that this sameness-of-reality assumption does for Descartes the philosophical work that the resemblance thesis does for the Aristotelians. Both Descartes and the Aristotelians understand cognition as a matter of sameness of structure in the cognizer and the cognized, and both understand sensation, in particular, as a process

---

[19] For further discussion of this passage see Carriero (2009), p. 446 (n. 23).

[20] "By this I mean that the idea of the sun is the sun itself existing in the intellect – not of course formally existing, as it does in the heavens, but objectively existing, i.e. in the way in which objects are usually [*solent*] in the intellect."

[21] Janet Broughton pointed out to me the distinctive character of the causal vocabulary that Descartes uses in connection with the production of sensory ideas.

whereby structure makes its way from the cognized thing to the cognizer. In this way, Descartes is still operating in what might be called a "sameness" framework, since what matters for sensory representation is sameness of something: when we sense, the same structure exists formally in the world and objectively in the idea.[22]

Still, it is clear from Descartes' criticism of the Aristotelian resemblance thesis that they disagree about something. Where Descartes and the Aristotelians part company, I think, is over whether we should understand this sameness of structure in terms of a shared (sensible) *form*. According to Descartes, there is, as a matter of fact, no sensible form in the red card; there is only a microphysical texture, a pattern of matter in motion. So when I have an idea of red, I am not made formally identical with the microphysical texture. I believe that when Descartes criticizes the Aristotelian resemblance thesis, he is mainly out to reject the claim that sensory cognition requires *formal* identity. When he denies that my sensory idea of red resembles the red in the referee's card, he is denying that there is a sameness of form in idea and thing.

Descartes opens up space for his view that sensory cognition requires sameness of structure but does not require sameness of form, through the claim that sensory ideas present the reality they contain in a confused and obscure way. He writes toward the end of the demonstration of body in the Sixth Meditation:

Perhaps, however, they [bodies] do not exist exactly [*omnino*] as I comprehend them by sense, for the comprehension of the senses is in many ways confused and obscure. (VI.¶10; 7: 80, 2: 55)

Corporeal reality is presented in our sensory ideas, but certain of its aspects are presented obscurely and confusedly. This makes it hard for us to say what is owed to the confusion and obscurity of the presentation and what belongs to the bodies that are being presented. It is difficult for us to determine what in corporeal reality as it exists in the world (i.e. formally) corresponds to the obscure and confused aspects of the objective presentation of that reality in our ideas.

How exactly Descartes thinks of the difference between the obscure and confused way corporeal reality exists in my sensory ideas and the way

---

[22] If so, notice that Descartes has a natural answer to the problem about proximal and distal causes faced by the covariance account: what makes my sensory idea of foot pain be of damage in the foot rather than some intervening event in my nervous system is that my sensory idea is foot damage existing objectively as opposed to some nerve motion existing objectively. This fact about the identity of the idea would, it seems, have to be prior to facts about the sorts of causal relations the idea enters into: it could not, it seems, be given through causal covariance.

it exists in the world, formally, is hard to say. But one thing that seems especially important to Descartes is the point that we cannot tell from a sensory idea to what extent it presents a reality or an absence of reality. To use an example he gives in the Third Meditation, we can't tell from our sensory ideas of hot and cold whether heat is a reality and cold is merely the absence of that reality, or cold is a reality and heat is merely the absence of that reality, or something else. Our sensory ideas of hot and cold present what reality they do too poorly for us to be able to determine this. In other words, when Descartes calls an idea obscure, one thing he has in mind is that one cannot read off the ontological situation (in terms of being and nonbeing) from the idea (or from what the idea makes available to the mind). Moreover, since *form*, in scholasticism, is a principle of *reality* or perfection, it would follow for a scholastic that one could not tell from the idea of hot or cold whether there is a *form* of hot or cold.

Descartes, then, while deeply indebted to Aristotelian ways of thinking about sensory cognition, develops the position in a novel way. Like the Aristotelians, Descartes thinks of a sensory idea as a matter of structure (reality) making its way from the world (where it exists formally) into the mind (where it exists objectively). But, unlike the Aristotelians, he does not think there is a sensible form that is shared by the mind and the world; he does not think a sensory idea brings about a formal identity between the mind and the thing sensed. Rather, according to him, sensory ideas bring enormously complex and intricate corporeal structure into the mind, but do so only obscurely and confusedly.

No natural tendency toward resemblance thesis

Paying attention to exactly what Descartes objects to in the resemblance thesis can help correct a widespread misunderstanding of what brings us to believe the resemblance thesis and what it takes to extricate ourselves from it. Many commentators seem to think Descartes holds that we have some sort of natural inclination toward the resemblance thesis.[23] A common view of the matter seems to be the following. Initially, our natures lead us to place in the world all manner of entities that do not belong there: a redness in the red card that is like my idea of it, a heat that is like my perception of a fire, and so forth. It is as if, in Hume's memorable phrase, "the mind has a great propensity to spread itself on external

---

[23] For instance, Gary Hatfield, in Hatfield (2002), pp. 154–55 and p. 262, understands Descartes to hold that we have a natural impulse to believe the resemblance thesis.

objects" (*A Treatise of Human Nature*, 1.3.14).[24] Subsequently reason corrects this mistake, pulling the objectionable entities out of the world and perhaps placing them in the mind. This correction may partly take place as the result of scientific investigation: science may teach us that there is nothing in the red card similar to my idea of it, only a surface texture.

There are places in the *Meditations* that might be taken to support this interpretation. Descartes does say that natural propensities are the sort of thing that can be overruled by intellect, and he offers an extended discussion of how it is possible that a natural tendency might on occasion lead us astray. And in any case it is hard to see why we would make this error – why we would think that sensory ideas are like their corporeal sources, or why we would place sensible qualities in the world in some objectionable way – unless we had some sort of instinctual leaning in that direction.

But this is *not* Descartes' view. As a purely philosophical matter, it would be very hard to explain why God would give us a natural inclination that would lead us to make the sort of very systematic mistake at issue, and Descartes never attempts such an explanation.[25] He does explain at length how local miscue is possible (in the discussion of dropsy in the final third of the Sixth Meditation), but never something this global. As an exegetical matter, ¶15 of the Sixth Meditation ought, I believe, to settle decisively the question of whether Descartes holds that we have a natural inclination toward believing the resemblance thesis.[26] The resemblance

---

[24] Hume (1975), p. 167.

[25] Indeed, one of the things to emerge from his discussion of how our natures occasionally lead us astray is that such errors are an unfortunate by-product of the "best system that could be devised" (VI.¶22, 7: 87–88, 2: 60).

[26] It is clear from III.¶8 that the meditator thinks of the resemblance thesis as something that nature teaches her:

But the chief question at this point concerns the ideas which I take to be derived from things existing outside me: what is my reason for thinking that they resemble these things? Obviously, I seem to have been taught this by nature [*Nempe ita videor doctus a natura*]. (7: 38, 2: 26)

I think the point of the *videor* is to make room for, in line with VI.¶15, the thought that this may be something that she only thinks that she has been taught by nature, but has not been really taught by nature. Admittedly, this sentence is difficult because the Latin *nempe* can mean either "namely" or something like "obviously" or "surely" or "evidently." If we take it as "surely" it can clash with "*videor*" (it appears to me that): "This is surely something that I have been taught by nature" as opposed to "This is something that I seem to have been taught by nature." I think the force of the sentence may be the following: "Surely (one of my reasons for accepting the resemblance thesis is that) this is something that I seem to have been taught by nature." I am grateful to Janet Broughton, who has expressed a preference for reading this passage in such a way that the *nempe* trumps the *videor*, so that it means "Surely nature has taught me this," for bringing this translation issue to my attention.

thesis is found in a list of things "which I may *appear to* have been taught by nature, but which in reality I acquired not from nature but from a habit of making ill-considered judgments" (7: 82, 2: 56; my emphasis). Further, ¶15 is constructed so as to link the origin of our commitment to resemblance to the origin of two other dubious beliefs, namely, "the belief that any space in which nothing is occurring to stimulate my senses must be empty" and the belief "that stars and towers and other distant bodies have the same size and shape which they present to my senses." With respect to this last belief, Descartes writes that there is no "real or positive propensity in me to believe [*realis sive positiva propensio ad credendum*] that the star is no bigger than the flame of a small light; I have simply made this judgment from childhood onward without any rational basis" (7: 83, 2: 57). I do not think this remark applies only to the mistake about size; I think Descartes would say the same thing about the other two items on his list of things that we mistake for teachings of nature – in particular, that we have no real or positive propensity to believe that there is something in the fire resembling the heat as it is presented by my idea of heat, or in the red card resembling the redness as it is presented by my idea of red.

If we do not come to the resemblance thesis by way of natural inclination, how do we come to it? Descartes tells us at the beginning of ¶15 that although we confuse the resemblance thesis with a teaching of nature, it is acquired "not from nature but from a *habit* of making ill-considered *judgments*" (my emphases). We may usefully distinguish two elements here, judgment and habit. We noticed earlier that in his Third Meditation reconstruction of his initial view, Descartes presents the basis of our judgment that sensory ideas resemble their sources as rather thin. He simply says that after having arrived at the conclusion that sensory ideas are caused by bodies, "the most obvious judgment [*judicem*] for me to make is that the thing in question transmits to me its own likeness rather than something else" (III.¶8; 7: 38, 2: 26). The picture is filled out a bit in the Sixth Meditation, where he explains that this judgment is first made early in life, while I am heavily dependent on the senses and before I have the use of reason. Descartes writes of that time, "Since I had no notion [*notitiam*: knowledge, information] of these things [viz. the things from which sensory ideas proceed] from anywhere else besides the ideas themselves, nothing else could enter my mind but [*non poterat aliud mihi venire in mentem quam*] that the things resembled the ideas" (VI.¶6; 7: 75, 2: 52).

If this were all there was to the account, it would be hard to see why we confuse our belief in resemblance with a teaching of nature,[27] or why, given the judgment's shaky character, it can prove hard to get rid of, as Descartes seems to think it is. This is where habit comes in. Over time, through a kind of repetition, our belief in resemblance becomes entrenched. The belief comes to exercise a nonrational hold over us – a hold that is independent of our seeing that something is the case. This is what, I imagine, makes it easy for us to mistake the resemblance thesis for a teaching of nature. From Descartes' point of view it is important not to make this confusion: at the root of my belief in the resemblance thesis is a faulty judgment; at the root of a teaching of nature is my unadulterated nature. What results directly from my nature is God's responsibility; what results from my judging activity is my own.[28] In order to extract ourselves from the resemblance thesis we need to combat entrenched habit, not to check our natural tendencies.

Resemblance and reality

So Descartes is claiming that we have no primitive natural tendency toward the resemblance thesis. But isn't this simply to misdescribe human psychology? Wherever philosophical reflection and scientific theorizing might lead us, isn't Hume simply right that our starting point is one where the "mind has a great propensity to spread itself on external objects"? And isn't Descartes' claim that we have a primitive tendency toward the sameness-in-reality assumption but not the resemblance thesis arbitrary?

---

[27] The meditator twice suggests that the belief appears to be a teaching of nature, at III.¶8; 7: 38, 2: 26 and VI.¶15; 7: 82, 2: 56.

[28] There is, on Descartes' telling, a certain inevitability to our becoming attached to the resemblance thesis, which makes the process seem natural, in a sense of natural meaning "what transpires in the normal course of events." I am not sure to what extent Descartes himself recognizes this sense of natural, but the discussion of dropsy (which, as Descartes construes it, involves a misfiring of our natural instincts) suggests that he would agree that God bears some sort of responsibility here. I think two things might be said in response from the point of view of theodicy. First, it is not clear how blameworthy Descartes takes us to be for becoming attached to the resemblance thesis. What we may be blameworthy for is not reflecting and working our way out of it when the occasion arises (e.g. by insisting that red cannot possibly be a microphysical texture because red must resemble my idea). Second, I think there probably is, lying in the background, a general reason for why God set things up as he did (this is the strategy Descartes follows in explaining why dropsy is allowed to happen). Descartes may hold, for example, that if God allowed our intellects to be bombarded with full information about our environment (that is, gave us clear and distinct sensory presentations of corporeal structure in all of its incredible detail instead of presentations that confused certain aspects of that structure), we'd all perish before we figured out what to do with this information.

Let's look at how Descartes describes what we ought not to believe concerning resemblance. This comes in VI.¶15. I used to think:

> that the heat in a body is something exactly resembling [*plane simile*] the idea of heat which is in me; or that in a white or green thing, there is the selfsame whiteness or greenness which I sense [*eadem albedo aut viriditas quam sentio*]; or that in a bitter or sweet thing there is the selfsame taste [*in amaro aut dulci idem sapor*], and so on. (¶15; 7: 82, 2: 56–57)

And here is what I now think:

> Similarly, although I feel heat when I go near a fire and feel pain when I go too near, there is no convincing argument [*nulla profecto ratio est quae suadeat*] for supposing that there is something in the fire which resembles the heat, any more than for supposing that there is something which resembles the pain. There is simply reason to suppose that there is something in the fire, whatever it may eventually turn out to be, which produces in us the feelings of heat or pain [*sensus caloris vel doloris efficiat*].

What seems targeted for discussion is whether there is in the white thing (presumably a body) the "selfsame" whiteness that I sense. Now, there is something about the way Descartes frames the issue that, I believe, may court misunderstanding. When he implies that I ought not believe that there is a whiteness in the white body that is the same as the whiteness that I sense, I don't think his point is that I ought to leave open the possibility that there might be two whitenesses, one in the world, which I don't sense, and another one in the mind, which I do sense. Rather, I think his point is that we ought not believe that the white in the body is the same as it appears to be, or that the obscure image of it that ends up in the mind, i.e. the sensory idea of the white, resembles the white in the thing. An analogy may be helpful here. I look at a tree in my backyard through uneven glass. Because of the unevenness of the glass, information about the shape is lost to me. We might say that the shape of the tree's trunk is not the same shape that I see, in that the trunk is straight and what I see is wavy. But this need not be taken to mean there are two shapes, the shape that I see and the tree's. Another way to describe the situation is that there is just one shape, the tree's, and that because I am onto it poorly, the shape is not the same as it appears to me.

So I take Descartes to be claiming here that I do not have a natural tendency to think that my sensory idea presents the whiteness the way it is, or, in other words, that I ought to leave open the possibility that my sensory idea of whiteness might present whiteness to me in a way that somehow distorts the whiteness present in the body. But that may sound odd. Why don't I have a natural tendency to think that the whiteness is exactly the way it is presented by my sensory idea?

The reason I have no such tendency is that I find my sensory idea of whiteness obscure and confused. As we saw, Descartes explains at the end of his argument for the existence of body that bodies "may perhaps [*forte*] not all exist completely such as they are comprehended by the senses [*omnes tales omnino existunt, quales illas sensu comprehendo*], for in many cases the comprehension of the senses is very obscure and confused." In contrast, "at least all those things are in [bodies] that I clearly and distinctly understand." I have a great propensity to think corporeal reality is being presented to me when I sense. In addition, or perhaps more specifically, to the extent that I find intelligible what is being presented to me – to the extent that I find what's being presented clear and distinct – I am inclined to believe that bodies are as they are presented; and, to the extent that I find what's being presented to me obscure and confused, I am not inclined to any definite views about exactly what is being presented. My sensory perception of color, Descartes thinks, ought to leave me open to different views about what white is and what green is and how white and green might differ from each other.

As noted above, of particular importance to Descartes is that I don't try to read off from a sensory idea the basic ontological situation of the thing presented through the idea. The resemblance thesis, as Descartes understands it, implies, for example, that if the idea of hot strikes me as "positive," hot is a reality as opposed to an absence of reality; and similarly, that if the idea of cold strikes me as "positive," cold is a reality as opposed to some species of nonbeing. Descartes thinks this is bad metaphysics. It will commit me to white and green as basic realities (as "forms," to use scholastic parlance). I come to this uncritical metaphysics, in his view, by way of "a habit of making ill-considered judgments" and not through an original natural inclination. And this does not seem so implausible.

IV CONCLUSION

In this chapter, I have considered two ways in which the meditator's views on the senses evolve over the course of the *Meditations*. I've argued that neither bespeaks a commitment to indirect realism.

First, the meditator comes to appreciate the need for an argument for the existence of body and finds argument that remedies that lack. But neither the need nor the argument shows a commitment to the thesis that our sensory cognition terminates at ideas rather than things in bodies.

Indeed, I think it is much easier to make sense of Descartes' argument if we see it as simply restoring our naïve trust, via the divine guarantee, in the senses.

Second, the meditator comes to reject the resemblance thesis. But this does not mean that the meditator abandons a picture of sensory cognition drawn in terms of shared structure in favor of a new theory based on causal covariance. Rather, what Descartes is really doing here is asking for a certain amount of latitude in how we construe the "resemblance" – i.e. enough latitude so that the reality that we sense can exist in our minds "obscurely" and "confusedly" and enough so that we don't find ourselves trying to read the basic metaphysics of sensory qualities off from our sensory ideas and wind up committed to hot and cold or white and green as primitive realities.

Although my focus in this chapter has been on the *Meditations*, I think that this is Descartes' consistent view throughout his writings. To be sure, analogies and remarks suggestive of a causal covariance model of sensory representation occur in his other writings.[29] But the Aristotelian "identity" framework is elastic enough, I think, that these remarks can be read as calling for its modification rather than its abandonment, and, whatever one makes of those remarks, Descartes never provides an argument for indirect realism or engages in the sort of rethinking of sensory cognition that would be necessary to articulate an alternative picture.

Finally, when I associate Descartes' teaching on sensation via his Aristotelian teachers with direct realism, I don't mean to imply that Descartes himself or his teachers were themselves interested in a controversy between direct and indirect realists. I don't think Descartes or Aquinas ever seriously entertained indirect realism.[30] My own sense is that the issues we now associate with indirect realism arise later in the tradition with Berkeley (and Reid).[31] Berkeley argues that if you give up on resemblance (as Locke does explicitly in the case of the secondary qualities) and replace it with causal covariance (as Locke's claim that the idea of a secondary quality simply represents the power to produce that sort of idea, could easily enough be read), you will be left, willy-nilly,

---

[29] Dennis Des Chene discusses some of these analogies and remarks in his (2010).

[30] By this I mean, for example, that *Summa Theologiae*, 1, q.85, a.2, for all the attention it has received over the years, has the feel of Aquinas' taking care of something straightforward and obvious as opposed to difficult and contested.

[31] Another tributary may be the controversy between Arnauld and Malebranche over ideas. The issues here seem to me rather different, though, inasmuch as they are not concerned with specifically how sensory ideas work, and inasmuch as they revolve about the peculiar commitments of Malebranche's system.

with indirect realism (a position that, in turn, Berkeley thinks is internally unstable and obviously inferior to immaterialism).[32] But getting to
"indirect realism" takes Berkeley some work – the better part of the First
Dialogue.

[32] Much of the First Dialogue seems to be devoted to teasing this out. I work out how it does this
in Carriero (2003).

CHAPTER 7

Descartes on sensory representation, objective reality, and material falsity

Gary Hatfield

Descartes' accounts of sensory perception have long troubled his interpreters, for their lack of clear and explicit statements on some fundamental issues. His readers have wondered whether he allows spatial sensory ideas (spatial qualia); whether sensory ideas such as color or pain are representations and, if so, what they represent; and what cognitive value Descartes attributed to sense perception. Some of these worries can be traced to the Objections published with the *Meditations*. They have received renewed scholarly attention in recent decades. These treatments take differing stands on the questions just mentioned, and also disagree over Descartes' account of the externalization of sensory qualities, on the origin and correct analysis of the "material falsity" he attributes to some sensory ideas, and on the value of the "teachings of nature."[1]

Such disagreement should not be surprising. Although sensory perception was an important topic for Descartes, to which he often returned, his treatment of these particular issues is not systematic – or at least not apparently so. Moreover, he seems abruptly to change his mind on some questions, such as whether sensory ideas represent: the *Meditations* in 1641 appears to say yes (7: 44), the *Principles* in 1644, no (*Princ.* 1.71).[2] Generally, there are no proof texts that unequivocally settle questions about Descartes' views on spatial qualia, the representationality of sensory ideas, their cognitive value, externalization, material falsity, and the status of the teachings of nature.

Earlier versions of this chapter were presented to the Oxford Seminar in Early Modern Philosophy, the Harvard Early Modern Workshop, the New York–New Jersey Early Modern Research Group, and the Quebec Seminar in Early Modern Philosophy; I am grateful for the lively discussions on these occasions. Thanks also to Sean Greenberg, Alistair Isaac, and Alison Simmons for comments and discussion on various versions.

[1] Works examining Descartes' theory of the senses and sensory ideas include Hatfield and Epstein (1979); Wells (1984); Yolton (1984); Bolton (1986); Chappell (1986); Hatfield (1986, 1992); M. Wilson (1990, 1993); Alanen (1994); MacKenzie (1994); Keating (1999); Simmons (1999, 2001, 2003); C. Wilson (2005); Wee (2006); Brown (2008); and De Rosa (2010).

[2] I cite Descartes' works in the Adam and Tannery edition (AT), by volume and page number, in accordance with the bibliographic conventions of this volume. Regarding translation, for the

Yet these questions and topics naturally arise from matters about which Descartes is explicit and (reasonably) consistent, regarding the role of the senses in philosophy and everyday life and concerning the nature of minds and ideas. It is, therefore, worthwhile to ask what his positions might have been. In this chapter, I develop answers by considering Descartes' systematic doctrines on the nature of the mind and its ideas and by combing his statements on sensation and perception for hints about how to apply such principles. In the next section, I review some key texts. In succeeding sections, I develop positions on representationality, cognitive value, externalization, material falsity, and the teachings of nature. Ultimately, I favor an interpretation in which, for Descartes, all sensory ideas represent by resemblance, different kinds of sensory ideas vary in cognitive value, externalization arises through spatial localization, and, with sensory ideas of color and the like, as materially false they do not intrinsically misrepresent but afford occasion for false judgments, which arise as merely apparent, and so not actually legitimate, teachings of nature.

SENSORY IDEAS AND THEIR VALUE

In the *Discourse*, *Meditations*, and *Principles*, Descartes brought the reliability of the senses into question through a combination of arguments, including the fact of sensory fallibility, the dream argument, and (in the latter two works) the hypothesis of an evil deceiver or deceiving God. In the First Meditation, after rehearsing these arguments Descartes asks the meditator to concentrate on the conclusion "that the sky, the air, the earth, colours, shapes, sounds and all external things are merely delusions of dreams" (7: 22). In the *Principles*, on similar grounds (briefly reviewed), he comes to suppose "that there is no God, no heaven, no bodies; and even that we ourselves have no hands, or feet, in short, no body" (*Princ.* 1.7).

As recent interpreters emphasize, these doubts serve a radical re-evaluation of the basis for knowledge and of the ontological categories into which things are divided, including the ontology of the senses.[3] The pure intellect, operating independently of the senses, is introduced in Meditations 3–5 as providing direct insight into the existence of God and the essence of matter. In the Sixth Meditation, the pure intellect purports to establish the mind–body distinction.

Dioptrics, *Meditations*, and *Passions*, I follow CSM; for the *Meteorology*, the Olscamp translation; for the *Principles*, the Miller and Miller translation (cited as *Princ.*, plus part and article number). Deviations from these translations are marked with an asterisk (*).

[3] Bolton (1986); Hatfield (1986); Dicker (1993), chs. 1, 5; Simmons (1999); and C. Wilson (2005).

Also in the Sixth Meditation, as in Part I of the *Principles*, Descartes rehabilitates the senses. In the *Meditations*, he contends that, since God is no deceiver, corporeal things must exist. He then allows that our knowledge of bodies by means of the senses is limited:

They [corporeal things] may not all exist in a way that exactly corresponds with my sensory grasp of them, for in many cases the grasp of the senses is very obscure and confused. But at least they possess all the properties which I clearly and distinctly understand, that is, all those which, viewed in general terms, are comprised within the subject-matter of pure mathematics. (7: 80)

Having noted the obscurity and confusedness of sensory perceptions, Descartes initially retreats to the properties of matter that can be known by pure intellect alone: the properties of extension, taken in general. But he continues by ascribing positive epistemic and cognitive value to sense perception, as regards both size and shape ("primary qualities," in the terminology of Locke and Boyle) as well as sensory qualities such as color and bodily sensations such as pain (ideas of "secondary qualities," along with bodily sensations):

What of the other aspects of corporeal things which are either particular (for example that the sun is of such and such a size or shape), or less clearly understood, such as light or sound or pain, and so on? Despite the high degree of doubt and uncertainty involved here, the very fact that God is not a deceiver, and the consequent impossibility of there being any falsity in my opinions which cannot be corrected by some other faculty supplied by God, offers me a sure hope that I can attain the truth in these matters. Indeed, there is no doubt that everything I am taught by nature contains some truth. (7: 80)

This last turn of phrase is particularly important. The "teachings of nature" were introduced in the Third Meditation by contrast with the epistemically powerful "natural light." They were ascribed to a "spontaneous impulse" and put aside (7: 38). Now, in the considered light of the Sixth Meditation, at least some "teachings of nature" are granted "some truth." We need to find out which teachings contain what truth, and how Descartes disentangles these from the obscurity, confusedness, and uncertainty that attend the sensory perception of (especially) secondary qualities.

Some indication of "what is true" in sense perceptions comes in the Sixth Meditation and *Principles*. The truths in question are (in effect) described as *legitimate* "teachings of nature"; they include the fact of mind–body union (7: 81) and the general reliability of bodily sensations (7: 80). But nature also teaches us about bodies outside our own body and allows us to distinguish them via sensory qualities:

[F]rom the fact that I perceive by the senses a great variety of colours, sounds, smells and tastes, as well as differences in heat, hardness and the like, I correctly conclude that the bodies which are the source of these various sensory perceptions possess differences corresponding to them. Also, the fact that some of the perceptions are agreeable to me while others are disagreeable makes it quite certain that my body, or rather my whole self, in so far as I am a combination of body and mind, can be affected by the various beneficial or harmful bodies that surround it. (7: 81*)

A similar point occurs in *Principles* (1.69–70). Both works note additional commonly made judgments about sensory objects, which the *Meditations* dubs "apparent" (but presumably not actual) teachings of nature and the *Principles* calls "prejudices" (*Princ.* 1.66, 71–72). These judgments may quite possibly be false (7: 82; *Princ.* 1.70–1). They include the notions that bodies possess properties that "resemble" the phenomenal manifestation of sensory qualities such as color, heat, taste, and the like, that empty space is truly void, and that distant bodies are truly small.

Some of these merely apparent teachings of nature engender metaphysical theses about the "essential nature" of bodies (7: 83). In Descartes' organon, such theses should not be drawn directly from sensory experience, but from the light of the pure intellect operating independently of the senses. Knowledge of the essential nature of bodies stems from a priori metaphysics (Hatfield 1986, 1993). Accordingly, Descartes distinguishes the maximally clear and distinct perceptions of the pure intellect from the entire class of sense perceptions (Simmons 2003). Nonetheless, sense perception remains valuable. Indeed, the meditator finds that "in matters regarding the well-being of my body, all my senses report the truth much more frequently than not" (7: 89). And regarding individual objects, by using more than one sense and also calling upon memory – that is, in effect, by engaging in deliberate observation – the meditator can put aside "any further fears about the falsity of what my senses tell me every day" (7: 89). Accordingly, we can accept that the senses reliably inform us of benefits and harms and of facts about particular objects, such as their size and shape, or that bodies which differ in experienced color truly differ in some way.

These last admonitions tell us what is appropriate and inappropriate in some judgments about sensory qualities, but they are not the whole story in evaluating the sensory qualities themselves. For, notoriously, in the Third Meditation (7: 43–44) and Fourth Replies (7: 232–34), Descartes says that sense perceptions can be "materially false" and that this falsity arises from their "obscurity and confusion." Material falsity is not the "formal" falsity of an erroneous judgment; rather, ideas are materially false if they "are such as to provide subject-matter for error" (7: 231). But how do they provide such subject matter? Descartes allows that a materially false idea can contain propositional content that is false even if not asserted, as when idolaters make up "confused ideas" of "false gods" (7: 234). In such a case, the ideas include propositional content (about the existence and properties of such gods) that is materially false, even if no formal falsity arises because the content is merely contemplated but not actually asserted in a judgment (Wee 2006, p. 35).[4] If that were the model of materially false sensory ideas, the material falsity of the idea of color could be ascribed to its representing external objects as possessing a color quality that resembles the phenomenally manifest color that we experience. Accordingly, sensory ideas would intrinsically misrepresent, even if we learned not to affirm their quality-ascribing content.

In the Fourth Replies, Descartes offers another model of material falsity. Sensory ideas are materially false because of their obscurity and confusion, which makes it impossible for the meditator to tell regarding a sensory idea "whether or not what it exhibits to me is something positive that exists outside my sensation" (7: 234*). The obscurity and confusedness of sensory ideas permits or perhaps entices the unreflective perceiver to make mistaken claims about the sensible properties of bodies. In this case, the false content would arise with an impulsive judgment, such as a judgment ascribing a "resembling" color quality to the external object.

Whence arises the obscurity and confusion? Is it merely a matter of childhood prejudices intruding upon the legitimate teachings of nature? That is, does the obscurity and confusedness arise only from confusedly joining the impulsive judgment with the sensory idea? It seems not: as perceptions of bodies, sensory perceptions (especially of secondary qualities) are themselves obscure and confused (7: 81–83; *Princ.* 1.46–47). Even if sensory perceptions are "clear and distinct enough" (7: 83*) for alerting us to potential benefits and harms, they remain somehow intrinsically obscure and confused, and so materially false (on the second model of that notion).

In preparation for examining the nature of this falsity, I first develop a general view of the status of sensory perceptions in Descartes' metaphysics of mind and mind–body union.

---

[4] This model of material falsity as arising from a "complex apprehension" is developed by Wee (2006), ch. 3, drawing on a text that Descartes cites (7: 235) from Francisco Suárez (*Metaphysical Disputations* IX.2.4, partial translation in Ariew *et al.* [1998], pp. 35–36). Wee holds that sensory ideas intrinsically misrepresent; I return to this issue below.

MIND AS AN INTELLECTUAL POWER

Outside the *Meditations* and *Principles*, Descartes discusses the anatomy, physiology, and mental operation of the senses in the *Dioptrics* and *Passions*, and, with special attention to nerve physiology, in the *Treatise on Man*. He also discusses sensory qualities in bodies in the *Rules*,[5] the *World, or Treatise on Light*, and the *Meteorology*.

These works fill out the natural philosophy of sense perception. They contain original developments in the theory of distance perception under a post-Keplerian conception of the eye as an image-forming organ with a lens that accommodates for varying distances. They offer clever proposals concerning the physiological basis for distance perception and they develop an account of what color is in objects. They reaffirm the "no resemblance" thesis for color and other ideas of secondary qualities, but they don't take us more deeply into the question of material falsity or the obscurity and confusedness of ideas of sensory qualities. For this, we must turn to the metaphysical works and consider Descartes' general conceptions of mind, ideas, and representation, and then interpret the natural philosophical writings in that light.

In the Third Meditation, Descartes lays down the principle that "there can be no ideas that are not as it were of things" (7: 44). He had earlier told us that ideas "are as it were the images of things" (7: 37). In the Sixth Meditation he explains that the mind itself is an "intellectual" substance. By this, I think he means that the fundamental character of all mental states is to represent (Hatfield 2003, pp. 187–89, 258–60). In addition, some thoughts involve an act of volition: these include judgments and desires (7: 37). These thoughts include both the "likeness of the thing" (the image or representation) and a further act of will (a judgment or volition). In the *Principles*, Descartes affirms that all "modes of thinking" fall under two rubrics: "perception, or the operation of the intellect," and "volition, or the operation of the will" (*Princ.* 1.32). He makes clear in both works that sense perception and imagination are simply "modes" of intellection or perception (7: 78; *Princ.* 1.32). On my reading, this makes them modes of the power of representation.

Descartes further develops the notion of ideas as images by explaining that differences in the "objective reality" of ideas amount to differences

---

[5] As the *Rules* predates Descartes' "metaphysical turn" of 1629–30 (see Hatfield [1993]), I do not rely on it for the metaphysics of sensory ideas; nonetheless, its treatment of the causal basis of color is compatible with his subsequent mechanistic program.

in what those ideas "represent" (7: 8, 40). The object of an idea, that is, what it represents, need not exist. We can think of a winged horse, even if there are none (7: 66). But if the object of an idea does exist, then for sensory ideas it does so in a way that relates to the objective or representational presentation of the object in the idea itself, on pain of God's being a deceiver (7: 79–80). That is, sensory ideas must tell us something about objects and their properties. The alternative is that sensory ideas are mere effects of substances or powers that they do not represent, produced in us by God himself or by some lesser immaterial being – hypotheses that the meditator rules out (7: 79–80). In the best case, properties in objects exactly correspond to the way in which they are represented. As Descartes explains in the Appendix to the Second Replies, "Whatever exists in the objects of our ideas in a way which exactly corresponds to our perception of it is said to exist *formally* in those objects" (7: 161). As we have seen, geometrical properties such as shape and size can exist in objects formally, that is, exactly as we perceive them (7: 80; also, *Princ.* 1.69).

In these passages, Descartes speaks of objects "corresponding" to the ideas that represent them. But he goes even further: in fleshing out the notion that an idea is like an image of a thing, he says that it contains "the likeness [*similitudo*] of that thing" (7: 37). I believe that this is Descartes' considered view of how ideas represent: by resemblance or similitude. In the *Meditations*, he tells us that the idea of God is perceived as a "likeness" or "similitude" between our mind and God (7: 51). He further suggests that when we ask whether bodies exist, we are in effect asking whether corporeal substance contains "formally everything which is to be found objectively or representatively in the ideas" of sensible things (7: 79).[6] In the *Principles*, he affirms that insofar as our sensory idea of matter presents us with "extension, shape and motion," that idea "comes to us from things located outside ourselves, which it wholly resembles [*similis*]" (*Princ.* II.1*). For Descartes, the paradigm of ideational representation is resemblance, and I maintain that he extends this paradigm, in one way or another, to all ideas, including those of sensory qualities such as color.

---

[6] In this quotation I include the phrase "or representatively" from the French version of the *Meditations* (9A: 63), which might have added it by following Descartes' own gloss of "objectively" with "or representatively" in *Princ.* 1.17, where he says, regarding the idea of an ingenious machine, that "all the ingenuity which is contained in that idea only objectively, or as if in a picture, must be contained in the cause of that idea, whatever that cause may be, not merely objectively or representatively, but in fact formally or eminently, at least in the first and principal cause."

There are apparent difficulties with taking Descartes at his word that ideas are like images that resemble their objects. First, images are spatial, but Descartes believes that an immaterial being such as God does not possess extension. How can an idea be an image of such a being? Here we must retreat to the more basic concept of "similitude." Our idea of God is like him inasmuch as we truly grasp the essence of God in our idea. The idea of God is just the essence of God existing objectively or representatively, to the extent that it can, in the idea (7: 105). Similarly, the idea of the sun is the sensory image of the sun, or perhaps the rationally calculated notion of the sun's size and shape, existing objectively in our idea (7: 39, 102). Other scholars have related Descartes' use of the notion of objective reality to extant scholastic notions, in a way that helps dissolve this worry.[7]

A second and more glaring problem for me concerns Descartes' repeated affirmation of a "no resemblance" thesis for sensory ideas such as color. How can it be that all ideas, including ideas of sensory qualities, have objective reality and represent by means of resemblance, if Descartes tells us plainly that ideas of colors are not resemblances, or, more accurately, tells us that it is a mistake to assume that experienced colors resemble real qualities in things? Here we need to distinguish between Descartes' analysis of the erroneous Aristotelian resemblance thesis[8] for color and other secondary qualities and his account of the representative character of ideas of secondary qualities inasmuch as these ideas are obscure and confused representations of objects. I contend that he can consistently deny that color qualia, taken as clear and distinct manifest images, actually resemble real qualities in objects, while also holding that those same qualia bear a resemblance relation to properties in bodies, which is a relation to the (micro) corporeal basis of color – even though we can't know the latter fact merely by contemplating our sensory ideas of color, because they represent the micro-property obscurely.

SENSORY IDEAS OF SIZE AND SHAPE

We have seen that Descartes' official notions of objective and formal reality encourage us to think of the ideas of extension as representing by means of resemblance. In the case of size and shape, our ideas present us

[7] Wells (1984) focuses on Suárez as a source for Descartes; Normore (1986) emphasizes Scotist sources. Wells (1984), n. 36, sees Suárez as seeking to reconcile Aquinas and Scotus on ideas or concepts taken objectively.
[8] On Aristotelian "real qualities," see Hatfield (1998).

sizes and shapes (contain sizes and shapes objectively or representatively), and objects possess the properties of size and shape formally (7: 35, 79–80; *Princ.* II.I). The sizes and shapes that objects possess can be found representatively and, at the macro level, phenomenally and manifestly, in our sensory experience of those objects. The phenomenal content resembles the external properties.

However, even here difficulties arise. In the Third Meditation, Descartes observes that the sensory idea of the sun, in presenting the sun as small, "is most dissimilar to it" (7: 39*) in comparison with the astronomer's conception that the sun is large. He says that both ideas cannot be "similar" to the sun, or perhaps, that they cannot both be similar to the sun as regards size (for both present the sun as round, even if the sensory idea presents it as round and flat). Even worse, in the *Dioptrics* Descartes criticizes the notion that the sense of vision operates by means of images that resemble their objects. He does not argue that there is *no* resemblance involved between the spatial forms of images in the eyes and brain and the spatial characteristics of the objects that they represent, only that the resemblance is partial or "imperfect." To illustrate this point, he considers the relation between an engraved image and the scene it represents:

[T]hey [engravings] represent to us forests, towns, people, and even battles and storms; and although they make us think of countless different qualities of objects, it is only in respect of shape that there is any real resemblance. And even this resemblance is very imperfect, since engravings represent to us bodies of varying relief and depth on a surface which is entirely flat. Moreover, in accordance with the rules of perspective they often represent circles by ovals better than by other circles, squares by rhombuses better than by other squares, and similarly for other shapes. Thus it often happens that in order to be more perfect as an image and to represent an object better, an engraving ought not to resemble it. (6: 113)

In this passage, Descartes does not rule out all resemblance of shape. The final line of the quotation, insofar as it pertains to the discussion of circles and squares in perspective, must surely be read as saying "ought not to resemble it exactly" or "in all respects," since Descartes has allowed that ovals and rhombuses resemble circles and squares "imperfectly," that is, to some extent.

Subsequently in the *Dioptrics*, Descartes affirms that the image or picture formed on the retina and transmitted into the brain retains "some resemblance to the objects from which it proceeds," but contends that it is not "by means of this resemblance that the picture causes our sensory perception of these objects" (6: 130). Rather, he invokes a relation "instituted by nature" (6: 130*) between brain states and sensory perception to explain the production of the latter. The sensory perceptions that he describes present to us objects in three dimensions, with "position, distance, size, and shape" and also "light" and "color" (6: 130). The institutions of nature take several forms. The perception of size and shape depends on the perspective properties of images, and so includes a limited form of resemblance between brain image and resulting three-dimensional perception, which Descartes allows in the engraving. Distance is sometimes perceived via perspectival relation, by taking into account the known sizes of objects in relation to their projective sizes (6: 138). But the perception of distance is also produced psychophysiologically, when states of the brain mechanisms that control accommodation (and perhaps convergence) directly produce ideas of distance (6: 137).[9] Light and color depend on "no resemblance" brain signs consisting of vibrational nerve processes that differ in their "force" and "manner." Color is perceived as being in objects at a distance presumably because the mind, through the processes of distance perception just scouted, localizes objects with colored surfaces at a distance. In this regard, "externalization" becomes a matter of localization via direction and distance (6: 134–37).

Descartes' discussions of resemblance in the *Dioptrics* allow us to specify more closely the ways in which resemblance and no resemblance come into play for him. He is, in the first place, intent to show that the processes of vision need not rely completely or fully on resemblance. For this purpose, he reminds us that non-resembling items can serve as signs that generate representations of things. As he explains, "our mind can be stimulated by many things other than images – by signs and words, for example, which in no way resemble the things they signify" (6: 112). In this connection, states of the brain that do not resemble the objects to which they correspond can make the mind form a representation of those objects.[10] In the case of partial resemblance, this happens when ovals make us see circles. Presumably, changes in the brain that signify distance, such as those controlling the accommodation of the eye, can make us experience distance, even though these changes need not resemble

---

[9] On judgmental and psychophysiological accounts of distance perception in Descartes, see Hatfield (1992, 2000); Wolf-Devine (1993), ch. 4; Vinci (1998), ch. 4.3; and Simmons (2003).

[10] The "sign" relation between brain states and sensory ideas is prominently discussed in the *Treatise on Light* (11: 4) and the Sixth Meditation (7: 86, 88). Yolton (1984), pp. 22–31, treats the sign relation as semantic: the mind "interprets" the signs. Slezak (2000) suggests that Descartes may have a merely causal relation in mind: that a brain state can cause a sensory idea that does not resemble the brain state. (Slezak then develops a further account of representation in Descartes, different from that I am developing.)

distance – although in fact Descartes specifies in the *Treatise on Man* that the central brain state that varies with distance is itself a distance, since it consists in the degree to which the pineal gland leans in order to control accommodation and convergence, with a greater lean forward indicating nearer distance (11: 183). Color is a clearer case of no resemblance between brain state and experienced quality. Here, the *manner* of brain motion causes us to see color. On the reading I am proposing, the resulting color quale that we experience does not, considered simply in its experienced or manifest qualitative character, resemble the object, nor does the experienced color quale obscurely and confusedly present the brain state; rather, it obscurely presents the surface texture that causes a spin on light particles that yields differing manners of brain motion, depending on the color.

These discussions contain two importantly different questions of possible resemblance or lack thereof. First, there is the question of whether brain states must resemble the objects to which they correspond. Second, there is the question of whether the sensory ideas that result in the mind represent via resemblance, and what they resemble (brain state vs. distal object). Once these two factors have been distinguished, we can see that various possibilities exist for Descartes. He could deny resemblance in both cases (brain state and idea), in one but not the other, or he could affirm resemblance in both cases. In particular, I note the possibility that a non-resembling brain state could yield an idea that represents distal objects via resemblance.[11]

These passages from Descartes' natural philosophical writings, and others from the *Treatise on Light* and *Treatise on Man*, expressly posit a partial resemblance between images in the brain and the spatial properties of things (11: 175–76), while also invoking "no resemblance" on occasion (11: 4). They do not address more fundamental questions about the nature of ideas as representations and whether representation itself relies on resemblance.

Taking into account what we have gleaned thus far from the metaphysical and natural philosophical writings, and looking forward to the next section, I propose a fourfold division of aspects of "resemblance" between ideas of objects, including between ideas of size, distance, and color and the properties in objects that these ideas represent. First, in the case of

---

[11] Keating (1999) rightly distinguishes no resemblance in mechanical cause from the question of representationality; however, she does not indicate that a non-resembling brain state might cause a resembling idea, presumably because she believes that ideas of sensory qualities do not represent and so is not interested in this conceptual possibility.

clear and distinct intellectual perceptions of the properties of extension, we can posit a complete resemblance. Objective reality (in ideas) and formal reality (in objects) exactly match.[12] Second, as regards sensory perception of size and shape, the resemblance is sometimes complete, sometimes not. Descartes acknowledged the phenomenon of size constancy (6: 140), in which the phenomenal size present in experience is congruent with the physical size of the object. But he observed that size constancy does not hold for far-away objects. Our ideas of those objects show only a partial resemblance: the objects may appear smaller than they are, or their shapes may not be accurately perceived (a square tower may appear round).[13] Third, ideas of color taken simply in their manifest or phenomenal image do not resemble anything in the world, consistent with Descartes' rejection of Aristotelian "real qualities." Fourth, I propose that, as representing the corporeal surface properties of objects, the very same sensory ideas of color are obscure and confused representations of spatial properties, which they resemble, however imperfectly.

The first and second instances, which distinguish purely intellectual representations from spatial qualia in sensory perception, are less controversial than the other two. The third and fourth instances require discussion.

IDEAS OF SENSORY QUALITIES: CLEAR AND DISTINCT, OBSCURE AND CONFUSED

In his discussions of sensory ideas such as those of color, Descartes explains that in some respects they can be viewed as clear and distinct, whereas in others they must be regarded as obscure and confused. This distinction can provide help with reconciling "no resemblance" with "representation through resemblance."

In the *Principles*, Descartes explains that sensations (along with appetites and affects) can "be clearly perceived if we carefully avoid making

---

[12] It is likely that the intellectual ideas of extended things do not present extension as a phenomenal image. In the Sixth Meditation (7: 72–73), Descartes distinguishes purely intellectual ideas of geometrical figures from those formed in the imagination and makes clear that, for some figures (such as a chiliagon), the shape is understood rather than imagined. In such a case, the intellectual idea of a circle would specify a curved line equidistant from a center point, and this intellectually grasped relation would perfectly match a material circle, if a perfect corporeal circle existed. Descartes does not offer an explicit phenomenology of intellectually grasped shapes.

[13] Although they are presumably not perceived as clearly and distinctly as purely intellectual perceptions of geometrical properties, Descartes allowed that sensible instances of size, shape, and motion can be perceived clearly and distinctly in sense perception (*Princ.* 1.69) and imagination (iv.200).

any judgment about them beyond what is exactly contained in our perception, and what we are inwardly conscious of" (*Princ.* 1.66). He further elaborates that "pain, and color, and the remaining things of this kind, are clearly and distinctly perceived when regarded as only sensations or thoughts" (*Princ.* 1.68). He gives some indication whence the lack of clarity and distinctness arises: it comes from failing to distinguish our sensations from habitual judgments that we make about them in accordance with childhood prejudices (1.46, 66) and from believing that our sensations allow us to perceive something that we don't in fact perceive (1.70).

In order better to interpret these passages, and to align them with the discussion of clarity and distinctness in the *Meditations*, let us recall Descartes' definitions of clarity and distinctness:

I call "clear" that perception which is present and manifest to an attentive mind: just as we say that we clearly see those things which are present to our intent eye and act upon it sufficiently strongly and manifestly. On the other hand, I call "distinct" that perception which, while clear, is so separated and delineated from all others that it contains absolutely nothing except what is clear. (*Princ.* 1.45)

Clarity makes the object of representation manifest to the mind; distinctness keeps other content out of the perception. By contrast, we may suppose that obscurity dims this perception, making it difficult to tell what exactly is being represented, while confusion mixes other things into the perception without our being aware of that mixture.

Descartes illustrates this distinction with the example of the perception of pain:

[W]hen someone feels some great pain, the perception of pain is indeed very clear in him, but is not always distinct; for commonly men confuse that perception with their uncertain judgment about its nature, because they believe something resembling the feeling of pain to be in the painful part. And thus a perception which is not distinct can be clear; but no perception can be distinct unless it is clear. (*Princ.* 1.46)

In the case of color, a sense perception is confused if we mix in a judgment that there is something in objects that is "exactly similar to" or that "resembles" the sensation (1.66, 68). We may falsely believe that we clearly perceive a resembling real quality in the object, when we do not. To the extent that we mix this false judgment about resemblance together with our phenomenally clear sense perception of color (our experience of a color quale), our perception is rendered confused.

Reference to the prejudices of childhood can explain how sense perceptions of color are confused, but it does not help us with clarity and obscurity. Descartes has told us that sense perceptions of color are both clear and distinct "when regarded as only sensations or thoughts." In accordance with the definitions of clarity and distinctness, they are distinct because they are not mixed together with other content, such as might be added by habitual judgments, and they are clear because, as phenomenal qualia, they are "present and manifest" to the mind. Are the color perceptions themselves obscure? In the *Principles*, Descartes says that from the perception of color, we are unable to tell what color is in objects, that is, "what it is for it [a body] to have color" (*Princ.* I.69), which suggests that, as a representation of a property in bodies, the perception is obscure (see also *Princ.* IV.200). He refers the reader to the *Meditations* for his account of what is true in "confused and obscure" sense perceptions (*Princ.* I.30), and in the *Meditations* he treats sense perceptions of color and the like as intrinsically obscure and confused (7: 80, 81, 83).

If sensory perceptions, as all thoughts, are representations, then their obscurity should arise if they do not make "present and manifest" what they represent in objects. This conception of obscurity is suggested by Descartes' discussion of material falsity in the Third Meditation:

[M]aterial falsity ... occurs in ideas, when they represent non-things as things. For example, the ideas which I have of heat and cold contain so little clarity and distinctness that they do not enable me to tell whether cold is merely the absence of heat or vice versa, or whether both of them are real qualities, or neither is. (7: 43–44)

This passage, which was targeted by Arnauld in his Objections, is often discussed in relation to whether Descartes thought that the idea of cold represents a non-thing as a thing, on the assumption that he believed cold to be a privation, consisting in lack of heat. By contrast to Aristotelian physics, in which cold is a privation, Descartes' physics treats heat and cold as degrees of motion, with hotter things having more motion of their particles (*Princ.* IV.29, 46; *Meteorology*, disc. I, II: 235–36). Cold is less motion, which, although privative in some respect, is surely not a non-thing.

In any event, with respect to material falsity, the case of cold is a red herring. For, no matter what Descartes thought about cold, he must also explain how the ideas of heat, color, and other sensory qualities can be materially false (7: 43, 234). Further, he must explain what it is that is true in such sensory ideas, since he tells us in the Sixth Meditation that they contain "some truth" (7: 80). In the passage just quoted from the Third Meditation, he does say that ideas are materially false if they "represent things as non-things" (7: 44). But he goes on to explain that, if they are true, then they represent something (7: 44), even if their objective reality is "slight" (presumably because they represent things obscurely). The problem with sensory ideas is that, from their phenomenal presence, we cannot tell what they represent.

As we have seen, taken merely as phenomenal qualia, sensory ideas of color are clear. They must, then, be obscure by comparison with some other standard, beyond their bare phenomenal character. I propose that this standard is whatever they represent, truly but obscurely, in objects. That is, their obscurity arises from a failure to make present and manifest to the mind the color property in bodies that ideas of color represent. Indeed, Descartes tells us that sensory perceptions such as that of color "provide only very obscure information" about the nature of bodies (7: 83), and that, regarding "qualities" of bodies such as "colors, sounds, and the rest," "their images in our thought are always confused, and we do not know what they may be" (*Princ.* IV.200*).

It is up to metaphysics to guide natural philosophy toward a correct interpretation of what color, heat, and other qualities are in bodies, and hence what the perception of those qualities represents obscurely in bodies. Descartes explains that these qualities in bodies consist of an "arrangement" of their particles, that is, in various arrangements of particles as regards their size, shape, and motion (*Princ.* IV.199). Hence, if color perceptions truly represent something in bodies – albeit obscurely and in a way not open to knowledge by means of direct inspection of the sensory ideas themselves – then they must represent the arrangements of particles on the surfaces of things, which impart varying spins to particles of light so as to cause in us sensory ideas of red, or blue, or another color. The sensory idea of red is an obscure representation of a surface texture. (A clear representation would be a clear image or understanding of the micro surface texture.)[14] In accordance with the institution of nature, God has made our minds such that the several surface textures of bodies give rise to differing sensations of color (6: 130–31), which I interpret as obscure representations. Accordingly, he has made our minds such that these

---

[14] Can this surface texture be clearly imagined? Or must any clear conception of it arise in the understanding alone? In *Princ.* IV.201–5, Descartes describes the rationale for attributing specific microstructures to visible things. The spin-inducing surface texture would be an instance. If imagined, wouldn't it need to be pictured as having color? Surely. But Descartes might have conceived the images of his posited microstructures as black and white, on the model of his illustrations in the *Dioptrics* and *Principles*. Black and white are still colors, but in the diagrams they serve the function of making known or illustrating the sizes, shapes, and motion-paths of subvisible particles, not their colors.

obscure representations of surface textures present themselves phenomenally as clear instances of phenomenal red (an experienced quale) – at
least to an attentive mind using healthy eyes in good light on a red object.
Obscure representations of variously shaped particles also yield tastes
and smells (depending on the nerves they affect, gustatory or olfactory),
obscure representations of vibrations are sounds, and obscure representations of motion in particles are sensory ideas of heat or cold.

There is an alternative interpretation that accepts part of this picture
but rejects the account of representation. One might hold (a) that sensory
ideas of color are obscure simply because in their phenomenal character they do not make manifest what color is as a property of bodies, and
(b) that sensory ideas represent the color properties in bodies (the surface
textures that spin light particles) by being arbitrary signs of them (as in
Alanen [1994]), not by obscure resemblance. The phenomenal color would
be a sign of the external color-property. This position agrees with my point
that phenomenal color does not reveal the physical color-property. But it
does not accommodate the notion that color ideas actually represent that
property in an obscure manner. Once the sign relation is understood, the
obscurity presumably is replaced by a clear understanding of that relation. Each color quality reveals to us that there is a distinct cause in the
object for that color but does not purport to tell us what that property is
and so does not represent that property obscurely. This position augments
representation-by-resemblance with a sign relation.[15]

On my reading, if we accept that sensory perceptions are "true" but
"obscure" representations of something in bodies, then metaphysics
tells natural philosophy that this something must consist in modes of
extension. From this hint, natural philosophy then develops the theory
that colors in bodies are differing arrangements of particles that cause
various spins in light particles, which variously affect the nerves, causing them to move in characteristic manners, which then cause perceptions of color in the mind. Because these perceptions are obscure with
respect to the surface textures, the specific surface-texture structure that
blue-ideas represent and how it differs from the structure that red-ideas
represent cannot be determined phenomenally. A sensory idea of red is a
blurry image of the texture that causes it. What makes it a blurry image

---

[15] As previously noted, I treat the sign relation as involving a causal relation, in which a
non-resembling brain state (the "sign" of II: 4) causes the mind to have a sense perception that
doesn't resemble that brain state (hence the arbitrariness of the sign relation between brain and
mind) but which may or may not, as further analysis would show, include content that represents external objects and properties by resemblance.

of a red-idea-causing surface texture rather another surface texture? The fact of which blurry image represents which texture is established by the institution of nature, which produces the blurry image of a red-surface-texture when certain brain motions are present, and a blurry image of a blue-surface-texture when other motions are present. (The institution of nature establishes what the obscure image is an image of.) Because representation occurs by resemblance, the perception should be regarded as itself an obscure presentation of the spatial structure of that surface texture. But, as it happens (and here is where some mystery lies), the mind experiences this obscurely represented microtexture as phenomenal red. Hence, the underlying resemblance is not detectable via contemplation of the phenomenal character of color. It must be posited through natural philosophical reasoning, guided by the metaphysics of matter (as in *Princ.* IV.189–200).

IDEAS, JUDGMENTS, AND REPRESENTATION

The position that I am proposing takes a stand on several disputed issues. It is in partial agreement with some interpretations and opposed to others. It puts several pieces together in a new way, especially in distinguishing the qualitative character of sensory ideas considered manifestly from the same qualitative character considered as the obscure presentation of a surface texture.

As regards the representationality of Cartesian ideas, I agree with those who have Descartes maintaining that all ideas are representations.[16] I do not distinguish between representationality and objective reality.[17] Hence,

---

[16] Chappell (1986) argues this position; Alanen (1994) ascribes to it, but treats sensory ideas of secondary qualities as representing differently from ideas of extension; ideas of extension-properties represent by resemblance, whereas secondary-quality ideas are mere signs of their causes. MacKenzie (1994), Keating (1999), and Brown (2008) hold that ideas of color and the like don't represent. Simmons (1999) finds that such ideas represent ecological properties but not by resemblance. M. Wilson (1990) maintains that secondary-quality ideas don't "present" objects but refer to them in accordance with a causal theory of reference. Bolton (1986) contends that sensory ideas all represent and that they generally do so by resemblance, but that secondary-quality ideas might resemble only in their relations (e.g. spatial placement) to other sensory ideas.

[17] Wells (1990) holds that all Cartesian ideas represent but distinguishes representation from objective reality, as does Normore (1986). I agree with these authors in allowing ideas to represent "pre-judgmentally" (as Wells puts it), that is, independently of judgment. The content of ideas can be spelled out propositionally (prior to any judgment that affirms the proposition) and in terms of represents-as: an idea represents body-as-extended, or that body is extended. My account treats the representational content of ideas of bodies as depicting those bodies as being a certain way. This sort of content shares something with Peacocke's (1992) scenarios and falls within a "descriptivist account" as invoked by De Rosa (2010), although the mode of description for me is pictorial and the descriptive content is not knowable through phenomenal character

I not only take Descartes at his word when he says that "the objective mode of being belongs to ideas by their very nature" (7: 42), but I also take him to be saying with this phrase that all ideas represent. The objects that ideas represent may themselves be true (possibly or necessarily existent) or false (can't exist).[18] I deny that entire kinds of sensory ideas intrinsically misrepresent, although individual sensory ideas may do so, as when a sensory idea presents a white thing as yellow (7: 145).[19] With Descartes in the Fourth Replies, I hold that kinds of ideas of sensory qualities merely provide material for error, or an occasion for error.[20]

At first blush, it may appear that Descartes holds that materially false ideas are indeed misrepresentations, because they "represent non-things as things" (7: 43). Descartes offers this gloss on material falsity in the Third Meditation. But he also offers a second position. In the Third Meditation itself, he considers the (exclusive) disjunction that materially false ideas are false and represent non-things or that they are true but that "the reality which they represent is so extremely slight that I cannot even distinguish it from a non-thing" (7: 44). Presumably, what is slight is the representation of the property of a body (he is not saying that the external property is slight). In the Sixth Meditation, he tells us that his sensory ideas, including those of color in bodies, must be regarded as presenting "teachings of nature" that contain "some truth" (7: 80–81), seeming to follow the second position. In the Fourth Replies, he concedes to Arnauld that if the idea of cold actually presents cold as a positive thing, then, assuming that cold actually is a privation, the idea "is not the idea of cold" (7: 234). He further explains that the material falsity of the idea consists not in a positive entity that it presents, but in the obscurity of the idea: "the obscurity of the idea is the only thing that leads me to judge that the

---

alone but is posited on metaphysical and natural philosophical grounds. I don't here take a stand on other questions, including how sensory ideas come to be of individuals, whether judgment is required for fully conceptualized perception (as the Second Meditation discussion of automata and human beings suggests, 7: 32), and more.

[18] Wells (1990) discusses ideas as apprehensions of objects that are true (possible) or false (impossible).

[19] Wee (2006), ch. 3, and De Rosa (2010) hold that sensory ideas (of secondary qualities) misrepresent. Alanen (1994) finds that material falsity arises from a resemblance judgment that is associated with kinds of sensory ideas; material falsity is constituted by the actual error of such judgments. When a jaundiced eye makes white things look yellow, if we withhold judgment, the idea itself may still be materially false, as in the false-gods example from above. But I interpret generic material falsity of sensory ideas as arising for Descartes from obscurity that permits false judgment, not from intrinsically false content, as in the positions of Wee and De Rosa. For me, types of sensory ideas normally possess material truth; color ideas obscurely represent a surface texture, before we judge, on metaphysical and natural philosophical grounds, that they do so.

[20] Wells (1984) and Bolton (1986) hew to this position.

idea of the sensation of cold represents some object called 'cold' which is located outside me" (7: 234–35) – perhaps an instance of an impulsive resemblance judgment. Accordingly, the sensory idea of cold would not present a non-thing as a thing, but would present whatever it represents so obscurely that we can't tell what sort of thing cold is.

Here in the Fourth Replies, as in the Sixth Meditation, Descartes invokes false judgments in his analysis of how we make errors with respect to sensory objects. This raises the larger and much-discussed question of the role of judgments in Descartes' theory of sense perception. At various points, Descartes invokes habitual judgments in accounting for sense perception, ascribing them a positive role (or at least sometimes positive) in the perception of size and distance and a negative role in cases of material falsity and the falsity of "ill-considered judgments" (7: 82). Further, some commentators attribute the externalization of sensory qualities such as cold, and their reference to bodies, as resulting solely from judgments.[21]

In the position I have developed, the only falsity that can properly be associated with materially false sensory ideas arises from the ill-considered judgments that ascribe "resembling" qualities – that is, qualities that resemble the manifest character of sensations – to bodies. Such judgments are not reflectively or wittingly made. In this regard, they are like the judgments underlying the perception of size and distance. These latter judgments, which are found in Descartes' "third grade of sense" (7: 437–38*), are partly responsible for the externalization of sensory qualities as appearing at a distance. But they are not the only mechanism for externalization. The referring of perceived qualities to objects, that is, the presentation of qualities such as red as belonging to objects in some sense, does not result solely from ill-considered judgments together with judgments in the third grade of sense, but also arises through the normal psychophysiological processes described in the *Dioptrics* and *Treatise on Man*.

We can better understand how judgments figure into "material falsity" by considering Descartes' explication of the term "material" as used here.

Since ideas are forms of a kind, and are not composed of any matter, when we think of them as representing something we are not taking them *materially* but *formally*. If, however, we were considering them not as representing this or that but simply as operations of the intellect, then it could be said that we were taking them materially, but in that case they would have no reference to the truth or falsity of their objects. (7: 232)

---

[21] Alanen (1994), MacKenzie (1994), and Keating (1999).

This passage is pregnant with implication. First, it distinguishes ideas taken "formally" from the same ideas taken "materially." The use of "formal" here is not the ontological notion of formal existence discussed above (which was contrasted with objective existence), but is a way of denoting the representational content of ideas. Accordingly, the distinction between considering ideas "materially" and "formally" corresponds to the distinction between taking ideas "materially" and "objectively" in the preface to the *Mediations* (7: 8).

More importantly, Descartes says that when ideas are taken materially, they have nothing to do with the "truth or falsity of their objects." Because they are not being taken objectively, they are not treated as intrinsically representing. And yet in our ill-considered judgments, we treat these same ideas as representing a resembling "real quality." That's part of what makes such judgments ill considered. It is because these sensory ideas naturally enter into judgments of this sort that they are materially false:

[T]he only sense in which an idea can be said to be "materially false" is the one which I explained. Thus, whether cold is a positive thing or an absence does not affect the idea I have of it, which remains the same as it always was. It is this idea which, I claim, can provide subject-matter for error if it is in fact true that cold is an absence and does not have as much reality as heat; for if I consider the ideas of cold and heat just as I received them from my senses, I am unable to tell that one idea exhibits more reality to me than the other. (7: 232–33*)

The appeal to the ideas of cold and heat "just as I received them from my senses" may be taken as an appeal to our immediate experience of these ideas, that is, to their manifest qualitative character. From the point of view of the metaphysical theorist, ideas so considered are treated merely as phenomenal sensations and not objectively as representations.[22] Taken

---

[22] Commentators who view Cartesian sensory ideas of secondary qualities as non-representational make much of some passages in which Descartes says that sensory ideas are "sensations" which "represent nothing situated outside thought" (*Princ.* 1.71) or that the materially false idea of cold is "a sensation which in fact has no existence outside the intellect" (7: 233). I read the latter passage, from the Fourth Replies, as concerning the idea of cold taken materially, hence not objectively or as a representation, in which case it is regarded as a mere mental state and so as merely in the mind and as not representing anything outside the mind. I read *Princ.* 1.71 as a developmental story, in which Descartes is saying that, when in the womb, sensations of taste, odor, etc., do not represent anything outside of thought because they are not produced by sensory stimulation of a normal sort. Later in development, the child mistakenly adopts the resemblance thesis. But in *Princ.* 1.68–70, Descartes explains that sensory ideas are actually perceptions of as yet unknown properties of objects; as perceivers accept Cartesian metaphysics and natural philosophy, they come to know that color, etc., in bodies are arrangements or motions of particles (*Princ.* IV.189–200).

as such, these ideas *do not* purport to represent objects as possessing "real" colors (as in an Aristotelian theory). But from the standpoint of the uninitiated child or the benighted Aristotelian, such ideas *seem* to present objects as possessing the very qualities manifestly present in the sense experience. Hence, uninitiates impulsively form the manifest resemblance thesis, that something which resembles cold as immediately and unreflectively experienced exists in objects as a "real quality." They "refer" the manifest quality to the thing.[23]

But what of the ideas of color, heat, cold, and the like, taken formally or objectively? I have said that they do represent, via resemblance, the corporeal counterparts to color, heat, and cold, that is, the surface textures or particle motions of bodies. Under this aspect, ideas of color are properly taken to represent the surfaces of objects and to reveal a property that is localized in that surface. That much is a proper teaching of nature (7: 81; *Princ.* 1.68–70). The uninitiated can correctly respond to this legitimate localization of sensory qualities in objects by avoiding the ill-considered judgment of manifest resemblance and simply affirming that something corresponding to color is found in the objects. The initiated can know that this something is a configuration of size, shape, and motion, that is, a surface texture. The initiated can further realize that ideas of color are obscure representations of that micro surface texture, so that phenomenal red arises not through absorption of a similitude or sensible species (a "form without matter"), but through the manner in which a surface texture is obscurely perceived.

In this regard, the referring of the quality to the thing comes about in the usual way that perceived sensory properties are localized for Descartes. In the *Meditations* proper, a simplified explanation of this reference is given through the institution of nature. As Descartes explains in the latter part of the Sixth Meditation, sensations such as pain are felt in

---

[23] De Rosa (2010), p. 28, quotes Descartes (7: 233) as saying that the idea of red "refers to something to which it does not correspond." In the passage, Descartes says that the idea of God "cannot be said to refer to something with which it does not correspond." When speaking of sensory ideas, such as that of cold, he uses the passive voice, saying that "an idea is referred to something other than that of which it is in fact the idea" (7: 233). He goes on to explain that, in such cases, the idea in question is merely "a sensation which in fact has no existence outside the intellect," a phrase that I read in the manner described above (the sensation is the idea of cold, described metaphysically in its material aspect as not representing, but is ill considered by children and Aristotelians and referred by them to external bodies under the guise of its manifest sensory quality). Thus, while I agree with De Rosa that Cartesian sensory ideas are all representations, I hold that in the analysis of material falsity, sensory ideas are regarded as mere sensations (so, not under their representational aspect). Such an idea does not, considered *qua* bare sensation, refer to anything.

the damaged part because that is the best arrangement for the preservation of the body (or the mind–body complex). The sensation-of-a-pain-as-
occurring-in-the-foot informs us of damage by phenomenally presenting
pain in the foot (7: 88). Extending to pain the view of sensory ideas as
obscure representations of corporeal states, the quality of pain should
now be seen as representing the damage; the spatial localization assigns
it to the foot. In this case, assigning the pain – or, inasmuch as the pain
is a representation, its object, bodily damage – to a location in space is
proper.[24] By parity of reasoning, the bodies in the environment that are
"the source" of sensory ideas of color and the like are perceived as possessing differences in their structures corresponding to those qualities (7: 81).
As long as we avoid the ill-considered manifest resemblance judgment, it
is perfectly correct to say that the sensory idea of red, in presenting a red
quality as in an object surface, obscurely presents what red is in bodies (a
surface texture).

REPRESENTATION AND BODILY SENSATIONS

According to this reading, sensory perceptions of colors and other secondary qualities do not intrinsically misrepresent their causes in objects.
They intrinsically represent objects as possessing a color property or other
property. The externalization of color qualia is not an error. It occurs in
a sensory system that has the purpose of presenting objects to us such
that we can, in useful ways, discriminate among them. Colors, tastes,
and the rest guide our practical interactions with objects. They do so by
obscurely representing properties by which bodies do differ. Our sensory ideas represent differences in corporeal microstructure as qualities of
color, taste, smell, sound, or touch.

   Is that the limit of what they represent? That is, do sensory ideas only
represent bare corporeal microstructure? Descartes suggests that they do
more, when he describes hunger, thirst, and pain as "confused sensations"
that play a similar role to that which a clear understanding of damage
would for a sailor surveying his ship. In a well-known passage, Descartes
says that nature teaches us that the mind (or the "I" considered as the
mind) is "very closely joined and, as it were, intermingled" with the body.
The passage continues:

---

[24] Contemporary philosophical discussions of pain have often treated it as a bare sensation that
    does not represent, an orthodoxy that has been challenged, e.g. in Tye (1995). Descartes himself
    is explicit on treating pains as "ordained by nature to indicate to the soul the bodily damage suf-
    fered" (*Passions*, 11: 400).

If this were not so, I, who am nothing but a thinking thing, would not feel pain when the body was hurt, but would perceive the damage purely by the intellect, just as a sailor perceives by sight if anything in his ship is broken. Similarly, when the body needed food or drink, I should have an explicit understanding of the fact, instead of having confused sensations of hunger and thirst. (7: 81)

If the sensations of pain, hunger, and thirst only represented, obscurely and confusedly, corporeal states, then the pain from a knife cut would dimly represent only cleaved skin and not a state of damage, and a feeling of thirst would only represent corporeal dryness and not the need to drink. But, in fact, these sensations also represent damage and needs.

Phenomenally, the inclinations produced by pain, hunger, and thirst appear as bare "teachings of nature." From a metaphysical standpoint, they result from an institution of nature, by which cleaved flesh is presented not merely as cleaved but under a phenomenal aspect of pain and damage, and a dry throat is presented not merely as dry but as indicating the need to drink, where these perceived warnings and needs are obscure representations of bodily states.

Here the resemblance underpinning for sensory representation is pushed to its limit, but it does not collapse. At minimum, a pain obscurely represents cleaved flesh, hunger emptiness, and thirst dryness. Whether these sensations can also confusedly represent damage and need depends in part on whether there are corporeal states of the body that intrinsically are instances of damage and need, rather than being corporeal states that the mind merely so interprets. This takes us to the metaphysics of bodily function, and whether Descartes believed, and had title to believe, that in the body considered as an organic being (as in animals, who have no minds) there are intrinsic properties of well-functioning, damage, and need.[25] Supposing that he did believe so (and leaving aside his entitlement), we may further ask whether it would be likely that there could be corporeal markers of well-being, damage, and need. Again, he likely believed there could be. Further, we might understand these markers in terms of the perfection of bodily organization. In this regard, we might speculatively suppose that the institution of nature includes a kind of blueprint of the well-functioning bodily machine. Feelings of healthful vigor are obscure representations (via resemblance) that bodily organization is in its proper state. Pain, thirst, and hunger would then

---

[25] On these issues, see Hatfield (1992, 2008) and Shapiro (2003).

be obscure representations (via resemblance) of deviation from proper order.[26]

Further discussion of this speculative interpretation lies beyond the scope of this chapter, in which I have sought to show the plausibility of Descartes' having held a resemblance theory of representation for ideas generally, paired with phenomenal clarity for sensations taken in themselves and intrinsic obscurity (but not error) as the relation between secondary-quality ideas and their representata in objects. This reading is supported by extending Descartes' account of representation by resemblance (based on an analogy with images) to ideas of secondary qualities. I don't claim that it is the only interpretation (sign-theories are an alternative), but it has the virtue of attributing a comparatively unified account of sensory representation to Descartes.

---

[26] This speculation is not as outlandish as it may appear. In the *Passions*, art. 5–6, Descartes effectively says that the soul leaves the body because the body is broken (11: 330–31). Perhaps the soul leaves when it perceives, via an institution of nature that implicitly relies on an innate schema of a well-functioning body, that the body has deviated from its proper order? In the Synopsis of the *Meditations*, Descartes implies that death results as follows: "a human body loses its identity merely as a result of a change in the shape of some of its parts" (7: 14), a picture that is suggestive of the soul as recognizing death through the body's deviation from proper shapes.

PART IV
The human being

CHAPTER 8

Teleology and natures in Descartes' Sixth Meditation

Karen Detlefsen

I INTRODUCTION

Here are three features of Descartes' philosophy relevant to the issue of teleology.[1]

Feature 1: Descartes famously rejects the use of teleological explanations in natural philosophy (7: 55, 2: 38–39; 7: 375, 2: 258; 8A: 15–16, 1: 202–3; 8A: 81, 1: 248–49; 5: 158, 3: 341).

Feature 2: In the Sixth Meditation, Descartes seems to give a teleological account of the sensations of the human mind–body composite, saying that it is perfectly legitimate to account for certain characteristics of the composite in teleological terms while, at the same time, rejecting the legitimacy of teleological explanations in the case of purely material systems including living bodies – a clock or a non-ensouled human body, for example (7: 82–85, 2: 575–9).

Feature 3: Descartes routinely makes use of teleological-sounding explanations in his biological[2] works where he describes and explains the functional behaviors of non-human living bodies as well as of the living human body considered (counterfactually) in isolation from its soul (e.g. 6: 46ff., 1: 134ff.; 11: 244; 11: 431).

Take any pair of these features and there is a tension – three tensions in all. My goal with this chapter is not to sort out all aspects of Descartes'

I am grateful for stimulating discussion with and questions from audiences at the following conferences and colloquia: The Life Sciences in Early Modern Philosophy: A Workshop (Princeton University), Johns Hopkins–Penn Early Modern Working Group (Johns Hopkins University), SPAWN 2009: Nature and Purpose in Early Modern Philosophy (Syracuse University), A Day with Descartes (University of Toronto), Annual Lecture Series, Center for Philosophy of Science (University of Pittsburg), Fordham University, and University of Massachusetts, Amherst. This material is based upon work supported by the National Science Foundation under Grant no. 0432156.

[1] I use the term "teleology" for ease of expression while being mindful that this term did not actually appear until Christian Wolff coined it in 1728 (Wolff [1728] 1983). I use it, as did Wolff, to designate that part of natural philosophy that deals with the ends of things or the purposes which they serve.

[2] I use the term "biological" to refer to Descartes' works in which he investigates living beings. For more on this, see section VI, below.

position on teleological explanations, human composites, and other living bodies; that project requires a more sustained discussion than I can give it here. Rather, my goal is to look more closely at the Sixth Meditation passage – especially in light of some helpful conceptual background – as a first step in gaining a global picture of Descartes' thought on teleology. Some of the more general, schematic conclusions near the end of the chapter indicate the more general picture I aim to develop in a longer, more sustained treatment of this subject in Descartes.

Thesis [handwritten marginal note]

[handwritten notes: "→ purpose sentence?" "gen. picture on Descartes though on teleology from the sixth meditation."]

II DESCARTES' SIXTH MEDITATION PASSAGE

Here is the Sixth Meditation passage, which seems to stand in tension both with Descartes' anti-teleology claims and with his teleological-sounding explanations in the life sciences:

I must more accurately define exactly what I mean when I say that I am taught something by nature … My sole concern here is with what God has bestowed on me as a combination of mind and body. *My nature, then, in this limited sense, does indeed teach me to avoid what induces a feeling of pain and to seek out what induces feelings of pleasure, and so on.*

[W]hen I consider the purpose of the clock, I may say that it is departing from its nature when it does not tell the right time; and similarly when I consider the mechanisms of the human body, I may think that, in relation to the movements which normally occur in it, it too is deviating from its nature if the throat is dry at a time when drinking is not beneficial to its continued health. But I am well aware that "nature" as I have just used it has a very different significance from "nature" in the other sense [as applied to the human composite]. As I have just used it, "nature" is simply a label which depends on my thought; it is quite extraneous to the things to which it is applied … But by "nature" in the other sense I understand something which is really to be found in the things themselves; in this sense, therefore, the term contains something of the truth.

When we say, then, with respect to the body suffering from dropsy, that it has a disordered nature because it has a dry throat and yet does not need drink, the term "nature" here is used merely as an extraneous label. *However, with respect to the composite, that is, the mind united with the body, what is involved is not a mere label, but a true error of nature, namely that the body is thirsty at a time when drink is going to cause the body harm.* (7: 82–85, 2: 57–99; emphases added; translation altered)

At this point, I highlight the following two initially crucial features of this passage. First, Descartes makes a clear distinction between a clock and a living human body on the one hand (and one can add any non-ensouled living body to this category), and the human being (or mind–body composite) on the other hand. Second, the latter but not the former is treated in self-consciously teleological terms. That is, Descartes here indicates

[handwritten notes: "↳ the passage in the sixth meditation ↳ sentence 2"] that certain physiological behaviors that typically fall under the purview of natural philosophy are *beneficial* or *harmful* to the mind–body composite, and that the sensations (e.g. pleasure and pain) are *functionally useful* in identifying those behaviors. We sense the world around us in the way that we do *so as to* be better able to preserve our bodies.

Unsurprisingly, this passage has attracted much attention, not least of all because of Descartes' pronouncements elsewhere *against* the reliance on teleological explanations in natural philosophy. Jean La Porte (1928) and Alison Simmons (2001) have both provided prima facie compelling readings of this passage, and I present critical features of these readings here. Simmons, for example, argues as follows. Descartes *does* take the mind–body composite to be a teleological system, uniquely so in the natural world (clocks, human bodies, and dogs, on the other hand, are not teleological systems). Certain features of the teleological system that is the human composite – sensation, especially, but other physiological processes such as digestion as well – serve the end of the mind–body composite. This end is survival, specifically the survival of the body in a state suitable to allow the mind to continue to be united with it (Simmons [2001], pp. 53 and 55–56).

Simmons, La Porte, and others are, of course, mindful of the possible problems that arise for this teleological reading of the Sixth Meditation passage, most notably the tension between this reading and Descartes' anti-teleology pronouncements (Feature 1, above). Roughly, Simmons resolves the tension as follows (Simmons 2001, pp. 64ff.). She first notes the medieval distinction between divine, rational, and natural teleology. Divine teleology is the attribution of ends to God, especially in his creation of the universe and its parts. Rational teleology is the attribution of ends to rational creatures in their conscious deliberation. Natural teleology is the attribution of ends to non-rational bodies and their parts. Simmons then claims that Descartes' anti-teleology passages banish divine and rational teleology from physics, but that these passages need not be read as banning natural teleology from physics. That is, as long as the attribution of ends to natural systems does not intrude in the search for the efficient causes of the behaviors under investigation, natural teleology is perfectly legitimate in Descartes' philosophy. Finally, Simmons argues both that the form of teleology that we find in the case of mind–body composites in Descartes is natural teleology, and that this natural teleology does not interfere in the search for the efficient cause of the behaviors in question.

Simmons does identify a potential problem with this approach. "In a theistic framework, it might seem a short step from proscribing divine teleology to proscribing natural teleology. If God creates the natural world, the thought goes, then surely any ends in nature are really God's ends" (Simmons 2001, p. 66). La Porte also identifies this problem and deals with it by offering the important distinction between the ends God has when he creates, and the ends he conveys to the things he creates (La Porte 1928, pp. 371–75).[3] Simmons picks up this distinction:

> There is an ambiguity lurking in this line of thought [which holds that pro-scribing divine teleology leads to proscribing natural teleology], for it fails to distinguish between (a) the ends that move God to create and (b) the ends of the things he creates. Perhaps God creates eyes because he wants his creatures to get around by seeing and he determines that the eyes are a means to sight … This is a matter of divine teleology about which Descartes claims the natural philoso-pher has no business making guesses. It is a further question whether the eyes that God creates serve the creature's end of survival. To be sure, it is God who decides that this sort of creature have the sort of means-and-ends structure that it does. God is thus the *source* of creaturely means and ends. But the creature's ends are not God's ends (except in the limited sense that he decides to create them); they are ends *with* which (not *for* which) God creates them. (Simmons 2001, pp. 66–67)

I think La Porte and Simmons are on to something crucial in highlight-ing this distinction, but it is not fully nor explicitly stated. As it stands, one might (uncharitably) reply to Simmons' defense just quoted as fol-lows. If we explain the harm done by dropsy, for example, to the human composite in terms of the ends of the composite that God bestowed upon that composite, we are ultimately making reference to God's purposes with respect to the composite, and this is illegitimate. That is, whether we refer to God's broader, theological ends, which urge him to create (such as his purposes with respect to the human's place in the universe), or we refer to God's narrower, physical ends, which are reflected in the living beings he has produced (such as his purpose to structure organisms in such a way that will permit them to function toward self-maintenance), we are ultimately making unwarranted reference to God's purposes.[4] Indeed, one can identify two possible misgivings one might have about the La Porte/Simmons approach at this juncture. First, as we shall see below, Descartes is opposed to any claims in natural philosophy which depend upon our supposing to know God's purposes vis-à-vis the natural world, and this presumably holds regardless of whether we claim to know God's

---

[3] La Porte notes that this crucial distinction is used by St. Thomas, and repeated by Gibieuf, whose work would have been the source of Descartes' own knowledge of the distinction.

[4] I take this to be Des Chene's conclusion with respect to teleology in Descartes as well. Des Chene (1996), pp. 391ff.

purposes directly and immediately, or indirectly and mediated by what we find in the mind–body composite. Second, and related, any explanation which relies upon making reference to God's ends (directly or indirectly), is an explanation which relies upon something "extraneous" to the mind–body composite (God) which runs counter to Descartes' explicit claims in the Sixth Meditation that the composite is different from everything else because of its intrinsic teleological nature – a nature "which is really to be found in the things themselves" – a nature which can *and must be* explicated wholly in terms of itself without any reference at all to anything outside of itself, including God.

III SOME HELPFUL CONCEPTUAL BACKGROUND ON TELEOLOGY

Teleological thinking is sometimes thought to belong to one of two main strains – what one might call "natural" teleology and "unnatural" teleology, with the former capturing a broadly Aristotelian approach and the latter capturing a broadly Platonic approach.[5] Aristotelian teleology is an immanent or intrinsic teleology according to which the goal or end is intrinsic to the being itself, which thus has an internal, end-directed principle of change. The being need not be conscious or aware of this intrinsic end. Platonic teleology is extrinsic or external teleology according to which the end or goal of a being is found in the mind of an external agent. The external agent is conscious and aware of this goal, and the end or goal is not the being's end or goal, but the agent's. The model of a craftsman who, with purposes in mind, builds an artifact that can fulfill those purposes is a typical example of Platonic teleology.[6]

In order to develop what I take to be the promising kernel in the La Porte/Simmons approach, and to therefore provide a more charitable reading of Simmons' quoted defense than the one offered at the close of the previous section, in this section I sketch some crucial elements of these two versions of teleology. I turn to Plato and Aristotle themselves not because these would have been Descartes' historical sources, but because the thinking of these two figures on teleology exhibits very clearly some *conceptual* principles helpful for thinking about Descartes' approach to the topic. Moreover, there are very few historically significant

---

[5] The term "unnatural teleology" used for the Platonic variety is James Lennox's. See Lennox (1985).

[6] For a more detailed treatment of these strains, see Lennox (1992), pp. 325–26.

versions of purely Aristotelian teleology that post-date Aristotle. Most versions of teleology that include Aristotelian elements also include Platonic elements.[7] And so it is helpful to turn to Aristotle himself to present the Aristotelian strand of teleology. One final remark: while a sustained treatment of our ancient figures is certainly warranted, here I merely draw some crucial, pertinent conclusions and working principles from their philosophies in order to return to a discussion of Descartes' Sixth Meditation passage.

General conclusions

(1) Plato and Aristotle both propose a need for teleology to account for certain features of the natural world – including living beings – because they believe that chance (taken in opposition to purpose) cannot explain these features. For Plato, the feature that cannot be explained by chance is beauty taken as that which is orderly and well-proportioned (*Tim.* 30a3–6 and 69b2–4), characteristics of the universe, which require intelligence and reason (*Tim.* 46e3–6). Aristotle's rejection of chance and his consequent embrace of teleology emerge from his rejection of the chance accounts of the generation of living beings given by his materialist predecessors such as Empedocles – accounts which Aristotle thinks are impossible because they cannot account for the facts of living beings such as their functional unity and their being alive (e.g. *Phys.* II, 8; 198b23–32).

(2) Aristotle makes a further teleological distinction between intrinsic and incidental ends (e.g. *Post.* I, 4; 73b10–15, and *EE* VII, 13; 1246a26–31). An intrinsic end is an end which accords with a being's own nature, while an incidental end is one that does not accord with a being's own nature. So, for example, a dog has both an intrinsic end, e.g. survival, which accords with its own nature, and an incidental end, e.g. fighting to the death with another dog to entertain humans, which does not accord with its own nature. According to Aristotle, living beings have both intrinsic and incidental ends, while artifacts have only incidental ends. This is related to the fact that artifacts *qua* artifacts have no intrinsic natures, with a nature

---

[7] Garrett (1999) thinks Spinoza has an essentially Aristotelian form of teleology. See note 9, below, for an example of blended forms of teleology.

in this instance being conceived of as an inner principle of change toward an end definitive of the kind of being it is (e.g. *Phys.* II, I; 192b33).

(3) According to Aristotle, only beings with intrinsic ends can be the subject of scientific study and scientific explanations (e.g. *EE* I, 5; 1216b10–18).

(4) If we think of living beings as constructed out of material parts by a craftsman – that is, if we think of them in purely Platonic terms – then an Aristotelian can conclude that living beings so conceived (a) have no natures *qua* living beings; (b) have only incidental ends; and (c) are therefore not the subject of scientific study and explanations.

Three useful conceptual principles to extract from the above conclusions

First, we ought not to conflate the distinction between a thing's *nature* on the one hand, and whether or not a *teleological account* can be given for that thing on the other hand. While related (as will come clear in the points which follow), these are two distinct issues.

Second, if a thing does not have an intrinsic nature to serve a specific end, a teleological account can still be given for it by making reference to something extrinsic to the thing, namely, to the mind and the goal within that mind, of the thing's builder or its user.[8] Such an account will not necessarily (though it could) tell us anything about the thing considered in itself. This point applies most obviously in the case of Platonic teleology.

Third, if a thing has an intrinsic end-referred nature, regardless of how it came to have that nature, then two different sorts of teleological accounts can be given for it:

(A) One sort of teleological account makes reference solely to the thing's nature (and to nothing external to it), and this sort of account necessarily tells us something about the thing considered in itself.

(B) The other sort of teleological account makes reference to the ends found in a mind extrinsic to the thing itself, and this sort of account does not necessarily tell us something about the thing considered in itself.

---

[8] See also Carriero (2005), p. 125, including n. 23.

This point applies most obviously in the case of Aristotelian teleology, or a blended form of teleology, which includes Aristotelian elements.[9]

IV REVISITING DESCARTES' SIXTH MEDITATION PASSAGE, IN LIGHT OF THIS BACKGROUND

In somewhat older literature on the seventeenth century, it is often suggested that the mechanical philosophy that dominated the century led to teleology being expunged from natural philosophy (e.g. Koyré [1950] 1965, p. 8; Taylor 1967; this is an attitude which even survives until more recent years – e.g. Clark 1995; Mackie 1995, p. 281). Recently, this assumption has been quite effectively challenged through studies of individual seventeenth-century mechanists who nonetheless allow room for teleological explanations in their natural philosophies (e.g. Garrett 1999; Simmons 2001; Carlin 2006; McDonough 2009),[10] and through more general accounts which (while perhaps not stating it in exactly these terms) demonstrate that mechanism in the seventeenth century and *Platonic* teleology are perfectly compatible even if mechanism and *Aristotelian* teleology (or forms of teleology which include an Aristotelian element) are not compatible (e.g. Osler 1996). For a mechanist, the immanent drive toward an end relies upon a form of efficient cause incompatible with mechanism, for this sort of efficient cause is not an unbounded, uniform inertial motion (as per the mechanist's efficient cause), but is a bounded motion aiming toward a specific end.[11] By contrast, Platonic teleology permits explanations of the behaviors of God-built machines wholly in terms of matter in inertial motion.

So, as a mechanist, if Descartes endorses any form of teleology, it has to be purely Platonic, or at least it cannot include any Aristotelian elements. Yet Descartes also clearly dismisses Platonic teleological explanations in natural philosophy, at least in cases where the external, conscious agent is God. This is clear in all of the anti-teleology passages found in Descartes' work where he alludes to purposes *external* to natural beings, found in the

---

[9] Aquinas offers such a blended account for he believes that God (the external agent as on the Platonic version of teleology) could have conveyed a metaphysically robust, intrinsic teleological nature (Aristotelian teleology) onto natural beings such that these beings are able to share in God's purposes while not, themselves, being intentional beings (e.g. Aquinas [1265–72] 1952–54, 3:36). On Aquinas' account of final cause, especially as it illuminates early modern concerns, see Carriero (2005).

[10] There are also dissenting views that argue against the inclusion of teleology, especially in the case of Spinoza (e.g. Carriero [2005] and Bennett [1984], pp. 213–30).

[11] See Carriero (2005), p. 121.

Descartes teleology has to be Platonic, but he also clearly dismisses the platonic explanations

mind of a conscious agent (God), but cognitively inaccessible to us. Here is a classic example from the Fourth Meditation:

[I]t is no cause for surprise if I do not understand the reasons for some of God's actions; and there is no call to doubt his existence if I happen to find out that there are other instances where I do not grasp why or how certain things were made by him. For since I now know that my own nature is very weak and limited, whereas the nature of God is immense, incomprehensible, and infinite, I also know without more ado that he is capable of countless things whose causes are beyond my knowledge. And for this reason alone I consider the customary search for final causes to be totally useless in physics; *there is considerable rashness in thinking myself capable of investigating the impenetrable purposes of God.* (7: 55, 2: 38–39; emphasis added; cf. 7: 374–75, 2: 258; 8A: 15–16, 1: 202; 8A: 81, 1: 248–49; and 5: 158, 3: 341).

If Aristotelian teleological explanations are eliminated from Descartes' natural philosophy because they are incompatible with mechanism and because Descartes is a mechanist, and if Platonic teleological explanations are eliminated from Descartes' natural philosophy because we cannot know God's purposes, then a number of possibilities arise. One possibility is that Descartes really does reject wholesale both Platonic and Aristotelian forms of teleology, and if these are the only two teleological options, then there appears to be no room at all for teleological explanations in Descartes' natural philosophy. This is, of course, suggested by the first feature of Descartes' philosophy with respect to teleology which I mentioned at the outset of this chapter and which is in tension both with his use of teleological explanations in discussing the human composite, for example, in Meditation Six (Feature 2), and with his teleological-sounding explanations of non-ensouled living beings (Feature 3). A second possibility is that Descartes in fact does not fully reject Platonic teleology, and I think this option represents part of the truth. A third possibility is that Descartes is committed to the use of teleology, he does reject Aristotelian teleology while also accepting some form of Platonic teleology, but there is another form of teleology which he might implicitly endorse, even if he does not fully articulate this form of teleology himself. I believe that this option, too, represents part of the truth. I deal with these two possibilities in sections V and VI respectively.

In this section, I will examine more closely the Sixth Meditation passage against the conceptual framework erected in the previous section. The first crucial point is that the Sixth Meditation passage *is not first and foremost about teleological explanations; it is first and foremost about the natures of things*, specifically, the nature of the human composite as opposed to

the nature of purely material systems (e.g. clocks and human bodies considered without a soul). Descartes' discussion of the natures of things has
implications for teleological explanations, to be sure. But as my first principle in section III, above, indicates, the natures of things and teleological
explanations of things are two distinct issues. And Descartes thinks so,
too, as Burman reports Descartes saying: "the knowledge of a thing's purpose never leads us to knowledge of the thing itself; its nature remains just
as obscure to us" (5: 158, 3: 341). Indeed, as I mentioned above, the crucial
distinction between the natures of things and teleological explanations of
things is implicit, even if not fully articulated, in the La Porte/Simmons
approach. Recall the central distinction Simmons highlights: "(a) the
ends that move God to create and (b) the ends of the things he creates."
In referring to the ends of the things God creates, Simmons *is* alluding to
the intrinsic, end-referred *nature* of creatures. A charitable reading, then,
of the La Porte/Simmons approach picks up on and develops the implications of this nascent acknowledgment that the fundamental issue in the
Sixth Meditation passage is the issue of the natures of things. My goal
here is to fill out this aspect of the La Porte/Simmons approach.

What the Sixth Meditation passage indicates, then, is that the human
composite has an *intrinsic* end-referred nature (which God has bestowed
upon the composite), while wholly material systems do not have intrinsic
end-referred natures (or they do not have such natures when we consider
their fundamental metaphysical nature, for that is the context of this and
related passages in the Sixth Meditation). Wholly material systems do
not have, metaphysically, intrinsic end-referred natures, because such systems are composed merely of matter which is moving in accordance with
descriptive laws of nature; there is nothing prescriptive or end-referred
about this. "Yet a clock [or any other purely material system such as a dog]
constructed with wheels and weights observes all the laws of its nature
just as closely when it is badly made and tells the wrong time as when it
completely fulfills the wishes of the clockmaker" (7: 84, 2: 58). The human
composite, according to the Sixth Meditation passage, is different *in its
nature* from merely material systems, for something within the composite
itself – something intrinsic to it – is end-referred, or teleological.

We can use the principles established at the close of section III, above,
to now connect the two issues of natures and teleological explanations
specifically with respect to Descartes' Sixth Meditation. The second principle is relevant to the case of purely material systems, and given my interest in living bodies (Feature 3 at the outset of the chapter), I discuss this
principle with respect to a dog. Dogs do not have metaphysical intrinsic,

end-referred natures according to Descartes. Dogs do have metaphysical natures, of course. They are, by nature, composed of extension that has the capacity to take on quantitative variations in their modes – variations in, for example, the size, shape, and speed of motion of their extended parts. The material parts of these bodies all obey the laws of motion (7: 84, 2: 58), and this is true of a dog whether or not its heart beats, for example. But this nature does not embody prescriptive ends; it is not teleological. Nonetheless, we can say that the dog is well functioning or not, and it makes sense to say so because this teleological account relies upon the goals vis-à-vis the dog which are found in the mind of either its maker or its user (or both) – and so such an account tells us about the dog's 'nature' as conceived in a mind extraneous to the dog itself. This is in keeping with the second principle: Descartes' position allows that we can give perfectly legitimate teleological accounts of non-ensouled material things, but that these accounts are not grounded in the metaphysical natures of the things themselves.

A crucial corollary to this principle is that, since the dog has no intrinsic nature to achieve specific ends, then there is no ground for saying one teleological account of the dog's use is better than any other. This is because the teleological account relies entirely upon making reference to purposes extrinsic to the dog, specifically, purposes in the minds of its maker or users, all of which are equally legitimate when there is no nature intrinsic to the dog constraining its proper use. To put it in Aristotelian language, all ends of the dog are incidental; none are intrinsic. This point deserves emphasis. In the case of living bodies, we may be tempted to say that the correct teleological account of them must make reference to God's mind and his purposes in creating them. But this approach is misguided, and not simply because we (perhaps) cannot know any of God's purposes. Suppose we *could* know that God intended a dog to behave biologically in order to survive (as we can know that a clockmaker intended his product to tell time). If there is nothing conveyed upon the dog's nature which reflects this purpose, it is just as legitimate to give a teleological account which says that the dog is for the sake of our entertainment in a fight to the death with another dog as it is to give a teleological account which says that the purpose of the dog is its own self-preservation and so it behaves in certain ways (e.g. avoiding unnecessary, violent situations) which contribute to self-preservation. Certainly, it may be an affront to God should I use the dog in a fight to its death, just as it would be an affront to a clockmaker were I to use his fine clock to prop open a door. But this would be a comment on our relations with God (or clockmaker), and it would not be a comment on what can be considered proper uses of the *thing* itself. My relationship with God (or clockmaker) does not impact the metaphysics of objects and what follows teleologically from that metaphysics.

The third principle at the close of section III, above, is relevant in the case of the human composite. In light of the third principle, two conclusions can be drawn about the relation between natures and teleological accounts of the human composite. First, we can give a teleological account of the human composite by making reference *only* to the composite itself, and this account will necessarily tell us something about the composite considered in itself. To put it in Aristotelian language, this would be an explanation based on intrinsic ends. In this sort of teleological account, we need not – indeed, we *cannot* – ground the account by making reference to the mind of a being *extrinsic* to the composite – the mind of God, for example, if God created the composite. So, for example, we may say that the composite has the sensory perceptions that it does in order to serve the end of self-preservation, and in order for this account to be grounded in the composite's *intrinsic* nature (thereby telling us something about the composite itself) it must somehow be cashed out only in terms of features intrinsic to the composite itself. This is the principal worry behind the uncharitable reading of the approach to teleological accounts of the sensations suggested by La Porte and Simmons. If the La Porte/Simmons account relies, even indirectly, upon reference to God's ends, then the teleological account of the composite thus given would be one based on something extrinsic to the composite. To give a teleological account of the composite that relies upon and elucidates the *intrinsic* nature of the human composite, we need to give an account of the composite which relies solely on features within the composite itself.

Second, despite the first conclusion just drawn, we can, nonetheless, give a teleological account of the composite by making reference to ends in a mind extrinsic to the composite; it is just that this account will not *necessarily* tell us anything about the composite itself. To put it in Aristotelian language, this would be an account potentially based on incidental ends. For example, suppose for now that Descartes does not preclude our knowing God's purposes. We could give a teleological account of the human composite by making reference to God's purposes when he created the composite. This second sort of teleological account might even tell us something about the nature of the composite itself – indeed, according to Descartes in the Sixth Meditation, this second sort of teleological account does tell us something about the composite because "God has bestowed [a nature] on me as a combination of mind and body." But this second sort of teleological account will not *necessarily* tell us something about the composite itself in the same way that the first sort of teleological account (the sort which relies only upon the nature of the composite) *will* necessarily tell us something about the composite itself.

This last point becomes clear when we consider a second example, that of a doctor who gives a teleological account of an ill human being whom she is trying to cure. For example, suppose the doctor has a patient who is extremely sensitive to bright light. The doctor may give the following teleological account of the patient's symptom: due to a mechanical fault in the eyes, the patient's pupils are not closing to the degree that is prescriptively normal for human eyes, they are therefore not functioning as they ought to, and so the patient's eyes will not serve as well as possible the human's end of self-preservation. Then the doctor would prescribe a cure in order to bring the patient's eyes back to as good a state as possible. This teleological account of the patient depends at least in part upon reference to the mind of the doctor and does not *necessarily* tell us something correct about the human being considered in himself, a point that would be underscored should he die of meningitis a few days later.

The foregoing forces us to face a question neither posed nor answered by Simmons – nor, indeed, by Descartes himself in the Sixth Meditation. What *is* the nature of the composite such that it uniquely has an intrinsic, end-referred nature?[12] It seems to me that to give a legitimate teleological explanation of the human being (the mind–body composite) without relying upon God's *unknown* and *extrinsic* purposes vis-à-vis the composite, it is in fact necessary to explicate the nature of the composite in order to show how it is the grounding of that legitimate teleological explanation.

V THE COMPOSITE'S NATURE

In this section, I consider three candidates for the composite's nature: (a) the composite is a hylomorphic substance; (b) the composite is a union of two distinct substances, mind and body, which retain their essential natures in the composite, and there exists a sort of satisfaction relation between mind and body such that mind *confers* value on the body which is, in itself, without intrinsic value; and (c) the composite is a union of two distinct substances, mind and body, which retain their essential natures in the composite, and there exists a sort of satisfaction relation between

---

[12] This point is also made by De Rosa (2007) p. 322n. 33.

mind and body such that mind *recognizes* value in the body. There are virtues and drawbacks to each of these options, though, in the end, I think the third option stands the best chance of easing all tensions identified at the outset of this chapter.

By acknowledging the fact that the human composite has an intrinsic end-referred nature, one might be enticed to endorse the thesis that Descartes has a hylomorphic account of the human being. The hylomorphic thesis holds that Descartes, in ridding his philosophy of Aristotelian ontology, nonetheless retains one substantial form – the human soul – and so maintains that the human being is a unified composite of form (soul) and matter (the human body). Paul Hoffman, who developed one of the earliest full defenses of the thesis, puts it as follows: "Descartes believes that mind inheres in body as form inheres in matter, and … this hylomorphism does real philosophical work for him … Descartes's account of the per se unity of his man compares favorably with medieval accounts of per se unity, and, indeed, is remarkably close to the views of Scotus and Ockham" (Hoffman 1986, p. 342; cf. Rodis-Lewis 1950, pp. 76–81; Grene 1986, 1991; Hoffman 1991). One might use the hylomorphic account of the human being to say that it is the process of the soul's actualizing the human body that lends the composite its intrinsic teleological nature. This does, indeed, seem to be the approach of at least some advocates of the hylomorphic thesis. Roger Ariew, for example, writes: "the human body, according to Descartes, unlike the body of an animal, has a real *functional indivisibility* and *internal finality* derived from its union with a soul" (Ariew 1983, p. 35, emphasis added; cf. Gueroult 1953, vol. ii, pp. 180–81).

One problem with the hylomorphic option is the fact that Descartes' biological works – including those which deal with the human body considered hypothetically in isolation from the soul, such as *Treatise on Man* and the fifth part of *Discourse on Method* – make clear that the soul does not actualize the body in any way typical of medieval hylomorphic theories. The living human body alone is able, through mechanical means, to achieve a great number of biological functions, including those which contribute to its continued unity, its continued life, and its self-preservative behaviors (cf. Rozemond 1998, pp. 170ff.) – the very teleological features supposedly realized by the presence of the soul. Consider also the case of sensation, which is especially interesting in this context, for animals share with ensouled human beings the first of the three "grades of sensory response" that Descartes identifies (7: 436, 2: 294). Given their behavior in reaction to their sensations which allows them to preserve a well-functioning disposition of essential parts and organs (which just is tantamount to biological survival), it seems this first grade is sufficient to account for the apparently end-referred behavior of self-preservation. Finally, whatever else might be said about Descartes' supposed endorsement of hylomorphism, it is certainly *not* the case that the human mind within the composite has purposes vis-à-vis the composite which permit it to survive biologically – purposes which it then actively carries out.

The second candidate for the composite's nature has the twin virtues of both paying due heed to Descartes' mechanizing of all living functions, including those found within the human body itself, and accounting for the intrinsic teleological nature of the human without thereby importing unwanted teleological explanations into natural philosophy. To recall, this is the first "satisfaction relation" sketched above, according to which the composite is a union of two distinct substances, mind and body, which retain their essential natures, and there exists a sort of satisfaction relation between mind and body such that mind *confers* value on the body which is, in itself, without intrinsic value.

According to this approach,[13] we acknowledge that the mind and body both retain their own essential natures within the composite. The body is essentially just extended matter moving in accordance with descriptive natural laws; there is nothing purposive about it. The mind's essential nature is to think, and this includes having sensations of all three grades, including mental perceptions of those sensations and judgments which follow on these perceptions. The body, as a living body, accomplishes all its living functions mechanically – that is, by matter moving in accordance with the laws of motion. The end-referred nature intrinsic to the composite comes about through a sort of "satisfaction relation" between the mind and the body. The mind has sensations due to its union with the body, and these sensations can be either pleasurable or painful. The teleological nature of the composite *just is* the fact of the soul's finding pleasure or displeasure in its union with the body. It is crucial to note that according to this option, the soul does not *recognize* that there is something beneficial or harmful occurring in the body. The soul is not *alerted to* the body's well-functioning or malfunctioning. The body is not the sort of thing that functions well or not; it is not the sort of thing in which beneficial or harmful events occur. It cannot be such a thing because it does not have an intrinsic

[13] I appreciate the discussions with Paul Guyer that led me to formulate this option.

end-referred nature, as Descartes explicitly says in the Sixth Meditation passage. Rather, we can think of the relation between the soul and body *as exactly symmetrical to* the relation between a user's mind and a clock. The user of the clock sees that it is keeping the time and says that it is functioning well. But the clock is not functioning well as a timekeeper. It is simply a pile of matter obeying the laws of nature. The teleological element in this relationship is in the user's mind. This is precisely what occurs in the case of the human composite according to the present option, only now, the body and soul are considered a unit and not two separate things, and so the soul's attributing normative claims to the (non-normative) body is intrinsic to that union, or to the relation which holds between mind and body in the composite. The intrinsic teleological character of the union comes about by the soul's conferring normative value onto the body due to the sensations it happens to have as a result of its relationship with it.

The two prime virtues of this account that I see are as follows. First, the non-teleological nature of the body is fully preserved. Thus, this approach involves no scientifically relevant teleological explanation, and so there is no tension between Descartes' general prohibition against teleological explanations and the Sixth Meditation claim about the human composite. The soul's attributing normative value to the body does no scientific work with respect to the body. The body and its behaviors are still fully explained in mechanical terms. Second, the tension between Features 1 and 2 of Descartes' approach to teleology is fully eased by referring to the composite itself and without making any reference *at all* to something extrinsic to that composite – God, for example. This is a version of Platonic teleology, but it is one in which the agent conferring purposes and value on the human body is not God, but the human mind within the composite.

There are, however, at least two drawbacks of this approach. The first – and this also applies to the second satisfaction relation below – is that were this Descartes' intention, he really ought to have said something in the Sixth Meditation passage about the nature of the union of mind and body since the human composite is treated as unique in that Meditation. The mind–body composite is different from any number of other composites one might imagine according to a satisfaction-relation approach: a mind–clock composite, a mind–dog composite, and so on without end. Unlike any other composite, for example, we do not have to think about the relation between mind and body for it to obtain, and it obtains for as long as we live.

As for the body which by some special right I called "mine", my belief that this body more than any other, belonged to me had some justification. For I could never be separated from it, as I could from other bodies; and I felt all my appetites and emotions in, and on account of, this body; and finally, I was aware of pain and pleasurable ticklings in parts of this body, but not in other bodies external to it. (7: 76, 2: 52)

What accounts for that unity? In the Sixth Meditation, Descartes does not say, and yet if either satisfaction relation were to be his considered position, he ought to have explained the nature of the union so as to not open the door to unending examples of composites.[14] The second drawback is that this approach solidifies the tensions between Feature 3 on the one hand, and the other two features of Descartes' thinking on teleology as noted at the start of this chapter. That is, living bodies – human or other – have no teleological natures at all, and so the teleological-sounding explanations that Descartes uses in his biological works pose an insurmountable difficulty for him. One may think this not at problem at all. That is, one may reply that the teleological-sounding explanations of Descartes' biology are just that – teleological *sounding*, but not truly teleological (Simmons 2001, p. 62n. 17). In the final section of this chapter, I return to this point, suggesting that Descartes might well rely upon quasi-teleological accounts of biological processes in all living things in order to secure a class of living beings to serve as the subject matter of his biology.

The third candidate for the composite's nature is a different version of the satisfaction relation. Recall that according to this version, the composite is a union of two distinct substances, mind and body, which retain their essential natures in the composite, and there exists a sort of satisfaction relation between mind and body such that mind *recognizes* value in the body, even if it sometimes fails to do so accurately. There are two obvious virtues to this approach. First, it has textual support, even if not in the Sixth Meditation. For example: "I consider it probable that the soul felt joy at the first moment of its union with the body, and immediately after it felt love, then perhaps also hatred, and sadness; and that the same bodily conditions *which then caused those passions* have ever since naturally accompanied the corresponding thoughts" (4: 604, 3: 307 emphasis added; cf. 11: 399, 1: 362; and 11: 407, 1: 365). Here *good* bodily conditions exist prior to, and are the cause of, the soul's reaction to those bodily conditions. The second virtue is that it at least opens the door to the resolution of the two tensions between Feature 3 on the one hand, and

---

[14] I thank Lisa Downing for drawing my attention to this difficulty.

the other two features of Descartes' thinking on teleology. Of course, it promises these solutions at a potentially great cost, and this is the primary drawback of this account of the nature of the human composite. This account seems to rely upon attributing an intrinsic teleological nature to the body itself, which is in explicit conflict with what Descartes clearly says in the Sixth Meditation passage. I now turn to this supposed great cost to see if Descartes must indeed bear it were this third approach to capture his intentions.

VI DESCARTES' BROADER 'BIOLOGICAL' PROJECT: NEXT STEPS

Recall Aristotle's distinction between intrinsic and incidental ends. Living beings have both sorts of ends, and they have intrinsic ends because they have natures (as in inner principles of change toward ends appropriate for the kinds of beings they are). They can therefore be the subject of scientific study and explanations. Artifacts, such as built machines, have only incidental ends, because they have no intrinsic natures in the form of an inner principle of change. Consequently, they cannot be the subject of scientific study and explanations. In the Sixth Meditation passage, Descartes draws a metaphysical line between human composites on the one hand and purely material bodies on the other. Purely material bodies, according to the Sixth Meditation account, do not have intrinsic end-referred natures, and so only teleological accounts based on what Aristotle would call incidental ends (purposes in an extrinsic mind) can be given for clocks, or dogs, or human bodies considered, counterfactually, in isolation from a soul. But this is a problem, and for broadly Aristotelian reasons.

First, the Sixth Meditation characterization obliterates what is distinctive about living bodies. An account of a dog that says that it serves the purpose of entertaining us in a fight to the death with another dog is equally legitimate against a consideration of the dog's nature as an account of the dog that says that its purpose is to survive through the exercise of certain biological functions. And yet, we intuitively believe that what makes a dog different from a clock is that it functions, and properly so, in ways unique to living beings. Dogs (and other living bodies) but not clocks generate offspring, undergo change in growth, can react to their environments in order to survive some environmental wear and tear, and thus preserve themselves. The implication of Descartes' Sixth Meditation certainly runs afoul of Aristotle's intuitions about living beings, but it also runs afoul of *Descartes'* intuitions that there is a distinction to be made between the living and the non-living even while they both may be machines. In June 1642, for example, in a letter to Regius he identifies living things as a *category*:

[Y]ou seem to make a greater difference between living and lifeless things than there is between a clock or other automaton on the one hand, and a key or sword or other non-self-moving appliance on the other. I do not agree. Since "self-moving" is a category with respect to all machines that move of their own accord, which excludes others that are not self-moving, so "life" may be taken as a *category* which includes the forms of all living things. (3: 566, 3: 214; emphasis added)

Second, if the distinction between living and non-living beings is obliterated, then this puts a study of organisms *as organisms* beyond the reach of science. If there were no such things as living bodies, then there can be no life science. Moreover, even if we were to ignore this problem and presume that there is something unique about living bodies for Descartes, we intuitively believe that a scientific study of them would want to account, for example, for their self-preservative behavior, but not for their ability to entertain us in a fight to the death with another dog. But Descartes' Sixth Meditation account, especially when seen in light of Aristotle's thoughts on teleology, cannot provide a way of grounding this intuitive belief in a theoretical scientific framework that would give rise to a science of life. Of course, we could give scientific accounts for the lawful behavior of particles of matter that make up a dog's body, just as we can give such an account for the particles of matter which make up a clock's body. But there seems to be no way for Descartes to ground a science of life per se. Once again, this runs afoul of Aristotle's understanding of theoretical sciences and their scope, and once again, this runs afoul of *Descartes'* approach to natural science. His life as a scientist is premised on there being a distinction between living and non-living beings, and on the assumption that the range of phenomena to be explained within a science of life do not include, for example, the ability of dogs to entertain us in a fight to the death with another dog. So, for example, on 18 December 1629, he writes to Mersenne that he was beginning a study of anatomy (1: 102), and by this, he means the study of the structure of plant, animal, and human bodies, not a study of the structure of clocks and fountains. From this date forward, his working life as a scientist would include a distinct study of living beings, the fruits of which appear in many of his written works. And the range of phenomena which occupied him in his study of living bodies were roughly those we would intuitively believe appropriate for a working life scientist: nutrition, growth, reproduction, embryology, and so forth (obvious examples of this are found in *Treatise on Man*, *Description of the Human Body*, and *Excerpta anatomica*). If we take seriously, as we should, the belief that "Descartes was a scientist before he was a metaphysician" (Hatfield 1993, p. 259), and that his metaphysics (such as appears in the *Meditations*, including the Sixth Meditation passage upon which I have been focusing) is designed at least in part to provide supporting foundations for his science (e.g. 3: 298, 3: 173), then Descartes' apparent inability to secure a science of life because of the demands of the metaphysics of the Sixth Meditation poses a serious problem for him.

One way of trying to mitigate this problem is to use what Aristotle calls incidental ends – ends found in a mind extraneous to living beings – to explain both how the things of the world are categorized and how the things of the world are then studied in the special sciences. So, for example, we may say that a Cartesian science of life depends first upon a life scientist dividing the things of the world into living and non-living by saying that the first sorts of things are those which strive for self-preservation and do so through specific kinds of functions (nutrition and so forth), while also recognizing that these characteristics are extraneous labels, dependent upon purposes found in her own mind and not in the nature of things in the world. And then she could go about studying these teleological behaviors, once again recognizing that she is studying purposes in the living being *as she conceives of them*, and not as they are actually found in the (so-called) living being itself. However, there is a problem with this approach, namely, that it is a violation of the general spirit of Descartes' approach to science, which is not meant to be an undertaking based in human convention (purposes within a human's mind vis-à-vis the things of the world) but which is meant to be an undertaking which uncovers the true nature of the world.

One way of muting this problem is to agree that only the human composite has an intrinsic, end-referred nature to preserve itself and thus stay alive; no non-ensouled living bodies have such a nature. But, we can extend our legitimate teleological conclusions about ourselves to other bodies we call living, such as those of animals, because of the structural similarities between the human body and such bodies.[15] Thus, all bodies we call living could be treated as if they had self-preservative natures, and

---

[15] Plants, too, may be seen to have similar structures to those of animals. On early modern and other historical attempts to find analogues of various essential animal organs in plants, see Delaporte [1979] 1982.

these natures could help to identify the class of bodies to be treated in a science of life. So while it is true that the life sciences would have as their subject a collection of beings identified by human convention, it would not be an *arbitrary* convention but rather one grounded in the structural similarity that living bodies have with the human body, which does have a genuine, intrinsic end-referred nature to preserve itself.[16]

I suggest a second solution to the difficulty – a solution I can only outline in the broadest of strokes, and which demands more careful treatment elsewhere. According to this solution, Descartes can allow (even if he does not do so explicitly) that purely material things have intrinsic end-referred natures, albeit not at the level of ground-floor metaphysics of matter; the metaphysics of matter is his focus in the Sixth Meditation passage. At the physical level, one might argue, living beings behave in certain ways that non-living things do not because of their physical *natures* as found in the specific disposition of essential organs and parts. Living beings function in specific ways (they grow, repair themselves, and so on), for the overall goal of self-preservation. This account is teleological in some way at least – the disposition of parts that bodies have allow them to function so as to preserve themselves.[17] On an especially bold account of this teleological nature of living bodies, the design and function can even come about by chance and environmental pressures, which is both suggested by Lucretius in his *On the Nature of Things*, which Descartes read, and in concert with Descartes' own chaos 'fable' of the origins of all things (11: 34–35, 1: 91; cf. 6: 42; 8A, 102–3).[18] That is, there can be a functioning design without a designer.[19]

This intrinsic end-referred *physical* nature may rely on a weaker form of teleology than does the metaphysical nature that human composites have, but it could be robust enough to categorize the things of the world according to features of the world itself (and not merely epistemological features of the categorizer), and to be scientifically useful. Descartes could then distinguish (physically) between, on the one hand, the intrinsic ends of self-preservation and the bodily functions which contribute to self-preservation which are grounded in the living being's nature, and, on

---

[16] I am indebted to Tad Schmaltz for drawing my attention to this solution. Carriero (2009), pp. 417f. suggests something similar as a way of explaining disorder in bodies.

[17] I take it Des Chene would dissent from my characterization of this kind of physical nature as teleological. See Des Chenes (2001), pp. 125ff.

[18] For a discussion of Lucretius' text and reception in the early modern period, including on this point, see Johnson and Wilson (2007).

[19] On this in contemporary philosophy of biology, see Kitcher (1998).

the other hand, mere incidental ends, such as entertaining us in a fight to the death, which are not grounded in a living being's nature but rather in a user's purpose vis-à-vis the living being. The former, but not the latter, would be the phenomena studied in the life sciences. This account would have the added appeal of showing that Descartes presages a crucial conceptual point in later biology, namely, that we can be reductionist in our explanatory accounts of living bodies without thereby eliminating the category of living beings.[20]

This approach would favor the third interpretation of the composite's nature explored in the previous section. The soul *recognizes* value in the body,[21] but the value is at the level of physical dispositions of parts, not the metaphysics of matter. It is a value shared by other physical things, such as dogs and other living beings. Thus, there are two forms of teleology at work in this account of the composite. First, the human body (as with other living bodies) has a teleological nature of the kind just described. It is teleology that could be non-Platonic (were it to arise without a designing mind having made it) and non-Aristotelian (there is no intrinsic, end-referred efficient cause or principle of change that accounts for the being's functions, all of which can be explained in wholly mechanical terms). Second, the human being (uniquely) has a Platonic teleological nature in that the human mind recognizes the value of the well-functioning physical machine that is its living body. But this is Platonic teleology of an innocuous kind for Descartes, because the mind recognizing the value of the machine is not God's mind, and so we are not making claims about God's purposes.

If I can establish that Descartes can leave room for intrinsic, end-referred natures at the level of the physical – I do not pretend that this is going to be an easy thing to show[22] – then all tensions would be solved. What Descartes says about non-ensouled living bodies in the Sixth Meditation (Feature 2) would be a comment about their metaphysical natures, and as such, they indeed do not have intrinsic end-referred natures. What he says about non-ensouled living bodies in his biological works (Feature 3) would be a comment about their physical natures, which do have intrinsic end-referred natures. Descartes' prohibition of

---

[20] Gaukroger (2000 and 2010) argues that Descartes is a reductionist but not an eliminativist about life.

[21] As Lisa Shapiro has pointed out to me, one element of this broad sketch that especially deserves attention is the nature of the "value" that the soul recognizes in a healthy body. On this, see Shapiro (2003). Hoffman's (2009b) account of conceptions of final causes of varying strengths is also helpful on this front.

[22] Helpful precedents for showing this include Hatfield (1992 and 2008).

teleological explanations in natural philosophy (Feature 1) is a prohibition against Platonic teleology where the mind of God (as maker) is the external agent. (He is also opposed to Aristotelian teleology.) Thus, there is no tension between this feature and his account of the intrinsic end-referred nature of the human composite (Feature 2), which relies on other forms of teleology. Similarly, there is no tension between his prohibition of very specific forms of teleology (Feature 1) and the different form of teleology he uses in his biological works (Feature 3). Admittedly, one significant problem would remain, and that is the problem of how to account for the *unique* unity of the human mind with its body. It is a problem that followed Descartes well into his later years, and turning to his work in those years may well be necessary to fully make sense of the Sixth Meditation on this point. → purpose

CHAPTER 9

The role of will in Descartes'
account of judgment

Lilli Alanen

I INTRODUCTION

Discussions of the account of judgment offered in the fourth Meditation tend to focus on its role in Descartes' epistemology and his response to skepticism. My concern here is not with the epistemological aims of the Fourth Meditation as much as the conception of will and its power of free decision there developed, and with the ensuing transformation of the concepts of belief or judgment. In my view commentators have not generally paid sufficient attention to the role Descartes attributes to the will, its independence in belief-formation and the consequences of this view for his conception of mind or reason and self-identity.[1]

In the Second Meditation Descartes, famously, discovers his existence and self as a thinking thing, that is, he explains, "I am a mind, or intelligence, or intellect, or reason" (7: 27, 2: 18). While many of Descartes' scholastic predecessors could agree that a mind can be described in those same terms, and is the most perfect part of man, few would identify the self with the mind alone, and few, with the exception of the Platonists, would follow him in concluding that none of the things he can invent or picture in his imagination – i.e. corporeal things – belongs to his self as a thinking thing or mind.[2] What was initially described as a mind or intellect or reason is soon expanded to include "willing and unwilling,"

[1] For recent discussions of Descartes' account of will and judgment see e.g. Lin (2004); Ragland (2006); Della Rocca (2005); Kambouchner (2008); Newman (2008); Shapiro (2008); John Carriero (2009) and Naaman-Zauderer (2010). I have examined Descartes' view of the will, its interpretation and its historical background more extensively in Alanen (2003), ch. 7 and Alanen (2009). In this chapter I defend and develop my earlier reading taking account of recent discussions, notably Ragland (2006) and Carriero (2009), whose insightful interpretations of Descartes' controversial account and valuable criticisms of my own view I am indebted to. Regrettably I could not benefit from valuable comments from Noa Naaman-Zauderer or respond to her recent reading of Descartes' account of the will in Naaman-Zauderer (2010), which came too late to my notice.

[2] "I thus realize that none of the things that the imagination enables me to grasp is at all relevant to this knowledge of myself which I possess, and that the mind must therefore be most carefully diverted from such things if it is to perceive its own nature as distinctly as possible" (7: 28, 2: 19).

and then, as an afterthought, "also imagining and sensing."[3] In a strict sense of a thinking being, the mind, as Descartes concludes in the Sixth Meditation, is really distinct from extended things and can exist without them (7: 78, 2: 54). Yet it is also, as he then goes on to argue, really united to the body and forms a whole with it. The self, or mind, or thing that thinks has faculties for these special forms of thinking, imagination, and sense-perception (7: 78, 2: 54), whose operation or use, as the Sixth Meditation purports to show, presupposes – God being no deceiver – that it also is united to or has a body (7: 79–80, 2: 54–56).

We can thus talk of the Cartesian Self in a strict sense as a mind, or in a wider sense as a mind embodied. While the latter is the real human being, the mind considered in the first, strict sense, in abstraction as it were from the body, is considered an individual self or entity.[4] It is the Self in this strict sense – the central abilities singled out as constituting what Descartes calls a mind – that we are concerned with here, and my aim in particular is to examine this entity in the light of the discussion of judgment and will in the Fourth Meditation. If willing and unwilling are included from the start among its essential core capacities – the instruments of the highest human perfection – the nature and operation of the will is not addressed until the Fourth.

That the will should be included among the mind's core abilities is nothing to remark about in itself. *Voluntas* is the Latin name for the desire of the highest part of the soul; any intellect comes with a desire or will of its own that tends to its proper object, its proper object being the true. The main focus of the Fourth Meditation is the true and the false (*De vero & falso*), and it completes the discussion conducted in the Second and Third Meditation about truth and falsity and the proper use of the truth rule.[5] In compliance with the Aristotelian–Thomistic tradition where the intellect is said to come with an appetite for the true that naturally makes it tend towards truth and away from falsity, Descartes takes mind or intellect to be naturally inclined to the true. What I find remarkable is the way Descartes redistributes the cards in making the will

---

[3] "A thing that doubts, understands, affirms, denies, is willing, is unwilling, and also imagines and has sensory perceptions" (7: 28, 2: 19).

[4] Descartes does not dwell on what individuates the mind, but seems to take for granted that it is an individual subject – the referent of "I" insofar as I, the very same subject who, sitting by the fire, engages herself in the project of the *Meditations*, is turning inward, away from her senses and body to inspect her "thoughts."

[5] Cf. Carriero (2009), pp. 223f. For a very helpful account of Aquinas' influential view of the will and the intellect that undoubtedly is in the background of Descartes', see Carriero (2009), pp. 243–49, and the references there given.

into a power of its own, attributing all the mind's motive tendencies and action to the will, leaving the intellect with a passive capacity to perceive and recognize the truth.[6] On the reading here defended, the view developed in the Fourth Meditation of the will as a distinctive power among the other core abilities making up the thinking thing or mind transforms this latter notion in ways that do not fit easily with standard pictures of Descartes as a mainstream rationalist.

To show this, I shall first summarize Descartes' view of the nature of judgment before examining more closely the account of the will unfolding in the Fourth Meditation, and the kind of indifference Descartes appeals to in defending his controversial doctrine of free choice. While Descartes' successors and critics like Spinoza and Leibniz saw him as defending a radical (and in their view ultimately unintelligible) conception of freedom of the will, modern commentators are divided on whether to read him as a compatibilist, or libertarian, using terms from later debates between necessitarianism and libertarianism. The kind of "determinism" Descartes would be concerned with in this context is ethical: determinism by the good, which is opposed to ethical "voluntarism." While there clearly are tensions between these two positions in his text – perhaps also a change of position – I argue that Descartes in the end does commit himself to a view that is radical indeed, but that it is not inconsistent. I try to unravel the complexities of his view by paying close attention to a distinction he makes between two kinds of indifference, and by separating (something Descartes does not do) the case of the pursuit of truth and the pursuit of the good. I suggest that although there is no room for exercising a two-way power (in the sense of being able in any given situation either to do something or not to do that very thing) in the former case, and the cognitive will by necessity is moved to assent by clear and distinct perception, the practical will retains a strong kind of indifference even when the good is clearly and distinctly perceived by the intellect. Insofar as truth is among the goods pursued by the practical will, this means that the latter

---

[6] It is easy to slip into faculty talk here, and think of the intellect and will as separate faculties. Yet Descartes opposes the scholastic division of the soul into separate faculties. In his view there is one undivided soul or mind and what used to be names for different faculties are different powers of one and the same thing (11: 364, 1: 346). When this faculty – what Descartes also calls a "potentiality" (8b: 361, 1: 305) or power of willing – is exercised, an actual volition occurs. Volitions are the mind's actions or activity properly speaking, while understanding and perceiving more generally is passivity of the mind. (See 3: 372, 3: 183.) In the *Principles* 1.32 Descartes lists "desire, aversion, assertion, denial and doubt" as "various modes of willing" falling under the class of thoughts called "volition, or the operation of the will" (8a: 17, 1: 204). For a clear presentation of this doctrine see Newman (2008), pp. 334–36.

has indirect power over the former, so is free (undetermined) in opting between making the pursuit of truth and knowledge part of its pursuit of the good or not. I end by considering some consequences of this view for Descartes' notion of self or mind, and the new kind of responsibility that the role given to the will with its power of free choice leaves us with in moral and cognitive matters.[7]

2 THE NATURE OF JUDGMENT: INTELLECT AND WILL

In the Fourth Meditation, Descartes argues that judgment depends on these two concurring causes: the power of cognition (*facultate cognoscendi*) and the power of choice (*facultate eligendi*), or what he also calls the freedom of decision (*liberum arbitrium*), that is "of the intellect, and at the same time of the will [*voluntatis*]" (7: 57, 2: 40).[8] The intellect is presented as a passive power of perception: it enables me to perceive (conceive, or understand) the ideas about which I can make judgments (7: 56, 2: 39). The intellect as such does not, as added in the French translation, affirm or deny these ideas (9: 45, 2: 39) – it does not make any judgments.

---

[7] Differently from Carriero (2009), pp. 244–45, who sees Spinoza's and Hume's criticism of the will to be the source of the undermining of the view of the will as a substantive faculty tending by metaphysical necessity to the good, I take the unraveling of this notion to begin with the very view of free choice that Descartes defends. While Carriero sees Descartes as basically accepting the doctrine of his Thomist teachers, I see him as breaking with it on decisive points, and claim that the view of the will he ends up defending is, perhaps, more in tune with those of the early medieval "voluntarist" critics of Aquinas. In any case, Descartes' contemporary opponents and successors were right in seeing something radically new and uncommon in Descartes' view. For an instructive account of the discussion of will among Jesuits contemporary to Descartes, see Schussler (forthcoming). Schussler takes issue with my tracing the roots of Descartes' position to medieval voluntarists when much closer and contemporary theories of the role of will in doxastic assent or judgment were at hand. Schussler importantly illuminates the Baroque background of discussion, but leaves – as one must – the question open of how much of this was actually on Descartes' horizon when developing his account. It is certainly even more questionable that Descartes would actually be influenced by earlier medieval voluntarists, and that is not what I have wanted to claim. My purpose in comparing Scotus' theory to Descartes', for example, was not to claim any direct influence, but merely to point out that there is a long-standing philosophical issue about the will and intellect that had already divided medieval philosophers and that Descartes seems to position himself on the side that emphasizes the role of the will as a self-mover with a certain independence relative to the intellect. Schussler's paper came to my attention too late for me to include a discussion of the very interesting alternative interpretation he proposes, which also helpfully locates Descartes' position with reference to contemporary discussions of doxastic voluntarism.

[8] Notice that choice or freedom of decision and will are here offered as different descriptions of the same power. Descartes associates freedom with the power of choice or decision, which is a power of the will. The English translation (CSM) obscures the distinction by using "freedom of will" for free choice of the will – *liberum arbitrium voluntatis*. For more detailed discussions of this see Alanen (2003), ch. 7, and Alanen (2009), from which part of the material here included is taken.

In the Third Meditation, Descartes traces error and falsity to the act of judging (7: 37, 2: 26), for ideas, when considered in themselves alone, cannot be false "properly speaking" (7: 37, 2: 26).[9] Considered as objects of mental acts, ideas that are clearly and distinctly conceived cannot be false in themselves, as long as they are not "referred" to something else, i.e. "to things located outside me." Judgment then is the product of the joint operation of the intellect and the will, where the latter, active, power affirms or denies what the (passive) intellect presents to it (7: 57, 2: 40; 8a: 18, 1: 204). In ascribing the ability to affirm (*affirmare*) or deny (*negare*) to the will, Descartes departs from the standard view according to which making affirmative or negative judgments is a function of the intellect alone, a view that he seems to have followed in his early writings (10: 421, 2: 45).

Descartes seems to follow the medieval scholastics, who distinguished between apprehensive and judicative notions. There is no falsity in merely apprehending or entertaining ideas, and *qua* merely apprehended, they do not constitute beliefs properly. A belief for Descartes presupposes, explicitly or implicitly, some judicative notion or judgment – that some idea or proposition, which could also be merely considered or entertained, is affirmed or assented to. I can fantasize about being in possession of my former agility, or to take Descartes' own examples of lunatics, being clad in purple or having a head of glass, but I do not – at least not as long as I have my wits – believe any of these things. Truth and falsity belong to judgments properly, which Descartes now claims depend on the will. What is it then that makes a judgment true and what goes wrong when we end up with false beliefs?

Descartes, who does not theorize about it, treats truth as a simple self-evident notion that we know by our nature as thinking beings. He accepts, as a nominal definition, that the word "truth" denotes the conformity of thought and object, and that when used of extra-mental things, it signifies that these things can be objects of true thoughts – God's or ours (2: 597, 3: 139). This, as Carriero points out, is all in line with the view of truth spelled out by Thomas Aquinas in terms of "adequation" of the intellect with reality: the intellect aligns itself, in making a true judgment, with how things are in reality. A judgment is true when what it affirms *is*

---

[9] "Falsity in the strict sense, or formal falsity, can occur only in judgments" (7: 43, 2: 30; cf. 7: 37, 2: 26; see also note 10, below). For problems with this view see Wilson (1978), p. 141, and the helpful recent discussion in Newman (2008), pp. 339–40. See also Alanen (2003), pp. 151ff. and p. 211n. 47. For a recent detailed account of positions taken on this issue by Descartes' immediate predecessors and contemporaries within the Jesuit camp see Schussler (forthcoming).

as it affirms. If I make a false judgment, on the other hand, then my judgment is not in conformity with things: things are not in reality as they are in my thought – hence falsity involves error.[10] I am in error, I make a false judgment, when I believe I have five bucks in my pocket but there are none, or when you suppose yourself to be a fair team leader when you are only driving your own interest, or, in general, when you ascribe better intentions to yourself than the ones you are acting on.

We still need a better understanding of what it is that goes wrong in false judgments. Ideas are representational states, which, in themselves, when not referred to anything else, cannot be false. Mistakes, for Descartes, are made in judging, in referring ideas – mere representations – to external reality, asserting that things are thus and so, when they are not. What worries him in particular is the scholastic theory of sense perceptions as likenesses of true properties of things: "[T]he chief and most common mistake ... consists in my judging that the ideas which are in me, resemble, or conform to, things located outside me" (7: 37, 2: 26). These mistakes are now explained as depending on our own will, more precisely, our misuse of the will and the freedom of decision we have been endowed with. The will in itself is our highest perfection. Differently from our intellect and the power of true judgment, which is limited in a finite mind, the power of the will is "extremely ample [*amplissima*] and ... perfect of its kind" (7: 54, 2: 40). The will can be extended to affirm things that the intellect does not clearly perceive. It is here, with the act of affirming or denying an idea (i.e. accepting its content or what it represents as true without having sufficient evidence), that falsity creeps in. Cognitive errors are caused by myself, by the fact that I, instead of properly limiting my will to what my intellect understands, extend it to things that are not distinctly perceived by the latter (7: 58, 2: 40). It is my will to affirm what is not perceived that alone accounts for my belief that I am, say, well liked by my colleagues, or in denial of some obvious fact, like the limit on my credit card. Not only in these examples of self-deception and wishful thinking, but in any false belief, whether habitually entertained, uncritically received opinions, or explicitly formed judgments about matters that are not evident, we apply our will beyond the clear and distinct perceptions of our intellect.

It is not clear, however, what the work of the will would be in the case of clear and distinct perceptions. Does Descartes not repeatedly insist

---

[10] For an insightful discussion of Descartes' indebtedness to the scholastic Thomistic tradition in his thinking about truth see Carriero (2009), pp. 226–32.

they are true and evident in themselves, and as such, impossible to deny (e.g. 7: 36, 2: 25)?[11]

Standardly, assent and denial would be seen as functions of the intellect, not of the will. But from the *Meditations* on, Descartes argues that all action in the mind, including assent and denial, depends on the will.[12] The intellect by itself or through sensory perception presents ideas of things to the mind. But these are purely passive, or inert, representations. They come to our attention, but they do not, as it were, do anything – they do not move us one way or other by themselves. All the causal power comes from the will, which in itself is a non-representational, purely conative mental state. The object to be judged has first to be perceived by the intellect in some way, but in order for a judgment to be actually formed, the will has to move itself to assent to or deny what the intellect so perceives. According to the doctrine Descartes here defends, whether or not the will moves, and how it moves, depends on the will itself, not on the intellect. These two kinds of faculties or modes of thought work together, but independently of each other. Let us now try to get clear about what the power of the will as an independent source of action could consist in, and what light the account of the operation of the will might shed on this unusual theory of judgment.

3 THE WILL

Having singled it out as our highest perfection, Descartes makes a series of perplexing claims about the will in the Fourth Meditation.[13] Consider the first two of the claims listed below:

(1) The will (*voluntas*) or freedom of choice (*liberum arbitrium*) is experienced as being without limits.

---

[11] Can one so much as perceive and understand an evident truth without at the same time assenting to it? Cf. Williams (1978), p. 183; Wilson (1978), p. 145; and Della Rocca (2005), pp. 148–52.

[12] See e.g. *Principles* (8a: 17–18, 1: 204) and *Passions* (11: 342, 1: 335), where the distinction between what depends on the mind itself and what does not is stressed. Clear and distinct ideas of things – although, as Karen Detlefsen pointed out, they seem to involve intellectual activity insofar as they are produced in the intellect or attended to by it – have their mind-independent nature, as have the things they represent. I would distinguish between acts of the intellect – ideas being actualized as objects of present attention – and acts of the will – the latter only involve the kind of mind-dependent action or, as it were, "motion" that Descartes attributes to the will or cognitive power. There are three ways the will "moves": withholding action, suspending judgment about what the intellect holds out for it, or assenting to or denying it.

[13] That the freedom of the will is known through experience was common ground in the Augustinian and voluntarist tradition that Descartes appears to be following on many points. For discussion and references see Alanen (2003 and 2009).

This fact that the will, in contrast with the finite intellect, is known to be without limits is taken as evidence that it is our property par excellence, one through which we are made to resemble God:

(2) It is through the greatness of my will that "I understand myself to bear in some way the image and likeness of God."

God's will is said to be greater than mine in virtue of his knowledge and power, yet considered in its essence (*in se formaliter & praecise spectata*), it does not seem greater than mine.[14] What is the essence of the will?

Descartes' notion of the freedom of the will is a matter of controversy among commentators.[15] Here, in the Fourth Meditation, he first describes the freedom of choice or decision as a power of choice between opposites, suggesting that this two-way power constitutes the essence of the will:

(3) The will consists in an ability to do or not to do something, i.e. (a) to affirm or deny, and (b) to pursue or avoid.

Many things are confusing here. First, as already noted, Descartes runs two different powers together, ascribing both to the will. Traditionally – at least in the Thomistic tradition – the ability to affirm or deny was ascribed to the intellect, the proper object of which is truth (understood in terms of adequation, so as something within the intellect itself), while the ability to pursue or avoid was reserved for the will, the object of which is the good.[16] In attributing both to the will Descartes makes what was seen as an inherent part of the operation of the intellect into a function of a separate power, thus reducing the human intellect to a passive capacity of reception and apprehension. The intellect in this narrow, new, technical sense is an aspect of the mind's operation – one of is core abilities – and the will is another.[17]

---

[14] (A) "It is only the will, or freedom of choice, which I experience within me to be so great that the idea of any greater faculty is beyond my grasp; so much so that it is above all in virtue of the will that I understand myself to bear in some way the image and likeness of God. For although God's will is incomparably greater than mine, both in virtue of the knowledge and power that accompany it and make it more firm and efficacious, and also in virtue of its object, in that it ranges over a greater number of items, nevertheless it does not seem any greater than mine when considered formally and strictly in itself [*in se formaliter et praecise spectata*]" (7: 57, 2: 40).

[15] For discussion and references see Alanen (2003), ch. 7; Ragland (2006); Kambouchner (2008); Newman (2008); and Carriero (2009), pp. 249–64.

[16] Carriero distinguishes between the cognitive good – a property of the intellect being aligned with things – and the practical good – a property of things to which the will tends, and he explains how Descartes may think there is a close connection between them (2009, pp. 226–27).

[17] Insofar as Descartes also continues to use "mind" as interchangeable with "intelligence," "reason" or "intellect" taken in a larger, more traditional sense (7: 27, 2: 18; see section 1), judgment could still be seen as a function of intellect in this larger, traditional sense. The will – as one of the sub-powers of the mind or intellect in this larger sense – is naturally attuned to its other part

But there is a second, and perhaps more serious, source of confusion in Descartes' account. Having defined the will as essentially a two-way power (sometimes called freedom of opposites), he goes on to describe it in terms of a capacity to follow reason or what has been called "liberty of spontaneity":

(4) The will consists in a capacity to follow reason or intellect in such a way that we do not feel determined by an external force.

Is (4) meant as an explication of (3)? Is the capacity to follow and align itself with reason the very essence or nature of the will, and the two-way power merely that whereby it operates, or is it the other way around: the two-way power constitutes its very essence? Is Descartes hesitating between different conceptions of the will – is he perhaps even confusing them? Two further claims are made in the same passage:[18]

(5) The perceptions of our intellect are followed by inclinations determining us internally.

(6) The indifference or the absence of reasons that leaves me inclined either way is the lowest grade of freedom. (7: 57–58, 2: 40)

The passage quoted above appears to offer two different characterizations of the freedom of the will – first in (3) as a two-way power suggesting a radical freedom of choice between opposites, which is then, in the paragraph introduced by "or, rather" (*vel potius*), explicated through (4)–(6) as freedom from external constraints. Can the two characterizations be made consistent? Two possibilities will be considered here.

The first is that Descartes interprets the notion of freedom involved in the freedom of decision or freedom of choice (*liberum arbitrium*) in (3) in terms of the capacity to follow reason in (4), where the will is essentially a rational desire, i.e. an inner inclination to follow the intellect that makes it tend naturally and spontaneously to whatever end intellect or reason presents as good – in cognitive matters, to align itself with reality

---

or sub-power – the intellect narrowly taken – so the will is by nature inclined to the good of the intellect, i.e. it is, by nature, moved by the truth. Yet, as will be seen, there is more to the will as a sub-power of intellect or mind than the power to act in accordance with its natural inclination and be moved by the cognitive good.

[18] The whole passage runs as follows: (B) "This is because the will simply consists in our ability to do or not do something (that is, to affirm or deny, to pursue or avoid); or rather it consists simply in the fact that when the intellect puts something forward for affirmation or denial or for pursuit or avoidance, our inclinations are such that we do not feel we are determined by any external force. But the indifference I feel when there is no reason pushing me in one direction rather than another is the lowest grade of freedom; it is evidence not of any perfection of freedom, but rather of a defect in knowledge or a kind of negation" (7: 57–58, 2: 40).

by producing true judgments. The will in the sense of a rational desire is necessarily determined by reason; this constitutes its very nature. Since reason is our highest faculty, we – our minds – are determined internally by our nature in following reason. This is a classic sense of freedom as autonomy or self-determination by reason. If (4) is what freedom of will consists in for Descartes, he would also hold this further claim:

(7) Freedom excludes indifference.

Here, in (7), indifference is taken in the sense of (6), as the lowest degree of freedom, which is really no freedom at all but rather shows "a defect in knowledge or a kind of negation." This reading gets support from the rest of the passage in the Fourth Meditation:

(C) For if I always saw clearly what was true and good, I should never have to deliberate about the right judgment or choice; in that case, although I should be wholly free, it would be impossible for me ever to be in a state of indifference. (7: 58, 2: 40)

When one sees clearly and distinctly the true or the good there simply are no alternate possibilities: the will, by itself, by its inherently rational nature, excludes any other options. On this reading, the two-way power would operate only in cases where the reasons are unclear or insufficient, i.e. when there are no clear reasons for preferring, say, A to not-A, so that the will may, at the same time, be equally inclined in opposite directions. (Buridan's ass!) Indifference here would be merely negative: a lack of power, due to insufficient perceptions, to choose the better.

This is a common reading of Descartes, favored by those who regard Descartes as a compatibilist in the sense used in later discussions of freedom of the will. It is supported by many texts, and also by the fact that the account of freedom it attributes to Descartes is a mainstream rationalist view (the "common doctrine of the school"), yet it cannot accommodate all the things Descartes says about the will.[19] Not only does it leave his claim about the greatness and unlimited power of the will rather mysterious,[20] it also seems to exclude another more radical kind of indifference,

---

[19] For a classic defense of the reading aligning Descartes with the rationalists, see Kenny (1973). I take issue with this reading in Alanen (2003), pp. 242–43. For recent discussion and criticism of Kenny's reading see Ragland (2006), pp. 76ff. A carefully argued recent defense of this line of reading is offered by Carriero (2009), pp. 249–64; cf. Newman (2008).

[20] Those who defend the reading just considered take the greatness of the will to be a matter of its scope – something that is suggested by *Principles* 1:35 (8a: 18, 1: 204). See e.g. Newman (2008), p. 339, and Carriero (2009). Clearly Descartes thinks there is no object that could not be the object of a human will, so that if only the human intellect were infinite like God's there would not be any difference between the human and the divine intellect. Yet it is not clear that this

which, differently from (6), is not based on any cognitive defect, and which Descartes acknowledges as a matter of evident inner experience.[21]

The second possibility, which I will pursue here, is to assume that Descartes works with a distinction between two different stages in the operation of the will that exemplify different kinds of freedom (and indifference). This reading gets it support from passages suggesting that the two-way power mentioned in (3) is a radical, positive power of choice, namely that of choosing or deciding between A or not-A independently of which of the two alternatives the perceptions of intellect inclines the will to chose. The will here is not seen as predetermined in its actions by its natural tendency to the cognitive good (the truth) or the practical good, i.e. it is not automatically carried away by such inclinations. It is seen instead as possessing a real power of self-determination with respect to its own nature and the end it pursues. Though this power is naturally guided by, and attuned to, the intellect, it is not, I have argued, necessarily determined by its natural inclination to the true and the good that God in creating the human intellect and will established as their natural object.

This means that there are important differences between the divine and the human will. The latter finds itself inclined by the true and the good that the former by its "supreme" indifference posits, so that nothing can be "thought of in the divine intellect as good or true, or worthy of belief or action or omission, prior to the decision of the divine will to make it so." Descartes explains:

(D) I am not speaking here of temporal priority: I mean that there is not even any priority of order, or nature, or of "rationally determined reason" as they call it, such that God's idea of the good impelled him to choose one thing rather than the other ... thus the supreme indifference to be found in God is the supreme indication of his omnipotence. But as for man, since he finds that the nature of all goodness and truth is already determined by God, and his will cannot be moved [ferri posset] towards anything else, it is evident that he will embrace what is good and true all the more willingly, and hence more freely, in proportion as he sees it more clearly. (7: 431–32, 2: 292)[22]

---

would be the main ground for the comparison given Descartes' unorthodox view about God's omnipotence and supremely indifferent will. Cf. Alanen (2009), pp. 90–91, and Alanen (2008a).

[21] I take the experience of freedom Descartes mentions in his reply to Gassendi's objection to the Fourth Meditation (7: 377, 2: 259) to be referring to this second kind of indifference. See also *Principles* I:17, 39, and 41 (8a: 11, 1:198), and the letter to Mesland of 9 February 1645 (4: 173, 3: 245).

[22] The claim "that there can be nothing whatsoever which does not depend on him ... applies not just to everything that subsists, but to all order, every law, and every reason for anything's being true or good." God's supreme indifference requires that there could be no prior reason for something being good determining God's preference. Unlike the human will, God does not resolve to

This is not to say that Descartes takes back his earlier characterization of the will's power of free choice or decision, experienced as "so great that the idea of any greater faculty is beyond my grasp" and that "in its essential and strict sense" renders us "in some way the image and likeness of God." The greatness we share with God, as I understand it, consists precisely in this ability we have through our will "to do or not to do something" (7: 57, 2: 40). The exercise of power by the human will differs of course from that of God's will, which is totally unconditioned. The human will is never unconditioned but restricted to opting for (or picking)²³ one or the other of pre-existing alternatives, and, in case one of them is distinctly perceived as good, for or against its inclination to pursue it. (I return to this below.)

Descartes stresses in the Sixth Replies that the human will does not share the essence of the divine will, for "no essence can belong univocally to both God and his creatures." Many have taken this passage as a straightforward denial of indifference as part of the human kind of freedom of choice. But the indifference of the human will that he here contrasts to God's is the first kind of indifference (6), which does not "belong to the essence of human freedom, since not only are we free when ignorance of what is right makes us indifferent, but we are also free – a indeed at our freest – when a clear perception impels to pursue some object" (7: 433, 2: 292). Indifference here is actually no freedom at all; more precisely, it is what Descartes earlier characterized as "the lowest degree of freedom," which is a weakness and not a perfection of any kind.

That the human will is restricted by prior alternatives does not affect the two-way power itself that the will "considered in its essential and strict sense" is said to consist in. The exercise of this power presupposes, however, a stronger sense of indifference than that of the indifference invoked in (6). If the human will consists in its essence in this two-way power, then, without making it share in God's incomprehensible, "supreme" indifference of will, it still has a positive power of indifference, which in spite of all other differences separating it from God's will, renders it analogous to or like God's will.²⁴ The true and the good, and the ensuing objective and unchangeable hierarchy of created perfections, depend entirely on God's will in creating them. The human will does

---

do things because they are good, but they are good because "he exercised his will to make them so" (7: 435–36, 2: 293–94). I discuss Descartes' view of the divine will in Alanen (2008a).
²³ Cf. the analysis of will and free choice given by Normore (1998).
²⁴ But see Ragland (2006), pp. 67–71.

not make truth or goodness, but retains unrestricted two-way power with respect to any of its naturally or externally caused inclinations, so is free to determine whether or not to align itself with the order of reasons established by God. It has the ability, even when it may never be used, to forsake this order by withholding assent from a clearly and distinctly perceived truth, just as it has the power not to pursue a distinctly perceived good.

To defend this claim, it is useful to separate the question of assent to the cognitive good and that of the pursuit of a distinctly perceived practical good, which Descartes unhelpfully runs together in his discussion of the will's two-way power. That the will actually would opt *not* to determine itself in accordance with its natural inclination to assent to a self-evident, distinctly perceived truth, is hard to conceive and, in fact, is hardly intelligible. There are many texts indicating that Descartes did not think the will had any power but to assent here: understanding the truth seems tantamount to affirming it.[25] But attributing a two-way power to the will with respect to a practical good clearly and distinctly perceived, is not unheard of. Indeed, many thinkers in the Augustinian, voluntarist tradition took it to be a matter of self-evident experience that we, through our will, have such a power.[26]

Let us concede that what is possible for the practical will is not possible for the cognitive will. The question to ask, then, is whether the two-way power Descartes ascribes to the will without distinguishing the two cases, even when its exercise in the former case seems excluded (i.e. denying a clearly perceived truth while so perceiving it), may still retain the ability to exercise this power *indirectly*. Some commentators have taken this line. Clear and distinct perceptions do not move the will unless they are attended to. As long as they are immediate objects of present attention, the will cannot but assent to them. But it takes some determination – work of the will – to keep them in focus. Other objects, considerations, or inclinations may obscure them. Once they slip out of direct attention, assent may be withheld. Attention may be turned (at will) to other motives. The

[25] In the Fourth Meditation (7: 58–59, 2: 41), for example. This, I have argued, is not a matter of psychological compulsion but more like a normative obligation (Alanen [1999]). If understanding a truth clearly and distinctly perceived involves affirming it, it is impossible not to assent to it while seeing that it is self-evident, or understanding the reasons and evidence in support of it. But there is nothing about evident perceptions that by themselves would make them objects of consideration. We take on an obligation *qua* cognizers to seek out, attend to, and thereby affirm as true only perceptions which meet the norm of clarity and distinctness, the mark of which is that we fully understand them so cannot but assent to them.

[26] See Alanen (2003), pp. 233–39.

two-way power here would be, at best, indirect or "derivative."[27] Support for this can be found in a letter where Descartes explains in what sense we can be said to retain our freedom to choose between pursuing good or evil even while admitting that it is impossible not to pursue the good which is clearly known *as long as* one attends to the reasons for it. He writes in the first of two letters on freedom to Mesland (2 May 1644):

(E) But the nature of the soul is such that it hardly attends for more than a moment to one thing, as soon as our attention turns away from the reason proving that a thing is good for us, and we merely retain in our memory the thought that it appeared desirable, we can represent to our mind some other reason that makes us doubt it, and so suspend our judgment. (4: 116, 3: 233–34; translation altered)

In this context the concern is with practical deliberation, and although Descartes seems to follow the "common" doctrine of intellectual or ethical determinism here, he may still be seen as leaving room for a two-way power working indirectly, either through attention or, as Ragland has argued, derivatively, through some earlier undetermined free choices shaping or determining one's character.[28]

I want to suggest a somewhat different way of understanding Descartes' doctrine: the radical two-way power and indifference can be applied directly but only in the case of the pursuit of the practical good, whereas it can be employed only indirectly or derivatively in the case of the cognitive good. The latter – the pursuit of the truth – is among the naturally pursued goods/ends of the practical will. Yet Descartes, whom I take to side with the Augustinians here, does not think the practical will is, by its nature, necessitated to pursue the good in the manner Aquinas' doctrine presupposes.[29] The pursuit of knowledge, consequently, is not necessarily or automatically among the highest goods of the practical will; it has to be endorsed. By its two-way power, the practical will can hold back from making the cognitive good its highest priority. Its power to withhold assent to distinct perceptions would here be indirect, derivative of a

---

[27] For a clearly worked out reading along these lines see Ragland (2006), pp. 80–90 (cf. Newman [2008]), although I am skeptical about Newman's solution, which does not seem so much to solve the difficulty as merely move it up (or down) to another level, for the same question of how attention can be controlled remains unanswered.

[28] That a truth is clearly perceived means that it is fully attended to. But Ragland (2006), pp. 83ff., ends up reading Descartes as a "moderate" libertarian, or "moderate compatibilist." The problem with this reading, as with the one defended by Newman (2008), is that the problematic, undetermined choice that these readings want to get around is merely pushed to another level, so remains in the end unexplained.

[29] See e.g. the texts from Aquinas quoted by Carriero and the ensuing comment (2009), pp. 244ff.

prior rejection of the cognitive good as highly placed on the list of ends to pursue. If you have no prior commitment to the search for truth – Descartes' main goal in the *Meditations* – you are not bound by epistemic norms governing the inquiry for truth, including the obligation to attend to the degree of distinctness of your perceptions. Thus, while not assenting is impossible in the presence of a clearly and distinctly perceived truth fully attended to,[30] assent can be withheld, indirectly, whenever the commitment to the cognitive good itself and the pursuit of knowledge is neglected or abandoned.

If according to the first possibility considered above (the "compatibilist reading"), the choice of the will can be said to be predetermined by its own nature, so that it is most free when it acts from and according to its innate, natural inclination to follow the intellect, its choice in the second case (a version perhaps of the "libertarian reading") cannot be thus determined by prior inclinations. Rather, it is a self-mover by nature, i.e. it has the power to determine whether or not to follow any given inclination, whatever its origin may be, or to pick the end it pursues. Nothing other than its own free choice, i.e. the will itself, can account for what final end it opts for or lets itself be moved by. If it goes for the lesser good, it is not through lacking clear perceptions of the better, but because it so wills to move itself. The will here is the end of explanations.[31]

4 TWO KINDS OF INDIFFERENCE

Descartes' explicit recognition of two kinds of indifference (or as he calls them "degrees" of freedom) in his second letter to Mesland supports this reading. Indifference in the first sense, he there explains, means absence of determining reasons and is the "lowest degree of freedom" (cf. passage [B] from the Fourth Meditation quoted above). I will refer to it as indifference$_{AR}$ – indifference in the absence of determining reasons.[32] Indifference in the second sense stands for a positive faculty of self-determination, and this, I have argued, is what Descartes thinks of as the essence of will when describing it as our "highest perfection." I will refer to it as indifference$_{SD}$ – a positive faculty of self-determination:

---

[30] See *Principles* I:45–46 (8a: 21–22, 2: 207–8).

[31] Cf. Augustine (1993), p. 105.

[32] (F) "I would like you to notice that 'indifference' in this context seems to me strictly to mean that state of the will when it is not impelled one way rather than another by any perception of truth or goodness. This is the sense in which I took it when I said that the lowest degree of freedom is that by which we determine ourselves to things which are indifferent" (4: 173, 3: 245).

(G) But perhaps others mean by "indifference" a positive faculty of determining oneself to one or the other of two contraries [*positiva facultas se determinandi ad utrumlibet e duobus contrariis*], that is to say, to pursue or avoid, to affirm or deny. I do not deny that the will has this positive faculty. Indeed, I think it has it not only with respect to those actions to which it is not pushed by any evident reasons on one side or the other, but also with respect to all other actions, so that when a very evident reason moves us in one direction, although morally speaking we can hardly move in the contrary direction, absolutely speaking we can. *For it is always open to us to hold back from pursuing a clearly known good, or from admitting a clearly perceived truth, provided we consider it a good thing to demonstrate our freedom by so doing.* (4: 173, 3: 245; my emphasis)

In the first letter to Mesland Descartes seems to acknowledge only one kind of indifference, and to endorse a compatibilist position (the common doctrine of the schools).[33] Passage (G) from the second letter acknowledges two senses of indifference, applying the second sense to the two-way power first mentioned as the essence of the freedom of the will (section 3). Here Descartes can be seen as reconciling the two kinds of indifference (and freedom) by referring them to different stages of deliberation and choice. They work at temporally and logically different moments in the operation of the will and power of choice.

The first moment is (i) before the actualization of the will, or in scholastic terminology, the "elicitation" of an act of will or volition, i.e. before the will has determined itself to one of two opposites, and the second is (ii) after the initial choice or decision has been made – i.e. after the act of will has been "elicited." Consider a case of deliberating about what good to pursue. The will may have a prior inclination in favor of the good clearly perceived by the intellect, but this inclination is not yet an actual volition, and the will may have other simultaneous inclinations as well, pulling in opposite directions. Think of Augustine in his early teens confronting the temptation to steal pears that he did not even want to eat in his neighbor's garden. He knew very well it was forbidden, and that it would be a good thing to abide by the rule prohibiting stealing – yet he delights in pursuing what he knows is evil precisely because it is evil, and because in so doing he manifests his self and his independence.[34] The will has this power or ability at all times according to extract (E), so it is always free to abstain from eliciting a prior volition to pursue a clearly perceived good even when nothing but the will itself could hinder this

---

[33] See (E) above in the text and the passage (G) from the second Mesland letter referring to the first quoted in the previous note (F). For an excellent discussion see Ragland (2006).

[34] Augustine (1992), II: iv–x.

volition from being actualized. Descartes may have some experience of this kind in mind in explaining the two different ways in which freedom of the will can be exercised:

(H) For a greater freedom consists in either a greater facility in determining oneself or in a greater use of the positive power we have of following the worse although we see the better. If we follow the course which appears to have the most reasons in its favour, we determine ourselves more easily; but if we follow the opposite, we make more use of that positive power; and thus we can always act more freely in those cases in which we see much more good than evil than in those cases which are called ... indifferent. (4: 174, 3: 245)

As we have seen, freedom in the first alternative, where we follow our natural inclination to affirm the true or to pursue the good, entails absence of indifference$_{AR}$, the lowest degree of freedom. Once a natural inclination is elicited and the volition to pursue the good is actualized or operative, it also excludes indifference$_{SD}$ consisting in the "positive faculty of determining oneself to one or the other of two contraries."[35]

Descartes' discussion of the will and its freedom is couched in scholastic vocabulary. What exactly does "elicit" mean? One can consider a volition to be a potential, non-active or "dormant" inclination, and we may have many such inclinations which are "externally" caused, passive tendencies until we decide to act on them. I may have desires and idle wants or wishes which I do not act on – for instance, spending a day by the sea, or hiking in the woods, or returning to the town where I grew up. I may presently desire different things that I cannot pursue simultaneously: I have this urge to take up smoking again but I also want to stay healthy and avoid polluting the environment if I can. Once I decide what to do – using this scholastic vocabulary – an act of my will is elicited: a passive state of willing or desiring becomes active or operative. If that passive desire was very strong, what now happens is that I simply cease to hold it back. If it was weak, but I wish it were stronger, I can do things to make it stronger and activate it – I can, as it were, strengthen it through various considerations. I can even work up inclinations I did not know I had. This happens through training and education. This is what Descartes' doctrine of the passions and learning to master them turns on. So inclinations of the will can be dormant or ineffective, and they can be causally active, actual volitions. In the latter case they have been, using Descartes' vocabulary, "elicited" through an act of assent that has no antecedent cause other than will itself.

---

[35] For Descartes' full discussion of this issue see (4: 174–75, 2: 245–46).

Commenting on what he wrote in the Fourth Meditation and in the first letter to Mesland (extracts [C] and [E]) Descartes goes on to explain in the second letter that when considering an act of the will in the first case (i) "with respect to the time before they are elicited, it entails indifference in the second sense but not in the first" (4: 174–75, 2: 245–46). So the free power of choice (the two-way power) entailing indifference in the strong sense of a positive faculty of self-determination is at work *before* an act of will is elicited. Although it is not possible to have two contrary elicited acts of will or volitions at the same moment, it is still possible, at the moment before the actual volition is formed, to elicit or not to elicit it. The more reasons we have for doing a thing, when perceiving it as very good, the freer we are in determining ourselves to pursue it. We can, on the other hand, follow an inclination that has fewer reasons going for it – we can choose the worse alternative, while seeing it as bad and having the power to choose the better. Suppose I choose to go for the worse while continuing to see the better. I will then also continue to have second thoughts and regret my choice, and in the absence of good reasons, I need to exert more of my (brute or arbitrary) willpower to stick with my decision and persist in my error. If I go for the better, the more reasons I see for doing so, the easier it is for me to stay committed to my choice, to the course of action I chose. In either case, the will elicits its own acts independently of what reason commands.

Even a very strong natural inclination to affirm a truth distinctly perceived or pursue a good clearly known, would, on this picture, have to be, as it were, activated to be and to remain operative. This seems implausible if taken to imply that we would be consciously deliberating at all times about our volitions, but that need not be the case. The point that seems important for Descartes is that whatever our actual volitions are, we could, at some point, have opted not to elicit them and so willed otherwise – for instance, we could have chosen, deliberately, to ignore the pursuit of the true and the good in order to gratify some desire of the moment (e.g. desires and inclinations caused by the passions depending on the mind–body union), ignoring the reasons speaking against this. Ignoring them here is not a matter of ignorance but depends on the will itself, whose power to choose alone prevents us from attending to them. It is only because of this power to control (directly or indirectly) what we assent to that we can be said to be both free and (internally) determined in following our rational inclination or impulse. This means that indifference₍D₎ is constitutive of the will and presupposed in any act of volition before its elicitation. It is also, I maintain, the sole ground for calling the will our highest perfection – that whereby we are made images of God.[36]

Descartes' problematic account of the will and its freedom is developed in an epistemological and theodical context, the aim being to warrant the truth rule and, perhaps even more importantly, to draw a line between God's and our own responsibility for our cognitive errors. The theodical context explains why judgment is treated as a case of moral action generally, the point being to show that we, through misuse of our will, are ourselves accountable for our false beliefs and theories just as we are for our actions or moral behavior and to some extent for our passions as well.[37] The result as we have seen, is a complex, and ultimately unstable, theory with what many have seen as a radically voluntarist doctrine of cognition control.[38]

5 BEING IN CONTROL OF ONE'S BELIEFS

Gassendi objected that the scope of the intellect cannot be narrower than that of the will, "since the will never aims at anything which the intellect has not already perceived" (7: 314, 2: 218), and always affirms what at the time seems most probable. If it goes wrong, it is not the will, but the imperfect perceptions of the intellect that are at fault (7: 315, 2: 219). If we want to use our judgment correctly we should "not so much restrain our will as apply our intellect to develop a clearer awareness, which the judgment will always then follow" (7: 317, 2: 220). Gassendi relies on a supposition that Descartes does not accept, namely, that the intellect has some activity of its own whereby it can determine itself to considering various things; in the case of obscure perceptions, to making them clearer. To the extent we can guard ourselves against error at all, Descartes argues, it is precisely because we have a will that is not automatically determined by what happens to be the clearest perceptions of the intellect.

Gassendi follows the common doctrine that the will is controlled by the intellect. Descartes holds that, although the will works in tandem with the intellect in the formation of our beliefs, its operation is not determined by the intellect. He does not hold, as many commentators have thought, that it could ever operate in the absence of prior perceptions, but that its assent to any particular perception depends not so much on its

---

[36] Compare also the account in the *Principles* 1:37 (8a: 18–19, 1: 205).
[37] Alanen (2009).
[38] See e.g. the literature mentioned in note 11, above, and references there given.

degree of evidence as on the will determining itself to endorse a particular belief (7: 376–77, 2: 259). If you judge that an apple, which unbeknownst to you has been poisoned, is good and healthy merely on account of its looks, smell, and taste, you extend your will beyond the limits of your intellect; you so believe because you will to believe it, not because you know it. You form the judgment – one you could have suspended – that eating it is good for you, basing your judgment on your desire and a false appearance. The will in itself is not at fault in cases like this, nor is the intellect itself at fault for presenting a false appearance. The blame is on you for affirming a belief there is little evidence for. You make a *leap* with your will – relying on nature, habit, your hopes, and expectations formed by earlier experiences. You act like the politicians and voters who favor expansion of nuclear energy even though the evidence for its long-term safety is feeble. They believe in it because they want cheap energy and can get away without counting possible disasters among its costs.

Descartes' point is that to the extent that the beliefs we hold depend not merely on the evidence perceived by the intellect but on the will, and because the will, differently from the intellect, is a self-mover, *we* are ultimately in control of and responsible for them ourselves. We can work on the will, and control, if nothing else, what kind of perceptions we assent to – what beliefs we accept and commit ourselves too.

Spinoza assimilates Descartes' notion of free will to the Stoic idea of free assent to propositions or appearances and sees them as products of utter self-deception. Not only does he deny the doctrine that the attitude or stance we take to our ideas could somehow be freely chosen, but goes to what may seem another extreme in rejecting any distinction between ideas and affirmations. Ideas or propositions come to the mind as affirmations or denials – as beliefs. We have no control whatsoever over our representations – indeed, there is no individual self or thinking subject over and above the sum of particular ideas composing it. Instead of being a "mute picture," an idea, insofar as it is an idea, involves an affirmation or negation.[39] Representations and volitions merge. Whatever activity there is in the mind, it is in the ideas themselves, and the more distinct or adequate the idea is, the more (affirmative) force or power it has. If Descartes turns beliefs (affirmations and denials) into actions that we do and cause, Spinoza turns ideas into active, dynamic states that are *not* caused by us, but are themselves caused by and causes of other ideas or beliefs. Their power of action (causal force) is determined not by any independent will

---

[39] Spinoza (1925), II: 49, scholium.

or agent, but by their very content and the context of other particular ideas and concurring causes.[40] The latter include the conatus or striving to persist that characterizes each individual thing (and idea), but there is no separate will in the sense of a real faculty or power with a force of action of its own over and above that of the individual ideas and their pattern constituting the human mind. Briefly, our representational states come as affirmations or denials, and the stronger they are, the more causal power they have in determining our cognitive stances and commitments. There is really nothing that we can do about this, and there is a sense in which we – our minds – are at the mercy of occurrent ideas and their interplay or associations, just as the body, whose idea the mind is, is at the mercy of external causes acting on its parts (Alanen 2011). Hume holds a somewhat similar view of ideas. Ideas or beliefs are more or less vivacious, they act on each other and our minds (which are collections of ideas) with more or less force. Their force determines what we believe and when we suspend judgment. We suspend judgment when there are no ideas clear and vivid enough to determine the mind one way or another.

Disregarding the "libertarian" streak of Descartes' view of the will, his account of judgment is not, in the end, as distant from that of Spinoza as one might think. Indeed, Spinoza's doctrine of ideas as including a conative, dynamic component can be seen as an important development of Descartes' account of volitions as part of judgments.[41] The most important step in Descartes' breaking with traditional views of the human intellect is in treating it as an external force with respect to the will that he sees as crucial in the process of determining the nature of the self. Once the idea of an inner agent – reason or will – is abandoned, the self – an idea among others – is at the mercy of the external forces acting on it.

6 ABSOLUTE AND MORAL POSSIBILITY

Many ingenious solutions to tone down Descartes' most radical claims have been advanced.[42] Carriero, who sees Descartes' account of the relation between will and intellect as ultimately aligned with the more

---

[40] Spinoza's notion of agency is very different from Descartes' and can be spelled out in terms of causation: the more effects a thing produces, the more active it is, and this holds for mental as well as physical causation (which really are the same thing). See Della Rocca (2003).

[41] This is not generally noted by commentators, who tend to focus on Spinoza's criticism of Descartes. One exception is Martin Lin (2004).

[42] See e.g. Kenny (1973) and more recently Newman (2008). For an interesting alternative see Kambouchner (2008).

"common doctrine of the school,"[43] offers an illuminating account of Aquinas' view of the will, and the ways in which Descartes' account of free choice departs from it. Among the views they share is the idea of the human will as a genuine faculty tending by nature to truth and goodness. While recognizing that Descartes' view of the divine will is different from that of Aquinas, since Descartes holds the radical view that God's will creates the true and the good (so that the good is not prior to but depends on God's will), Carriero points out that Descartes never abandons the Aristotelian–Thomistic view that the will of a created human being who finds goodness and truth determined by God, "cannot move [*ferri*] toward anything else" and "will embrace what is good and true all the more willingly, and hence more freely, as he sees it more clearly" (7: 432, 2: 292; Carriero 2009). In my view, Descartes is, at best, of two minds about this. That he agrees that goodness and truth are determined by God explains his willingness to subscribe to what he calls the common doctrine of the school, but it also helps us understand where precisely he goes beyond it, and what he may have in mind in claiming that although it is "morally speaking" impossible for us to "hold back from pursuing a clearly known good, or from admitting a clearly perceived truth," we still have the ability to do so "absolutely speaking."

A straightforward reading of this claim that I favor is that as long as our will is ordered as it should, i.e. as long as we continue to will what God who created us disposed our will to move towards, namely, the true and the good clearly perceived, it is "morally" impossible for us not to do so, nevertheless it is "absolutely" or metaphysically speaking possible for us to hold the will back from so moving itself. The human will is not determined with absolute or metaphysical necessity to the good – in general or in particular – in the way Aquinas thinks it is, since whatever particular inclination it may have, it does not move to action unless elicited by its own free power. This gives it the ability to hold back any given motion and opt out of pursuing any presently perceived good, including the good set for it by its maker. Insofar as practical deliberation is concerned, this means that it can, absolutely speaking, move for the worse while seeing the better, and in the case of the cognitive good, that it can ignore it by not embracing the truth distinctly perceived, just as it can affirm something it does not clearly know or understand. Though we would not in normal circumstances have any use of the power to withhold assent from

---

[43] The one Descartes himself professes to follow in some contexts. See e.g. Second Replies (7: 166, 2: 117), and the letter to Mesland of 2 May 1644 (4: 115, 3: 233).

clear and distinct perception, Descartes seems to hold that it is only by this power that we can follow God's command as free agents, and so deserve credit when using it well.[44] → using our will well.

Two considerations speak in favor of this reading. One turns on how to understand Descartes' comparison between the divine and the human will, and taking this comparison seriously has already been discussed. The other is Descartes' view of God's power and our total dependence on our maker, with the ensuing problem of God's responsibility of our errors discussed in the Fourth Meditation (7: 55, 2: 38). Realizing, to his regret maybe, that he is not the supreme being, since he finds himself lacking in so many respects, Descartes reverts to a common theodical move. The imperfection, evidenced by his fallibility, means that he participates in non-being or nothingness, something that does not require a cause and so does not constitute a threat to God's perfection. He treats error as Augustine treats sin: "error as such is not something real which depends on God, but merely a defect." He explains this defect by his own misuse of two faculties that are in themselves perfect. The defect is the outcome of the application of a faculty – the will – which is unbounded and constitutes our highest perfection, to a faculty – the intellect – which, although perfect in itself, is finite by nature. He does not, however, rest content with the traditional explanation of the origin of evil, turning it – sin or error – into mere lack of being or nothingness requiring no cause. He talks of privation rather than absence or non-existence, and the privation here is the absence of knowledge that we or our minds, created as thinking, rational beings, are due or entitled to.[45] It is not God or our God-given faculties that deprive us of it, but we (the cognitive agent) deprive ourselves, by a free act of will, of whatever knowledge we could have had and are entitled to by birthright, or whenever we lack clear and distinct perfection, of the lucidity we might have with respect to our cognitive limitations.

The ensuing complex account of judgment with what appears as its exalted view of a free power of decisions or choice provides a metaphysical basis for Descartes' moral psychology and ethical doctrine, which places a heavy burden of responsibility on finite agents and cognizers.[46] Descartes is well aware that the rational will would not take us very far in life and matters of practical decision, however. *Qua* embodied, our nature is not merely intellectual; our will is moved by other than rational inclinations,

[44] See again the passage from the *Principles* 1:37 referenced above in note 36.
[45] See Gombay (2007), ch. 4.   [46] Cf. Svensson (2011).

like those tending to the preservation of the body and the mind–body union. The latter, which are followed by instinct and habit, in fact determine a large part of our beliefs.[47]

This brings us back to the question of the nature of the mind or self raised at the beginning of this chapter, where a distinction was made between the self in the strict sense of the mind apart from the body – a pure cognitive agent – and the self in a larger sense of an embodied mind, subject to passions and inclinations caused by the bodies and external thing acting on it. Given the God-given core abilities of the self in the strict sense (a passive intellect and a self-moving will), the embodied mind or self retains some measure of control over its beliefs and inclinations, and is, to this extent, master over its own nature, i.e. it determines freely, directly and indirectly, what road to follow in life, for instance, to strive or not to strive for greater knowledge and perfection. Omit the independent mind and its free-wheeling power of self-determination, and you end up with what looks very much like Spinoza's picture of *Natura naturata*. There is no individual self in control any more – at best, there is a community of thinking things sharing, through some of their ideas, in common reason that ideally would move them, but who in reality are governed by their random affections and passions, and through them by more or less enlightened prophets.

---

[47] See e.g. the letter to Mersenne about two kinds of nature and natural instincts, one we have *qua* human beings and which is purely intellectual and is always truthful, and one we have *qua* animals and which should not always be trusted (2: 599, 3: 140). However, in the Second Replies, Descartes notes that we in fact may have to act on even less than probable beliefs, and not only on what is clearly perceived, in matters of conduct of life (7: 149, 2: 106).

CHAPTER 10

God and meditation in Descartes' Meditations on First Philosophy

Jorge Secada

> … human kind
> Cannot bear very much reality.
> T. S. Eliot, *Four Quartets*

This chapter looks at Descartes' *Meditations on First Philosophy* as a guide to meditation on God. The proposed reading will uncover key aspects of the text, providing insight into its philosophical contents and answering central questions regarding what Descartes intended to do with it and how it should be read. One way to put this is to say that I take seriously the title of the work: meditations on first philosophy in which the existence of God is made manifest, displayed, or demonstrated (7: 17: "*Meditationes de prima philosophia in quibus Dei existentia … demonstratur*").[1] I will begin by briefly laying out some interpretative assumptions. After that, we will follow the order of the text and articulate our reading around three moments of the meditation on God: initial consideration of the idea in the First Meditation; ascent to grounded belief in his existence in the Third Meditation; further discovery of the divine within us, and, in the Fifth, final intuition of his nature and existence. My presentation is narrative, seeking to lay bare a structure and contents not always properly grasped. Such narration is not linear, mirroring the layered unfolding of the text itself, while progressively unveiling its structure.

HERMENEUTICAL PRELIMINARIES

Descartes' *Meditations on First Philosophy* is not a treatise or essay (see 7: 157, where Descartes writes that the *Meditations* is neither "Disputations" nor

---

[1] All references to the works of Descartes are to volume and page in AT. When a reference would repeat the last one, it is omitted. I have used the English translation by Cottingham, Stoothoff, Murdoch, and Kenny. I have also used the fine translation by Moriarty (2008). However, I have amended and altered the translations as I have seen fit, and occasionally I have translated a passage wholly anew.

"Theorems and Problems"). The unity and coherence of this work is not exclusively or even principally that of rational argument.[2] The *Meditations* is instead a therapeutic manual. It offers a course of treatment for a cognitive illness inherent to human beings, resulting from the embodiment of the human mind, which as a result is prey to passions, feelings, and emotions and must rely on sensation and imagination to know the world around it. For Descartes, this epistemic therapy is essential if one aims to find something "unshakeable and permanent in the sciences" (7: 17). Not unrelatedly, the *Meditations* is also a manual for meditation on first philosophy, and in particular on the self and on God.[3] Not only is cognitive therapy required for meditation, but meditation is indeed the proper exercise of the therapeutic process. Of all the meditative exercises, it is meditation on God that constitutes the most demanding and pristine use of purely intellectual perception, since reflection on the self, though easier to pursue, does not put the meditator in contact with an object completely alien to sensation and imagination. The meditative nature of the *Meditations* has been brought to light; but its implications have not been sufficiently explored.[4] Philosophers' focus on argument and doctrine makes it difficult for them to keep the meditative character of this work in mind, or to apprehend securely its full consequence. Here, we will lay out some of its significance and use it as the context within which we discuss our central concern: God, the discovery of his existence, and the ascent to the contemplation of his nature.

Readers of fiction usually distinguish between the voice of the author and the different voices within a story, be they the voices of characters or of impersonal or third-personal narrators. These distinctions are particularly important when interpreting this meditative text. One must not take

---

[2] Contrast Gueroult (1953). For a critique of Gueroult's approach see my introduction to the Spanish translation, Gueroult (2005), vol. I, pp. vii–xliii. Other examples of similar misreadings are Dicker (1993) and Almog (2002). A particularly unfortunate example, given its many other virtues, is Rubin (2008). See my review of Rubin's book, Secada (2009).

[3] In 1640 Descartes wrote that the *Meditations* does not deal with "God and the soul in particular, but in general with all the first things that may be known by philosophizing" (3: 235). I do not take this to deny that these two objects are the meditative focus of the *Meditations*. Descartes is instead stating that this work will deliver the complete metaphysical foundations of science and knowledge.

[4] The point was made by Étienne Gilson and other commentators in the earlier part of the last century; see e.g. Gilson (1975), p. 186. For more recent statements see Marlies (1978); Wilson (1978), pp. 5–11 (Wilson, however, appears to come short in her discussion of the meditational "I" on pp. 4–5); Garin (1984), ch. 4, section 11; the section entitled "Skeptical Therapy" in Garber (1986), pp. 91–97, and especially his n. 36 on p. 113; Kosman (1986); Rorty (1986b); Vendler (1989); Janowski (2000), pp. 109ff.; and Nolan (2005).

Worthy of special mention is the rich and insightful essay Hatfield (1986; published in a shorter version, Hatfield 1985). See also Hatfield (2003).

the "I" of the body of Descartes' *Meditations* ever to refer to its author or to be its spokesperson.[5] A more plausible identity for the first-personal meditator is the reader.[6] Descartes hoped that readers of his meditations would actually be meditators living through the meditative process, a transformative process (7: 34, and 162–63). The *Meditations* does not describe this undertaking; rather, it aims to become the expression of the reader's own transformation. From Descartes' point of view, the intended reader and the meditating ego are living through the same transformative process: the *Meditations* is its expression and it is supposed to be sung by both in unison. Yet, we, contemporary readers, can no longer oblige its author. We cannot wholeheartedly take on the meditator's garb because we can no longer believe Descartes' promise of scientific advance, nor his diagnosis. We know too much that Descartes did not know, and this makes taking the *Meditations* as he intended impossible. So we must apply the literary distinctions between author, meditational character or narrator, and reader, keeping in mind that the distinction between the latter two was not originally intended but results from historical accident and distance.

The *Meditations* follows upon a diagnosis; and the meditative exercise will only work for those who come prepared to approach it in a certain way (see 7: 9, 130, and 158).[7] The meditator will undergo a treatment of cognitive cure and her belief-forming dispositions will be profoundly transformed. She will emerge not only with a considerable body of certain knowledge about the nature of things, but also, most importantly, armed and ready to march on to the frontiers of knowledge and science and help expand them securely. The illness, if we may call it so, that the meditative therapy seeks to mitigate is dependence on the senses; and the cure will enable the mind to exercise its purely intellectual perception. On the one hand, this dependence is necessary and good for human beings. Humans are not angels. We are embodied minds who must attain eternal salvation by leading good lives, and this requires sensorial perception: "[a]ll the conduct of our life depends on our senses" (6: 81; see 8A: 35–36). On the other hand, sensorial perception induces error when inquiring into the nature of things; it is an obstacle if our aim is to know ourselves as we truly are and the things around us as they are in themselves (see 7: 157; see

---

[5] Cf., for example, Dicker (1993), p. 3: "In *Meditation I*, Descartes doubts ... his previous beliefs."

[6] Of course, I do not intend to deny that the meditator sometimes expresses Descartes' own views, or that her views may reveal Descartes' own.

[7] Notice the implicit selection of meditators Descartes effects by writing in Latin: "it would not be helpful to give a full account ... in a book written in French [i.e. the *Discourse*] ... read by all and sundry... [and even] weak intellects" (7: 7).

also 8A: 34–38). From this perspective, sensorial dependence is an illness. Amongst its symptoms are our lack of progress in acquiring knowledge of ourselves and of the world around us, and the unending disputes amongst the learned in almost any discipline but mathematics.

Now, the proposed meditation is not merely instrumental, as would have been understood by readers familiar with the meditative tradition and genre. Nonetheless, nowadays many who recognize a meditative character in Descartes' masterpiece then go on to put it at the exclusive service of natural science as if it were just the metaphysical propaedeutic for physics.[8] Descartes believed only a select few would be able to perceive the conceptual and argumentative foundations of science with the supreme clarity and distinctness with which he could grasp them, and that most (even when we refer only to those few who engage in these pursuits) would have to accept them somewhat on faith. My point now is that the meditative undertaking has a further aim, one that unlike the former is of little, if any, use to anyone who cannot fully engage in it. These prospective readers will honestly submit to the requirements imposed by the author driven by the desire to meditate about ultimately real and significant objects. From its very title this work promises the fruits of such meditation – amongst others, as the meditator puts it in the course of a quasi-mystical rapture at the very center of the *Meditations*, "the greatest joy and fulfillment [*maximam … voluptatem*] of which we are capable in this life" (7: 52; in 9A: 42, the French version has "*le plus grand contentement*").

Not surprisingly, this promise is not mentioned at the start of the text itself, even though it is present in the title: these are meditations. The perceptive reader will receive the invitation to meditate and seek to attain the contemplation of self and God, a non-instrumental enterprise which is not only valuable in itself but which has the dialectical structure proper to those activities which endow human existence with meaning.[9] Others will engage in this meditative enterprise only incipiently, resting content to move on to pursuits more suited to the human mind, such as scientific inquiry into the workings of bodies and human souls.

Descartes' *Meditations on First Philosophy* embodies a conception of philosophy that is deeply anti-scholastic and anti-analytic.[10] It offers

---

[8] As is shown by many of the pieces mentioned in note 4, above.

[9] On the nature and structure of such dialectical activities see Brewer (2009), ch. 2 and *passim*.

[10] Indeed, there is a connection between the underlying conception of the subject and the genre used to engage in it in writing. The import of this fact for Cartesian scholarship is missed when the *Meditations* is treated as something akin to an essay.

an understanding that is not the finalized result of argument but an unending activity indistinguishable from meditation itself. Though we, contemporary readers, will find this promise more difficult to uncover than the promise of success in the sciences, it is here that we can find a voice that speaks to us, difficult as it may be to make it our own. Here we find a conception of philosophical inquiry that, regardless of whether ultimately we agree with the Cartesian stance on it, may engage us who can no longer take Descartes' scientific promises seriously. It is within this context that I propose we approach our topic.

THE INTRODUCTION OF GOD IN THE *MEDITATIONS*

From the perspective of the meditation on God, the purpose of the First Meditation is to introduce the meditative object. After leading the meditator to complete doubt regarding the reality and existence of the world around him which he thought he knew through his senses, Descartes has him pause and consider certain disciplines and propositions which do not rely on sensation and so appear to withstand doubt. The meditator refers to "arithmetic, geometry" and to "two plus three equals five, and a square has no more than four sides" (7: 20). A possible extension of the doubt to those and other "such obvious truths" is mentioned at that point. It is then that the notion of God makes its appearance and is introduced into the meditative process. Descartes reminds the meditator of an "opinion held for a long time that there is an omnipotent God who created me as I am now" (7: 21). The object presented for consideration is that of a supreme entity or God who is omnipotent. Since the meditator is appealing to a mere "opinion held for a long time" (a phrase reminiscent of the beginning of the meditation in 7: 17: "years ago I was struck by the large number of falsehoods that I had accepted as true since childhood"), and she is by now aware that many if not all such opinions are subject to doubt, we should take this as nothing more than an invitation to consider the matter. The issues raised are whether the notion of such entity makes sense, whether it could exist, and what relations it has to the meditator and any other entities there may be.

There are three interrelated processes in the early meditations. Descartes wants to lead the meditator's "mind … away from the senses" (7: 12). She will be made to deploy arguments designed to help in this process by casting doubt on sensory experience or by making manifest the certain truth of matters not falling under the scope of sensorial perception. Descartes wants the meditator to exercise her purely intellectual perception. And he

1) bring forth skeptical argument
2) bring out whatever truth may be in them
3) refute them

will lead her to a discussion of whether her intellect can be trusted. The meditator will undertake, that is, a further project of validating reason. Finally, the meditator will confront skeptical arguments, rescue whatever truth they may contain, and refute them. *— what the meditator does.*

These three projects (withdraw the mind from the senses; validate reason; refute the skeptic) have different purposes and standing within the *Meditations*. The first is a precondition for meditation, since proper meditation is the act of a pure intellect, detached from sensory perception. Beyond helping secure the mind's purely intellectual gaze, the second line of argument is an important component of the grounding of science. As the meditator releases the pure perception of her mind or intellect with which she will be able to grasp the true nature of things, a question naturally arises for her: is this clear and distinct perception trustworthy? Both these thematic lines have a place within the meditations on self and God. The validation of reason, of course, crucially appeals to God. As these two projects are pursued, the meditative objects will be apprehended with greater confidence, and they will reveal unsuspected riches. Finally, the refutation of the skeptic is merely a tangential consequence of the former, central concerns (see 7: 171–72). It is noteworthy only on account of the fact that so many have fallen prey to skepticism. Let us now look at these undertakings and the interweaved meditation on the self from the perspective of our main interest, the meditation on God. *= what Secada plans to do.*

While in Descartes' considered view there is truth to doubt of the senses and he did think that to some extent our waking experience is like a dream populated by unreal entities, like colors and tastes, he believed there is no truth to the thought that clear and distinct purely intellectual propositions may be false. Further, doubt regarding such propositions has *— the* little hold over the meditator. Beyond its introduction and the passages *deceiving* in the Third Meditation when it is recalled, taken up for examination, *God hypothesis* and discarded, such radical doubt does not figure in the *Meditations*. The *is not a* meditator is never shown to engage in it, to be under its grip.[11] Given the *valid reason* extent to which commentators have discussed Cartesian radical doubt of *for doubt* reason, one might wonder why the text does not do more to display it and use it! I propose that instead we see it as primarily serving two purposes: *— I say* it raises the issue of whether and how reason or intellect can be validated; *bauthor*

---

[11] Summarizing the state and scope of doubt at the start of the Second Meditation, the meditator states: "I … have no senses at all; body, shape, extension in space, motion, and place itself are illusions. What truth then is left? Perhaps this alone, that nothing is certain" (7: 24). After that, she moves to a first intellectual perception of her self.

Secada's proposed use of the Cartesian
radical doubt
1) raises the issue of whether and how reason
or intellect can be validated
2) introduces the meditator to reflection on
the idea of god.

and, most importantly for our interests here, it serves to introduce the meditator to reflection on the idea of God.

Consideration of God has various roles to play within these three strands. God reinforces doubt about the senses. But such function does not require the supremely perfect being which Descartes wants the meditator to consider; Putnam's scientist manipulating a brain in a vat would do. The meditator himself considers some alternative hypotheses: that she is the result of "fate or chance or a continuous series of events" and not design; or that there is "an evil spirit, most powerful and equally cunning" intent on deceiving him. (7: 21 and 22; 9A: 17, the French translation of the latter passage reads *"un certain mauvais genie, non moins rusé et trompeur que puissant."*) However, doubt regarding the simplest and most evident propositions, such as "2 + 2 = 4" or "a square has four sides" or "something even simpler, if anything simpler can be imagined," appears to require at least an omnipotent deceiver who created me with a nature that makes me go wrong even about those things.[12] In the *Meditations* this radical doubt is never actually and fully granted. Whether it should be granted or not depends on whether a supreme deceiver, an omnipotent and deceitful God, could, for all we know, exist. This issue is not resolved in the First Meditation. Its examination must wait until the Third. Engaging in this doubt and allowing it to possess the meditator serves no purpose, and at best it is based on ignorance. So it is introduced and then put aside until the matter can be more carefully considered.

Note the following passage in the course of introducing the possibility of a deceitful God: "perhaps God has not willed that I be so cheated, for he is said to be supremely good. But if it were incompatible with his goodness to have created me such that I am perpetually deceived, it would seem equally inconsistent with that quality to permit me to be sometimes deceived. Nonetheless, I cannot doubt that he does permit it" (7: 21). Descartes presents the meditator with an issue that will be

---

[12] It is striking that in spite of the attention devoted by commentators to the Cartesian "malignant demon [*genium malignum* or *mauvais genie*]," this famous being is clearly mentioned only once in the text of the *Meditations* (7: 22, and 9A: 17). The entity is introduced en passant towards the end of the First Meditation to reinforce doubt regarding the senses. Towards the start of the Second Meditation the meditator refers to "some God or whatever he should be called" (*aliquis Deu, vel quocunque nomine illum vocem*; in the French this is changed to *quelque Dieu, ou quelque autre puissance*) (7: 24 and 9A: 19). There may be perhaps two subsequent, indirect references in the Second Meditation. They both occur shortly after: "some deceiver or other, most powerful, most cunning" and "some deceiver, who is most powerful, and, if one dare say so, evil" (7: 25 and 26). The hesitation to call the deceiver evil may indicate that the meditator is not clearly distinguishing between a very powerful demon and a deceiving God. The evil genius does not ever appear, directly or indirectly, in the context of doubt regarding reason.

resolved much later in the course of the meditative exercise. It is only in the Fourth Meditation that she will address the problem raised by her having established that God exists, that he cannot be a deceiver, and that she falls into error. When the issue is first mentioned, in the cited passage, the meditator is not prepared to deal with it. She is not clear even about whether there could be a God or not. More to the point, she does not have the necessary epistemic means to address it successfully.

Descartes does this repeatedly. He plants a seed in the meditating reader that anticipates a subsequent discussion and which it would be premature to consider when it is first broached. In this way, he prepares the meditator, who will start thinking about the matter and will keep it in the back of his mind as the meditation progresses. As we shall see in a moment, this constant anticipation of issues makes sense given Descartes' conception of meditation. I propose that while the matter of the meditator's capacity for error given the existence of a good God is an obvious case of such anticipation, the question of whether there are good reasons for doubt regarding the simplest of intellectual matters is another.

From the perspective of the meditation on God, an object is offered for consideration: a supreme or most perfect being. The supreme character of the entity is underscored when he is described as "the source of truth" (7: 22 and 9A: 17: "*fontem veritatem*" and "*souveraine source de verité*"). The meditator is invited to reflect on the nature and attributes of God, his unbounded omnipotence, and his possible goodness; he is asked to ponder on God's relation to the meditator herself and to other entities. Is he her "creator," and if so, could he be a deceiver (7: 21)? Could such an all-powerful entity endow me with a nature that ensures I go wrong even about the simplest, most evident matters? Could he be not good?[13] The meditator will also reflect on the actual or even just merely possible existence of this entity, this "supreme fountain of truth." The meditator is never led to actually engage in radical doubt about the intellect, beyond considering its possibility. Yet he is presented with an object for examination: the idea of God. A pertinent hermeneutical question to ask is why consideration of this object (and the related issue of whether radical doubt regarding intellectually perceived, clear and distinct propositions is warranted) must wait until the Third Meditation. The answer, briefly, is that the Second Meditation is a necessary propaedeutic for proper consideration of God.

[13] Cf. Wickes' claim that "at the very end of the Third Meditation there is a sudden switch to the use of 'perfection' as a moral term, involving benevolence and veracity" Wickes (1994), p. 21.

One of the aims of the Second Meditation is methodological: it takes the meditator from radical distrust of the senses to a secure hold of his capacity for purely intellectual perception. The meditation starts with the meditator in the grip of complete doubt about her sensory experiences: "I suppose ... that everything I see is false. I believe that nothing ever existed which my deceitful memory represents. I have no senses. Body, shape, extension, movement and place are chimeras" (7: 24). It ends with him fixing his purely intellectual gaze on non-sensory objects: "I have now learnt that bodies themselves are perceived not, strictly speaking, by the senses or the imaginative faculty, but by the intellect alone ... I clearly acknowledge that nothing can be perceived by me more easily or more clearly than my own mind" (7: 34). It is only then, in the Third Meditation, that the meditator will be made to explicitly consider the idea of God.

There is a final point to make before we move on to examine the Third Meditation. When reflecting on the piece of wax in the latter half of the Second Meditation, the meditator uncovers an infinity within her. Her grasp of the piece of wax reveals a power to apprehend it through "innumerable changes" (7: 31). This capacity is only one item amongst "so much else within the mind itself" (7: 33). A world of ideas within the self, modeled on the Platonic archetypes within God, is first suggested when arguing that this power to grasp a piece of wax and objectively judge about it is the working of the pure intellect alone (see 7: 181 and 134, and 5: 160). Grasp of the corporeal world, whether that world be real or not, reveals the objective presence in us of the infinity of extension: "a thing extended, flexible, mutable ... capable of more variations in extension than I will ever encompass with my imagination" (7: 31). Such infinities are far removed from the infinity of God; they are not supremely perfect and their infinities are merely negative, a never-ending succession of the same finite reality. Still, in the order of meditation, where the mind is slowly ascending to contemplation of God, reflection on our understanding of the corporeal world, undertaken as part of the methodological securing of the mind's purely intellectual vision, serves as an initial step. Furthermore, this is a first intimation of a point Descartes will make to Elizabeth of Bohemia some years later: "the greater we deem the works of God to be, the better we observe the infinity of his power" (4: 315).

CARTESIAN MEDITATION AND THE IDEA OF GOD

At the start of the Third Meditation, the meditator is finally ready to turn her attention to the idea of God within her, and to begin reflecting on it. As she is entertaining the rule of truth, she is reminded of the "pre-conceived opinion of God's supreme power" and the hypothesis that she could have been made "so as to be deceived even about what appeared most obvious" (7: 35 and 36). So she resolves to "examine whether there is a God and if there is, whether he could be a deceiver" (7: 36).

Before we can appreciate the meditator's progress, some general comments about the Cartesian conception of meditation are in order. Descartes took understanding to be a kind of perception: "All the modes of thinking that we experience within ourselves can be brought under two general headings: perception, or the operation of the intellect, and volition, or the operation of the will. Sensory perception, imagination, and pure understanding are simply various modes of perception" (8A: 17). To understand is to clearly and distinctly perceive a non-sensory, purely intellectual object. Accordingly, he took meditation to be the contemplative perception of pure intellect. Metaphysical meditation consists in the contemplation of the objects of first philosophy. Yet meditation differs from a mere act of discrete, contained, clear and distinct understanding. The contemplation it involves is peculiarly dynamic and open-ended; it is neither completely passive nor static, nor is it ever completed. As the pure intellect is freed from embodiment, it comes to perceive itself and the purely intellectual contents within. These objects are gradually revealed to the mind's gaze, but such perception demands attention and discipline. As we pointed out earlier, it is an unnatural activity. This is why Descartes himself rarely engaged in it. It is not an enterprise recommended to the many, nor is it one that should be undertaken regularly.[14] Nonetheless, "once in her life" the meditator will be asked to "spend some time" in the contemplation of God (3: 695 and 7: 52). It is then that she will acquire the "very necessary … knowledge of God" as best it can be had in this life (3: 695). Furthermore, this contemplative activity is worthwhile on its own.

These objects, self and God, are each infinite in their own way and thereby inexhaustible. Their contemplation is an open-ended activity through which the meditator gains not only increasing information about the object, but a deeper understanding of it. She progressively grasps its nature more fully but neither aims to attain nor could ever achieve a final complete grasp of the object. As the meditator acknowledges in the Fifth Meditation: "Much remains to be investigated regarding the attributes of

---

[14] I return to this matter below in the last section, where the relevant texts are cited.

God, much about the nature of myself, or my mind; but perhaps I will take this up again some other time" (7: 63).[15]

Though meditation is fundamentally a form of passive perception, the meditator is not passive through this process. As Descartes states elsewhere, "understanding is the passivity of the mind and willing its activity" but "we scarcely ever understand something without at the same time willing something" (3: 372; cf. 11: 342). These objects, God and the self, cannot be perceived without engaging the will, which will actively seek to remain directed to them. If love arises "when something is represented to us as good with regard to us, that is to say, as being beneficial for us," then there can be no greater love than the love of God (11: 374).[16] As Descartes explained to Queen Christina, "God is the supreme good ... incomparably more perfect than any creature" (5: 82). The meditator will be moved by this judgment "to join [herself] willingly" to God, and so she will strive to make herself one with him, part of a whole of which God is the other part (11: 387; compare also 5: 56). Still, she will have to struggle to ensure that sensation and the natural inclinations of her embodied mind do not loosen her grip on this purely intellectual, infinite object. Her will is engaged both by the efforts required in order to bring this all-perfect object into focus and then to persist in its perception, and also by the love this contemplation elicits in her. The contemplation of God, though a function of the intellect, leads the meditator to a state of "maximal joy [*maximam voluptatem*]" in complete involvement with the "beauty of the immense light" of its object (7: 52). It puts the meditator in a state of fulfillment comparable to the "happiness [*faelicitatem*]" of beatitude in the afterlife, though of course "much less perfect."

The meditator perceives God as "a perfect being who is already wholly present though never wholly grasped by the human mind."[17] Meditation on God will transform the meditator as it displays its infinite, ultimately fulfilling, object. Though the meditator is active in the exploration of her object, engaging in argument and actively considering conceptual distinctions and connections, as the contemplative state is attained, it is the object which increasingly reveals itself, unfolding and displaying its infinity. The meditator engages in intellectual activity, guided by the object itself, in order for it to unveil. She is like the archaeologist digging a buried site, which gradually makes itself manifest, guiding his labors to expose it.

---

[15] See Devillairs (2004), pp. 103ff.   [16] See Marshall (1998), pp. 131ff.
[17] Brewer (2009), p. 60.

Descartes repeatedly anticipates the objects and themes of later meditation to bring them to the meditator's attention. They are apprehended gradually. Descartes introduces them to start the process: at first dimly grasped, the object has revealed itself within the meditator. He will slowly become more familiar with it, better grasping it, allowing it to manifest itself. The process is analogous to a process of recollection. Knowledge forgotten and buried in the mind is gradually recalled. A first clue, a sign, starts this gradual process of recovery. We should add two qualifications to this analogy. The first is that there never is complete recollection. The object is never fully possessed, for it is infinite and beyond the grasp of finite minds.[18] Any sense of full comprehension will soon be displaced by new, infinitely rich horizons to explore through previously unsuspected paths. The second is that the meditative process requires use of a purely intellectual gaze, which itself requires exhausting attention and discipline, and which, though refined and enriched as it is exercised, will prove impossible for an embodied human soul to sustain indefinitely, or indeed for any considerable length of time. Cartesian meditation is a kind of intellectual mysticism.[19]

One further point before we move on. There is an underlying conception of philosophy at work here. When Descartes advises against devoting too much time to metaphysics, he is pointing to a notion of metaphysics that is distinct from that concerned exclusively with the argumentative and conceptual foundation of science. This enterprise, more proper of angelic pure intellects than of embodied humans, consists not in problem solving, nor in the formulation of a doctrinal corpus backed by argument. In this metaphysical undertaking, argument, doctrine, and conceptual analysis are all at the service of a never-ending, never finalized activity, the activity of contemplative meditation, helping secure grasp of its objects. In this context, philosophical progress is not measured by success at answering questions but by the activity itself of understanding and meditation, in its progressive but never finalized enrichment.[20] This metaphysics can be seen as an activity worthy of a lifetime, worthy of the whole history of humanity. If progress has a place

---

[18] We shall revisit this notion of a human mind both finite and infinite in the last section.

[19] One can find a similar intellectualized mystical meditation, though not philosophical in that it does not appeal to argument and rational analysis and articulation, in the first of T. S. Eliot's *Four Quartets*, "Burnt Norton." See Eliot (1971), pp. 13–20. I owe the insightful suggestion of such a reading to Ms. Hedera Greaman and Dr. Korohito Kozinawa, in conversation.

[20] See Frankfurt (1978), p. 27, and p. 39n. 1. Cf. the "Concluding Meditation" in van Inwagen (2009), pp. 273–75.

in this context, it is in terms of deeper understanding and an enriched intellectual life.

I do not deny that Descartes viewed philosophy as seeking to deliver a complete and true account of the real, an account which definitively answers our philosophical questions and which is in a continuous spectrum with science. What I am proposing is that underpinning this conception there is a different one. We know that what he took to be final, definitive answers to questions that still occupy us were not so. We also know there are many related and prior issues he did not address. And, notwithstanding the considerable self-confidence of philosophers, few honestly believe these questions are soon to be conclusively answered. So it is with this other conception where, to some extent ironically, Descartes' more interesting contribution in this area may lie. I should stress that I am not claiming that Descartes himself perceived this fact or its significance.

Earlier we identified three strands in the first three meditations: turning the mind away from the senses and securing its purely intellectual gaze; validating reason; and refuting skepticism. At the start of the Third Meditation, the last two of these strands are still being developed. The meditator is already in possession of the purely intellectual perception that will allow her to carry them out successfully. The skeptic will be refuted as the idea of God is uncovered and it becomes manifest that he never did offer a reason to doubt reason, since his argument is seen to be incoherent and based on mere prejudice. And in due course reason will be validated with an argument, valid and persuasive, establishing that it is trustworthy.

After recalling the radical doubt of reason and deciding to examine whether there can be a deceiving God, the meditator considers the contents of her mind, in particular those ideas that are "like the images of things" (7: 37). She notes that those ideas are all equally modes of her mind, but then focuses on their objective or representative contents. In this regard they differ considerably. Some "contain in them, so to speak, more objective reality" than others, "that is to say, they participate representatively in a higher degree of being or perfection" (7: 40; the latter phrase is added in the French translation in 11: 32). In this context she mentions the idea of "a supreme God, eternal, infinite, omniscient, omnipotent, and the creator of all things" (the French translation adds "immutable" between "infinite" and "all-knowing"). This idea, she notes, "has in it more objective reality than those by which finite substances are represented."

Some pages later, the meditator explicitly and self-critically articulates his idea of God: "By the name 'God' I understand an infinite, independent, supremely intelligent, supremely powerful substance, by which I myself and whatever else was created, if anything else does exist" (7: 45; again, the French translation, in 9: 35–36, differs slightly, adding "eternal, immutable" between "infinite" and "independent"). In subsequent discussion, the meditator mentions that there is "absolutely no potentiality" in the idea of God; that God has "from himself the power to exist" (that is, that he is necessary or self-caused or such that his nature entails his existence); that the "unity, simplicity, and inseparability of all those things that are in God is one of the principal perfections that ... inhere in him"; and that God's infinity is actual perfection and not indefinite boundlessness (7: 47, 49–50, 50, and 51).

As this examination of the idea of God advances, the meditator articulates two causal arguments for his existence.[21] One starts from the very idea of God as an effect in need of causal explanation. It argues for the conclusion that God exists through a causal principle specifically about the objective reality of an idea: the total cause of an idea must account for its representative or objective content. The other argument is a version of Aquinas' Second Way. As I have shown elsewhere, both arguments contain an indispensable reference to the idea of God that is progressively displayed in the meditation.[22] They both require, that is, premises to the effect that God is a (possible) infinite, all-perfect, maximally great, or greatest conceivable, hence necessary, being. Though the argument from the idea of God itself was Descartes' own, in his version of the Second Way he was following in the footsteps of a tradition that included Duns Scotus and Suárez, a tradition that had discussed and modified the original Thomistic argument to include consideration of the idea of God.[23] Aquinas' scholastic successors had argued that only certain causal relations would allow for the demonstration of God, causal relations which required the notion of a possible most perfect and necessary being to stop an infinite regress. More generally, unless the proof included a definition or quasi-definition of God as a supremely perfect being, it could not be

---

[21] For a discussion of the causal arguments in the Third Meditation see Secada (2000), ch. 6. For a discussion of the structure of the Third Meditation and St. Anselm's *Proslogion* see Galonnier (1997), pp. 293–306. Also see Nolan and Nelson (2005).

[22] Secada (2000), pp. 160–66.

[23] See Scotus (1966); and Suárez, *Metaphysical Disputation* XXIX, in Suárez (1960–66), vol. IV, pp. 241–314. Suárez is at odds with Descartes in denying that we can reach God "starting from the operations of the rational soul and its essence" (*Metaphysical Disputation* XXIX, section 1, paragraph 19; in Suárez [1960–66], vol. IV, pp. 256–57).

said to have shown that God, as opposed to some other being, an imperfect creator or some other lesser entity, exists.

In the course of reflecting on God, the meditator fixes on the notion of infinity as utmost perfection. This is the unifying aspect of her idea of God, the defining characteristic of the divine being. This positive infinity is taken to be primary, both ontologically and epistemologically, to all other reality, which in one way or another is its negation (7: 45ff.).[24] The Third Meditation is focused on the issues of "whether there is a God, and, if there is, whether he can be a deceiver" (7: 36). Towards the end of the meditation, the meditator is persuaded there indeed is a God; and his grasp of the nature of this supreme being is sufficient to assure him that he is all good and cannot be a deceiver (see 7: 51–52). Knowledge of the existence of a substance requires, in Descartes' eyes, knowledge of its essence. He explicitly adopted such essentialist doctrine, and made clear that he believed it applied in the particular case of God (see 3: 273 and 7: 107–8).[25] By the end of the Third Meditation the meditator has some grasp of God's infinite nature, sufficient to support knowledge of his existence.

Yet that grasp is imperfect, even if judged exclusively by the standards of the limited understanding of the divine essence that we embodied, finite intellects can attain while in this life. For, in Descartes' view and as we shall discuss in a moment, by itself a fuller grasp of God's nature would assure the meditator of God's existence, as in the Fifth Meditation (also 7: 166–67 and 8A: 10). Two-thirds of the way into the Third Meditation, the meditator confesses that "when my attention wavers, and the images of sensible things blind the eye of the mind, I do not remember so easily why the idea of a being more perfect than myself necessarily proceeds from some being that is truly perfect" (7: 47). All the same, the Third Meditation establishes the existence of God, even if only initially and insecurely. Most importantly, it places the meditator in the presence of the clear and distinct idea of God within him, in such a way that he can grasp it unencumbered by prejudice. At the end of the meditation God is understood not by means of a discursive listing of attributes, but as "the very being the idea of whom is within me, that is, the possessor of all the perfections which I cannot comprehend, but which I can to some extent reach in my thought, and who is subject to no defects whatsoever" (7: 52). After a brief concluding reflection on the fact that God has placed this idea of himself within the meditator, who is made in God's "image and

---

[24] See Ronald Rubin's most interesting discussion in Rubin (2008), pp. 69–72.
[25] See Secada (2000), ch. 2.

likeness" and who thereby perceives this idea with the same pure intellectual faculty with which she perceives herself, the meditator decides to "remain for a while in the contemplation of God himself."

THE LIKENESS OF GOD IN THE MEDITATOR, AND THE INTUITION OF GOD'S EXISTENCE

If the *Meditations* is read as an essay engaged in refuting skepticism and securing the foundations of science, the quasi-mystical rapture at the end of the Third Meditation is surely most surprising:

I wish to pause here and spend some time in the contemplation of God himself, to ponder on his attributes, and to gaze on, wonder at, and worship the beauty of this immense light, as much as the eye of my understanding, shrouded as it is in darkness, is capable of doing. For just as we believe by faith that the supreme happiness of the other life consists purely in the contemplation of the divine greatness, so we find also by experience that this contemplation, though far less perfect, affords us the greatest joy and fulfillment of which we are capable in this life.

From the perspective of the *Meditations* as a manual for meditation on God and self, on the other hand, this passage makes perfect sense, coming at exactly the right moment in the meditator's ascent to the contemplation of God as best it can be had in this life. He is now in fairly secure possession of his purely intellectual intuition; he has come to understand God's nature adequately enough to ground the causal arguments for his existence that are the focus of the Third Meditation. He is thereby assured of God's existence. The contemplation at the end of the meditation goes beyond that assurance and understanding, involving the whole of the meditator, who is overcome by supreme pleasure, both purely intellectual and bodily, as he is wholly possessed by the divine object.

Earlier, in the course of considering the causal arguments, the meditator is introduced to the notion of materially false ideas, coextensive with the proper objects of sensory perception, ideas whose objects cannot exist on their own, even if they are presented as if they could (see 7: 43–44).[26] A moment later, the idea of God is placed in relation to those materially false ideas:

Nor can it be said that perhaps this idea of God is materially false ... For on the contrary, since it is supremely clear and distinct, and contains more objective reality than any other, there is no idea that is truer in itself ... This idea ... is ...

[26] See Secada (2000), pp. 91–102.

supremely true … It is also supremely clear and distinct; for whatever I clearly and distinctly perceive that is real and true and that contains some perfection is all included within it. And this remains no less true even though I do not comprehend the infinite, or even if there are innumerable other attributes in God that I can neither comprehend, nor even perhaps touch in the slightest by my thought … Provided that I understand this … the idea I have of him will be the truest and most clear and distinct of all my ideas. (7: 46)

The full extent of this claim, that the idea of God stands at the other end of a spectrum generated by materially false ideas and is the uniquely truest of all ideas, is not something the meditator fully grasps when this is stated in the text. This is, once again, a case of Descartes, the author, planting a seed in the meditator's mind, anticipating something she will only perceive much later after the seed has grown to yield its fruit. If materially false ideas present objects which can exist only embedded in acts of perception, the "truest of all ideas" presents an object that exists with supreme independence and necessity. That, however, will not be appreciated fully until the Fifth Meditation.

In between those two moments, when the idea of God is first said to be the truest of all ideas and when the significance of this claim comes to be properly understood, the meditator's grasp of the nature of God becomes considerably deeper and more secure. The rapture at the end of the Third Meditation is one important moment in that process, which is informed by the recognition of the meditator's divine likeness. We have seen the meditator dwell on this likeness just before that climax. It will be further manifested and explored when addressing an issue that is overtly raised at the start of the Fourth Meditation. At the beginning of that meditation, the meditator reviews the ease with which she can now "withdraw her mind from the senses" and direct it "towards those things which are purely intelligible" (7: 52–53). But an issue resurfaces then that can interfere with her perception of God, clouding her clear and distinct grasp of the divine idea: if God exists and "it is impossible that he should ever deceive me," how can it be that "I am prone to countless errors" (7: 53–54)?

Resolution of this issue will lead to a further recognition of the meditator's divine likeness, and to a fuller and more intimate understanding of the divine nature. Error is present only in judgment, when the will affirms as true a proposition presented to the mind, and the proposition happens to be false. In a sense, the scope of the will cannot exceed the scope of the intellect or perceptual faculty, since the will can only be exercised over an object that is present to the mind through perception. But "understanding" is an equivocal term, with both a neutral and a commendatory sense. On the one hand, it may refer to the mere intellectual perception of an object, whether it be clear and distinct or not. On the other, it can refer to the clear and distinct perception of purely intellectual objects, when the mind is said to truly understand them. In this latter sense, the will can exceed the scope of understanding, and judge to be true something it does not actually perceive clearly and distinctly to be so: "when you judge that the mind is a kind or rarefied body … the proposition that it is one and the same thing that thinks and is extended is one which you certainly do not understand" (7: 376–77). Gassendi, whom Descartes was addressing with this statement, of course perceived or considered or entertained what he was asserting. But he could not, Descartes claims, understand it, since it is contradictory.

Error results from misuse of the unbounded power of the will, which when joined in us to a finite intellect, can lead to false judgment by asserting as true what the intellect does not correctly perceive to be so (see 7: 56–60). The will is irresistibly driven to assent to what the intellect clearly and distinctly perceives to be true. This, however, is no limitation on its power. If anything, Descartes tells us, this natural inclination, and God's grace which inclines the will towards the good, "do not ever diminish freedom, but instead increase and strengthen it" (7: 58). That is, the will is no more free or autonomous when it acts in the face of an indifferent object, than when it does so compelled by truth or the good. For its freedom does not consist in being able to do otherwise; it consists wholly in its capacity for self-determination.

We are endowed with an infinite power: the power to causally determine our acts of volition with complete independence. A free will is the only true cause other than God. This is the single limit Descartes imposes on an occasionalist causal ordering.[27] Indeed, he makes the human will causally God-like regarding its own free acts:

[A]lthough God's will is incomparably greater than mine, both in virtue of the knowledge and power that accompany it and make it more firm and efficacious, and also in virtue of its object, in that it ranges over a greater number of things, nevertheless it does not appear any greater than mine when considered as will in the essential and strict sense … [T]he will consists simply in the power to do or not do something; or rather, it consists simply in the fact that when the intellect puts something forward … our inclinations are such that we do not feel we are determined by any external force. (7: 57)

[27] For Descartes on causation see Ott (2009), Part I, and in particular ch. 9.

The will's absolute "power to do or not do something" consists solely in that it alone is the causal determinant of its free acts, even when it is compelled to assent by its perception of the truth. The omnipotence of God, which is conjoined to his omniscience, and which extends to the whole of reality, created and conserved by him, is mirrored in our capacity to independently determine our free acts of will: "free will is in itself the noblest thing we can have, since it makes us in a way equal to God" (5: 85).

At the end of the Fourth Meditation the meditator is finally in firm possession of the rule of truth, having undergone a strenuous process of cognitive therapy and meditation (see 7: 62). It is at that point that she can move, in the Fifth Meditation, to the final, fuller contemplation of God's nature and existence.[28] After a brief survey of simple geometrical natures, the meditator goes on to display her now secure and deep understanding of God. As I have argued elsewhere, in this context she articulates a version of a modal ontological proof of God's existence, moving from a definition of God as a necessary being, through the claim that he is possible, to the conclusion that he exists.[29] This proof, we can appreciate now, is intended to culminate a process of consideration of the idea of God. It can be reduced to a clear and distinct intuition of God: the intuition of the possible and therefore necessary and actually existent nature of a most perfect or supreme being. This is how it is first laid out early in the meditation: "my understanding that it belongs to his nature that he always exists is no less clear and distinct than is the case when I prove of any shape and number that some property belongs to its nature" (7: 65). In the rhetorical question after the argument has been presented, the full import of the claim that the idea of God is the truest of all ideas is displayed: "what is more self-evident than the fact that the supreme being exists, or that God, to whose essence alone existence belongs, exists?" (7: 69).

In the course of this meditation the meditator states: "Since I have been accustomed to distinguish between essence and existence in everything else, I find it easy to persuade myself that existence can also be separated from the essence of God, and hence that God can be thought of as not existing" (7: 66). As I have shown elsewhere, Descartes followed Suárez in claiming that between the essence and the existence of a creature there is only a distinction of reason (see 7: 116 and 5: 164–65).[30] The point the meditator

---

[28] Cf. Donald Cress' difficulties understanding the place and function of the Fourth Meditation when seen from the perspective of an order of reasons, in Cress (1994).

[29] See Secada (2000), pp. 230–35.

[30] See Secada (2000), pp. 214–30.

makes here is not that there is any greater distinction than that, or, to put it differently, that existence is a real property, but that the essential definition of any creature does not entail that the creature exists. Creatures are contingent. The idea of God, however, is peculiar. When properly understood we see that its object must exist necessarily: "when I concentrate more carefully, it is quite evident that existence can no more be separated from the essence of God than the fact that its three angles equal two right angles can be separated from the essence of a triangle" (7: 66). We see that "there is no impossibility in the nature of God; on the contrary, all the attributes which we include in the concept of the divine nature are so interconnected that it seems to us to be self-contradictory that any one of them should not belong to God. Hence, if we deny that the nature of God is possible, we may just as well deny that ... he who is actually thinking exists" (7: 151).

Underscoring that this object of contemplation, of understanding, desire, and love, is what determines and thereby moves the soul towards it, the meditator adds that "it is not that my thought makes it so, or imposes any necessity on anything; on the contrary, it is the necessity of the thing itself, namely the existence of God, which determines my thinking in this respect" (7: 67). She explains that "whenever I do choose to think of the first and supreme being, and bring forth the idea of God from the treasure house of the mind as it were, it is necessary that I attribute all perfections to him, even if I do not at that time enumerate them or attend to them individually." Later she underscores that "this idea is not something fictitious which is dependent on my thought, but is an image of a true and immutable nature" (7: 68). The only possible entity that the meditator can clearly and distinctly conceive to be necessary in this way is God; only an infinite or supremely perfect being is such that, if he exists, he exists necessarily. That being is unique, and in its idea "I perceive many other attributes of God, none of which I can remove or alter." Descartes believed that after the cognitive therapy and the meditational process, the possibility and necessity of God will be evident to the intellectual gaze of the meditator: "as regards God, if I were not overwhelmed by preconceived opinions, and if the images of things perceived by the senses did not besiege my thought on every side, I would certainly acknowledge him sooner and more easily than anything else" (7: 69). The meditative process uncovers an infinite, supremely perfect object and allows it to reveal itself unobstructed.[31]

---

[31] I agree that these texts appear to manifest "a rather too optimistic assessment of the problem of consistency" (Cargile [1975], p. 72). My hesitation arises from the fact that Descartes does

A Kantian point emerges here. The causal proofs of God's existence require consideration of the idea of God. Furthermore, they require that its infinite objective reality and, therefore, its possibility, be recognized. This is evidently so in the first argument, the one starting from the very idea of God as effect. It is also clear in the second argument, which must use the idea of a necessary being in order to resolve the seemingly intractable issue arising from the claims that nothing exists without a cause and that there cannot be an infinite regress of causes and so there must be a first cause. Moreover, both arguments must use the idea of God to fix the object of demonstration. It is the essence or nature of God, in the limited way in which humans can apprehend it, that secures the identity of the being whose existence is in question. An accidental description, one that happens to apply to God, could not do this. In this case the object of inquiry is determined essentially and wholly a priori, so a description that *could* apply to an entity with a different essence cannot serve to identify it. If we are to prove God's existence, an essential definition of God, at least to the extent that we can formulate one, must be a premise of our proof.

If this is so, and the causal arguments (and indeed all arguments) for God's existence require reference to an adequate idea of God, then, since proper consideration of this idea suffices to establish the existence of God, it follows that all the causal apparatus and any other premises are redundant. If the meditator did not realize this in the Third Meditation, it is only because he did not then have as secure and sufficient a hold on the idea of God as he in fact needed for the purposes of those arguments themselves. Once that is attained, a simple intuition of the mind will suffice to establish the existence of God; and the rest of the apparatus of the causal arguments can be dispensed with.

MEDITATION, GOD, AND THE HUMAN CONDITION

In a letter to Jean de Silhon of the spring of 1648, Descartes discussed the relation between perception of the idea of God in this life and the beatific vision of the blessed in heaven.[32] This letter sheds light on the text at the end of the Third Meditation; and it serves to qualify some

suppose that the meditator has undergone a process that few of us have. I am not prepared to rule out that a successful meditator is in a better position to determine the possibility of God than someone who has not.

[32] Interestingly, in 1626 Silhon (1596–1667) had published *Les deux véritez ... l'une de Dieu et de sa providence, l'autre de l'immortalité de l'âme*. This text has been reprinted in Silhon (1991).

of our earlier comments. Descartes distinguishes between "intuitive knowledge" of God and the contemplation of him through perception of his idea by a finite, human mind (5: 136). The former "is an illumination of the mind, by which it sees in the light of God whatever it pleases him to show it by a direct impress of the divine clarity on our understanding," while the latter depends on "reasoning and discursive inquiry" to fix its object (5: 136–37). The knowledge we have of God through consideration of the innate idea of a supreme being is discursive, moving "from one attribute to another; or, to speak more accurately, using the natural (and consequently comparatively obscure) knowledge of one attribute of God, to construct an argument leading to another attribute of God" (5: 138–39). This knowledge of God

[I]s deduced from ... faith ... or ... comes from the natural ideas and notions we have, which even at its clearest are only gross and confused on so sublime a topic ... [I]n this life you do not see, in God and by his light, that he is unique; but you deduce it from a proposition you have made about him, and you draw the conclusion by the power of argument. (5: 137 and 139)

The intuition of God in heaven, when the mind is "detached from the body, or has a glorified body that no longer hinders it," is "a pure, constant, clear, certain, effortless and ever-present light." It stands in contrast with the earthly "troubled and doubtful perception, which costs us much labor and which is enjoyed only momentarily once acquired." This heavenly intuition is similar to the intuition the mind has of itself, expressed in "the proposition 'I am thinking, therefore I exist'" (5: 138).

Human perception of God in this life is a finite mind's perception of an infinite object within it. There are two sources of problems here: one has to do with the existence of an infinite object within a finite mind; the other has to do with the finite mind's perception of this infinite object within. Focusing on the former, some have rejected the claim that a true infinity, even if only objective, can exist within the finite human soul.[33] Writing to Silhon, Descartes focuses on the latter. He stresses that our grip on the infinite idea of God is ineliminably discursive. For instance, however much we "labor" to intuit his unity, we cannot fully overcome the distinction between his attributes. God is an elusive object. Truly present within us, we can reach him only discursively. Though we can

---

[33] See Malebranche's *Search after Truth*, bk. III, pt. ii, ch. 6 and ch. 7, section 2; and bk. IV, ch. 11, section 3; and *Dialogues on Metaphysics*, Dialogue II, sections 2–10; in Malebranche (1991), pp. 437–47 and pp. 449–50; Malebranche (1967), pp. 56ff.; and Malebranche (1980a), pp. 45–53.

uncover the idea of God in us, we are constantly in need of argument and conceptual elucidation to secure our intuition of it.

Descartes is not withdrawing his claim that this idea of the infinite or supreme God contains infinite objective reality and thereby demands a formally infinite cause. Nor should we take him to be casting doubt on the claim that "the contemplation of God" via our idea of him is "the greatest joy and fulfillment of which we are capable in this life" (7: 52). We are then, indeed, considering an infinite object that elicits "wonder and adoration." He is, however, pointing out that this contemplation of God while embodied is not of the same kind as the contemplation of God "in the next life." The difference, he tells us, lies in that while one is the intuitive, immediate, direct perception of God, akin to the perception of the self in self-consciousness, the other has to fix its object in inevitably discursive ways. The former requires no discursive activity on our part: our understanding is "simply ... a receiver of the rays of divinity" (5: 136). The latter requires that we actively reason in order to secure our perception of the infinite object within us. In doing so we move from attribute to attribute, aspect to aspect, one truth to another, even if in doing so we are guided by the object itself, which shapes our understanding and overpowers our will.

A letter of 1647 to Pierre Chanut sheds further light on this matter, confirming our reading of the text at the end of the Third Meditation and the letter to Silhon. In it, Descartes directly addresses the question "whether the mere natural light teaches us to love God" (4: 601). He distinguishes between "the love which is purely intellectual or rational, and that which is a passion. The first ... is nothing else than that when our soul perceives some good ... which it judges convenient for itself, it joins itself to it willingly, that is to say, it considers itself and the good as the two parts of a whole." An embodied soul in this state will hardly fail to feel "the other kind of love, which can be called sensual or sensuous" and which arises from certain bodily events (4: 602). Indeed "usually, these two loves will be found together" (4: 603). He then asserts that he has "no doubt that we can truly love God by the sole power of our nature ... [W]ith regard to this life, it is the most delightful and useful passion we can have; and it can even be the strongest, though only if we meditate very attentively, since we are continually distracted by the presence of other objects" (4: 607–8). Descartes goes on to lay out how it is that the soul can attain this state, through a process of consideration of the nature and origin of the soul in relation to God (4: 608–9). He explains that "the love we have for objects above us is ... by nature ...

more perfect, and makes one embrace with greater ardor the interests of what one loves" (4: 611). Given the infinity of God and our own insignificance relative to him, "it is evident that our love for God must be, beyond comparison, the greatest and most perfect of all" (4: 612–13).

If we make appropriate room for differences of vocabulary, we can place Descartes within a tradition including "Plotinus, Gregory of Nyssa, Augustine, and Aquinas" according to which there are desires which are "intimation[s] of a concrete instance (or possible or apparent instance) of some kind of goodness or value. Such intimations incite efforts both to gain a clearer understanding of the goodness in question and to respond in some appropriate way to that goodness."[34] What will count as an appropriate response to such desire will not necessarily consist in bringing about some good in order to satisfy the desire. The contemplation and love of God is one such response that "moves from vague intimations of the activity's proper form or end, towards more determinate and satisfying apprehensions of the end."[35] The meditator of the *Meditations* displays such a process, from the initial recollection of God in the First Meditation to the rich intuition of his nature and existence in the Fifth.

It is not surprising that Descartes would find value in the activity of meditation itself. Nor should it surprise that the rapture at the end of the Third Meditation be the expression of a line of thought which tends to be missed when the *Meditations* is seen as concerned exclusively either with the metaphysical foundations of science and knowledge, or more generally with establishing metaphysical doctrines through argument. The meditative reading I have articulated coheres with the Cartesian conception of human nature as embodied intellect, a conception he developed in part in *The Passions of the Soul* and which stresses both the fact of embodiment and the intellectual nature of the soul. The human mind is a finite intellect that must rely on the body in order to know the world in which it lives: it has direct intuition only of itself, and must argue from its innate ideas or the perceptions that its body occasions in it to knowledge of the real beyond it (see 5: 137–38 and 341). In fact, the human mind is designed, cognitively and morally, for its embodiment. It must live in this extended world, in relation to other souls via bodies, pursuing virtue as it acts according to its uncertain, fallible judgment, and in close union with its body.

[34] Brewer (2009), p. 15.   [35] Brewer (2009), p. 98.

Repeatedly, the human mind encounters its finitude. The best validation of the rule of truth it can find is through a clear and distinct argument concluding that its clear and distinct perceptions correspond to things as they are in themselves. Such argument is not worthless. Nonetheless, it is reason that validates reason. Though strictly inconceivable, a logic at odds with our reason looms beyond the bounds of its grasp. In pursuing its validation reason makes it own limits and our radical finitude manifest. There is no absolute self-grounding of human reason (see 7: 144–45 and 146).[36] Still, the finite human soul contains infinities within it, some merely negative but one, its idea of God, positively infinite or supremely perfect, even if only objectively. Moreover, human free will is actually infinite and God-like. If suitably endowed, and adequately disposed and trained, the mind is capable of an anticipation of a vision of the infinite, albeit inadequate and poor when compared to the beatitude of the after-life. The greatest good for humans is not of this world, and can only be loved and enjoyed by them if they go against their natures. Unlike Plato, the Christian Descartes does not see the human soul as incarcerated in the body. It is instead naturally suited for it, even though attaining its ultimate end will require either a disembodied existence or embodiment in a "glorified" body. There is a tension in human nature: human souls are naturally suited for embodiment, which they need in order to live well and attain a state of blessedness; but they reach their ultimate fulfillment only if freed from their bodies. Human beings are finite entities that tend towards and indeed contain the infinite.

This helps account for the tension in Descartes' writings regarding the activity of meditation on the objects of first philosophy and, in particular, God. We can now see how the many passages in his correspondence and other writings, which cohere with the meditative undertaking of the *Meditations*, are to be read side by side with texts such as the following. In 1643, Descartes wrote to Elizabeth that

[T]he chief rule I have always observed in my studies … has been that I have never spent more than … a few hours a year on those [thoughts] that occupy the intellect alone … I think … that it would be very harmful to occupy one's intellect frequently in meditating upon [the principles of metaphysics, God, our

---

[36] I agree with commentators who, like Harry Frankfurt (in Frankfurt [1978]) and Howard Wickes (in Wickes [1994]), argue that Descartes did not believe in reason's capacity to attain absolute self-validation, while yet aiming to provide more than a demonstration merely of its coherence. On my view, Descartes thought he had attained a rational validation of reason as provider of certain knowledge of things as they are in themselves. This comes short of absolute validation on account of this possibility which, though somehow grasped, cannot be articulated discursively.

soul], since this would impede it from devoting itself to the functions of the imagination and the senses. (3: 692–93 and 695)

Some years later, in conversation with Frans Burman, Descartes is reported to have said that:

[O]ne should not devote so much effort to the *Meditations* and to metaphysical questions ... Otherwise they draw the mind too far away from physical and observable things, and make it unfit to study them. Yet it is just these physical studies that it is most desirable for people to pursue, since they would yield abundant benefits for life. The author did follow up metaphysical questions fairly thoroughly in the *Meditations* ... so everyone does not have to ... spend time and trouble meditating on these things. (5: 165; see also 1: 350; 4: 613; and 5: 139)

Underpinning these claims there is a complex conception of human nature and of philosophy as meditation.

Whatever our stance on the various issues we have touched upon in this chapter, and however we assess Descartes' own take on them, recovery of the Cartesian conception of philosophy as meditation is a worthwhile enterprise. Examination of the conceptions of God, human nature, and the ultimate ends of human existence which underlie it opens up a field for inquiry that promises not only to enrich our grasp of Descartes' thought, but also to contribute to our understanding of philosophy and its place in human life.[37]

[37] This chapter has benefitted from conversations with Ivy Arbulú, Tal Brewer, Roque Carrión Wam, and Antonia LoLordo.

CHAPTER II

Cartesian selves

Lisa Shapiro

[handwritten annotations: "we know what the essay is about as an essay is an answer to a question. – she opens with a question." and in left margin "standard answer"]

I

What is Descartes' account of self? Within contemporary philosoph-ical discussions of personal identity it is altogether common to invoke a 'Cartesian' notion of the self, which is, not surprisingly, attributed to Descartes. On this view, the Cartesian self is nothing other than that immaterial substance constituting a thinking thing, and we are the same self over time just insofar as we remain the same immaterial thinking substance.[1] Contemporary philosophers either inveigh against this sub-stance account of self so as to better motivate an alternative psychologistic account of personal identity or they staunchly defend the notion.[2] In this chapter, I aim to problematize this reading of Descartes. I do not want to deny that Descartes maintains that the self is a thinking substance. Indeed, in section III I will outline the textual basis of this reading.

Descartes himself does not offer a well-theorized account of the self and its identity over time. We are given little other than the first-person narrator of the *Meditations* as the basis ascertaining his views on these matters. Nonetheless, there is quite a lot packed into that 'I'. The narra-tive structure of the *Meditations*, and the way in which its central char-acter develops both intellectually and morally within it, can give us some insight into just what Descartes takes to be involved not only in being a thinking thing but also in continuing as the same thinking thing over time. I aim to highlight two features that go unremarked by both detrac-tors and defenders of the Cartesian self, and indeed by most commenta-tors: the psychological continuity afforded by memory and conformity to a norm. With these two features in mind we are left with a much more complex story about Cartesian selves.

---

[1] In what follows I refer to this view as 'the standard reading.'
[2] See for instance: Evans (1982); Foster (1991); Cassam (1997); and Rudder Baker (2011).

II

Let me first consider some other key features of the substance account of self often assigned to Descartes. First, the self on this view is disembodied. Insofar as the self is an immaterial thinking substance, it is separable and so really distinct from extended substance or bodies. As the self is independent of the body with which it is united during a human life, our continued existence is also independent of the existence of this body. Second, if the self is disembodied in this way, it would seem that it is also doomed to isolation. There is no prospect for distinct selves to engage in direct interpersonal exchanges, for it is not clear how one thinking substance can communicate with another thinking substance in an unmediated way. Indeed, it is not clear how one thinking substance can even recognize that there is any other thinking substance out there.[3]

Critics of the 'Cartesian' self take these features to be devastating shortfalls of the account, but it also has at least two well-recognized advantages. Theological considerations of salvation, damnation, and resurrection demand a soul that can exist without a body and whose identity as the same soul does not depend on the body. The standard reading of the Cartesian self as an immaterial thinking substance allows for an easy assimilation of this self and the soul of the theologians. Second, and less often remarked, taking the self as an immaterial thinking substance effectively strips it of qualities associated with body, and in particular of any sex. What we are – our selves – is thus not essentially male or female, and equally, our faculty of reason admits of no sex-based differentiation. Men and women are equally capable of rational thought. This insight provides the fulcrum on which arguments for women's education and ultimately for political equality of men and women pivot. It is a question whether a revised understanding of Descartes' account of the self can preserve these advantages.

III

The standard reading of the Cartesian self has a clear textual basis in the Second Meditation. Therein the meditator emerges from the radical

---

[3] At best, the self might be able to draw an inference from certain bodily signs, especially the use of language, that there is another self in another body. The two selves could then potentially communicate with each other indirectly through the mediation of their respective bodies. But it is hard to imagine just what would ground the initial inference from bodily signs to the existence of a self. Might we not just as easily conclude that parrots have selves just like our own?

doubt of the First Meditation to assert that "this proposition, *I am, I exist,* is necessarily true whenever it is put forward by me or conceived in my mind" (7: 25, 2: 17). Immediately, the question arises of "what this 'I' is, that now necessarily exists" (7: 25, 2: 17). It is natural to take this question to be about the nature of self, and below I will show that this presumption is warranted. But first consider the answer:

I am, then, in the strict sense only a thing [*res*] that thinks; that is, I am a mind, or intelligence, or reason – words whose meaning I have been ignorant of until now. But for all that I am a thing [*res*] which is real and which truly exists. But what kind of a thing [*res*]? As I have just said – a thinking thing. (7: 27, 2: 18)

A paragraph later the conclusion is repeated: "But what then am I? A thing that thinks [*Res cogitans*]" (7: 28, 2: 19). This 'I' is a thing, a *res*, and *res* is the term Descartes uses to refer to substances in the *Meditations*. Moreover, this thing is thinking and non-extended as made explicit in the Sixth Meditation (7: 78, 2: 54); it is an immaterial thinking substance.

That this immaterial thinking substance is indeed a self is clear from the rhetoric of the Second Meditation. Within Latin grammar there is no need to utilize a separate first-person pronoun – the first person is indicated straightforwardly in the declension of the verb – but it is hard to move from the first-person verb form to a notion of self. '*Ego*' is used rhetorically, to emphasize the first person and so to point to a self. Whereas within the First Meditation, *ego* appears but once, within the Second Meditation alone there are seventeen instances of the term, out of thirty-one instances in the whole of the work. And unsurprisingly it appears at precisely those points where the meditator is coming to recognize his nature as a thinking thing.[4] The 'I' is thus a self, and recognized to be a thinking substance.

While the Second Meditation clearly establishes that the Cartesian self is a substance, the standard account of the Cartesian self maintains further that it is the self's substantial nature that both individuates it as a particular self and that accounts for its persistence as the same self over time.[5] The textual basis for this claim derives from Descartes' answer to a query about whether the various doubts, affirmations, denials, willings, imaginings, and sensings on display in the beginning of the *Meditations*

---

[4] See 7: 24, 2: 16; 7: 25, 2: 17.

[5] A 'self' that has but a momentary or episodic existence is hardly a proper entity, let alone a self, at all. Hume relies on this point in *Treatise* 1.4.6, "Of Personal Identity," in denying that he can find in any one perception in the stream experienced an idea of self and in searching for an account of how the fiction of self is construction. A similar point in Parfit (1971) has shaped much contemporary discussion of personal identity.

all belong to him (7: 28, 2: 19). It seems clear that each of these thoughts occurs at a different moment in time, and so the question of whether these thoughts belong to the same self is the same as the question of whether that self – that thinking substance – persists over time. The answer seems to be that it is indeed that same self that has had all these thoughts, because the thoughts are all modes of one and the same substance. So while thoughts of a thinking thing change over time, it remains the same substance and its being the same substance provides the conditions for its preserving its identity over changes of thought.

It is worth highlighting that little in this explanation of the identity of the Cartesian self over time depends on how the relation between substance and mode is understood. Descartes sometimes refers to modes as inhering in a substance (7: 78–79, 2: 74–75).[6] The language of inherence can suggest that the condition of the identity of a thing with properties that change over time is just the sameness of the substance where these different properties combine.[7] On this view, the substantial nature of the self explains how thoughts occurring at different times can belong to the same thing: they simply share the same locus of inherence: the same immaterial thinking substance.[8] Alternatively, Descartes can also be understood to take inherence to be the relation between a particular determination (a mode) and the determinable (a substance) of which it is a determination. That is, a thinking thing is a determinable thing, something with the potential for thought, that is then determined to be the particular thing it is (a thing with the thoughts it has) in thinking the thoughts it does.[9] On this view, too, the sameness of the substance, of the determinable, through the changing determinations of that thing over time provides the condition of the identity of that thinking thing.

To sum up, the standard account of the Cartesian self as a thinking substance seems completely uncontroversial. That account seems to be well founded in the text of the Second Meditation, by Descartes' pointed use of 'ego' to mark out an entity properly called a self, his identification of that entity as a *res cogitans*, and his accounting for the persistence of

he gives a long analysis of the standard answer but concludes that it ↑

6 See also: 8A: 25f., 1: 212f.
7 This account of the identity conditions of substances can be found in some scholastic accounts.
8 Of course, what allows us to identify a thinking substance as the same thinking substance is unclear on this account, since we are to think of a substance divested of its modes. Locke would seem to be criticizing this sort of account of the identity conditions of particular things insofar as he maintains that pure substance in general cannot serve as a principle of individuation for any kind of particular thing. Though some contemporary readers ascribe this sort of view to Descartes, it does not seem that Descartes himself holds it.
9 See Secada (2000) and (2005) for a defense and development of this view.

the word seems is an invitation for deeper exploration, for investigation. As philosophy students we should know this.

that entity as the same thing over different episodes of thought just by its being a *res* or substance.

It is a central feature of the *Meditations* that they are meditations, and while this somewhat obvious aspect of the work was ignored for some time, over the past quarter-century commentators have not only recognized this dimension of the work but also brought it to bear on our understanding of the philosophical content contained in it.[10] Within the meditational tradition that Descartes is drawing upon, the process of meditating is supposed to effect in the meditator some sort of progress: in the weaker conception of meditations, a meditator is to achieve some contentment by coming to a better self-understanding through meditation; on the stronger conception meditating is supposed to effect a transformative change in the meditator. While I am inclined to think that Descartes adopts the stronger conception of meditation, for the purposes of this chapter, it is only important that the meditator makes some sort of progress from the beginning to the end of the meditations.[11] In what follows I examine the role of memory in the meditator's intellectual progress and the normative dimension of her progress towards epistemic virtue. I suggest that a substance account of self masks the irreducibly psychological dimension of the way the meditator actually develops as a self, the same self, over the changes evidenced in the *Meditations*.

Intellectual progress: the role of memory

The meditator clearly makes intellectual progress over the course of the *Meditations*. She begins from a position in which she recognizes reasons for doubting all her former beliefs and from there slowly claws back the prospect of knowledge until she can claim that "the exaggerated doubts of the last few days should be dismissed as laughable" (7: 89, 2: 61). Along the way, the meditator comes to recognize a set of truths – that she exists

---

[10] Hatfield (1986); Kosman (1986); Rorty (1986a); Shapiro (2005); Wee (2006); and Carriero (2009).

[11] Much of the discussion that follows can actually be deployed as part of an argument that Descartes holds a stronger conception of meditation. Nonetheless, even if we think that Descartes' meditator only has an improved self-understanding through his meditations, considering how that self-understanding is achieved and what it comes to can serve to unsettle the common reading of the Cartesian account of self.

insofar as she is thinking, and so that she is a thinking thing; that God exists as the cause of her existence *qua* thinking thing and of her idea of God; that she will avoid error in affirming only those ideas perceived clearly and distinctly, and withholding judgment on others; that material things are essentially extended and non-thinking; and that she is a true union of mind and body. Though I will return to this last truth later in this chapter, I will generally not be concerned here with understanding the content of these truths or with the lines of reasoning through which the meditator arrives at them. Rather I want to highlight the role memory plays in the meditator's intellectual progress. For in five of the six meditations remembering drives the meditator's reasoning forward.

In a certain way the *Meditations* begin with the meditator's recalling what she took to be true and juxtaposing those beliefs with her current doubts. And indeed, once the meditator has concluded her skeptical arguments, she "must make an effort to remember" that all her beliefs can be called into doubt. Nonetheless, the meditator's memory of her former beliefs threatens to get the better of her in her project to arrive at certainty, overwhelming her memory of her more recent conclusions (7: 22, 2: 15). However, it is also memory that helps her move forward to emerge from radical doubt. The Second Meditation begins from the meditator's memory of the findings of the First (7: 23–4, 2: 16) and from this renewed view of her skeptical conclusions, the meditator moves to recognize that first truth, that which must be the case whether the basis for her doubts is true or false. The Third Meditation in turn begins with the recollection of both the doubts of the First and the insight of the Second, and the meditation moves forward from a recognition of a tension between the positions of each of these previous meditations. The meditator begins by reviewing the discovery that she is a thing that thinks, "that is, a thing that doubts, affirms, denies, understands a few things, is ignorant of many things, is willing, is unwilling, and also which imagines and has sensory perceptions" (7: 34, 2: 24), and remarks that the certainty of this truth might well signal a general rule for arriving at certainty: if I perceive an idea clearly and distinctly, then it must be true. But the validity of this rule is undermined by the memory of the First Meditation's skeptical arguments. She notes: "Yet I previously accepted as wholly certain and evident many things which I afterwards realized were doubtful" (7: 35, 2: 24), and in particular the worry that God might be a deceiver threatens the stability of the rule. It is not the simple fact that she recalls raising the doubt that God is a deceiver in the First, it is the impact that this recollection has on the stability of her recalled result of the Second Meditation and the tension between the two moments of recollection, that moves her forward in the rest of the Third Meditation to prove that God exists and is not a deceiver.[12]

Before looking at the role of memory in the subsequent meditations, it is worth noting an interesting feature of the meditator's recollection here of her prior conclusions. Though the reconstruction of her skeptical arguments certainly tracks those in the First Meditation, some points do get highlighted here that were not in the First. For instance, the meditator couches the final skeptical argument of the First Meditation, that which undermines the validity of those truths we take to be self-evident, as a concern about her *nature*, a term not invoked in the First Meditation.[13] Equally, though the Third Meditation enumeration of the modes proper to a thinking thing resembles the list proffered in the Second Meditation, they are not identical. (Compare 7: 34, 2: 24 and 7: 28, 2: 19.) And further, the meditator introduces a whole taxonomy of ideas and asserts that she has been taught by nature that her ideas resemble those things outside her from which they are derived, as if these were assumed from the outset, and the example used to illustrate this point – her idea of herself sitting by the fire – is the same one as in the First Meditation. Yet neither a resemblance thesis nor a taxonomy of ideas was ever there articulated.

I will return to why these differences between the meditator's original thoughts and her recollections of them are significant, but let me resume the summary of the central role of memory in the *Meditations*. The Fourth Meditation too begins with recollection of what has come before (7: 52–53, 2: 37). With her conclusion that God exists and is not a deceiver fresh in her mind, the meditator can finally properly understand the general rule put forward provisionally at the beginning of the Third and, with this understanding, can affirm its validity: that we cannot err if we affirm only those ideas perceived clearly and distinctly. The Fifth Meditation is more forward-directed, looking to "the most pressing task [of] try[ing] to escape from the doubts into which I fell a few days ago, and see whether

---

[12] Though I am not interested here in the role memory plays in the arguments of the *Meditations*, it is worth noting that a distinction between current attention and memory has been taken to help Descartes avoid arguments of circularity in his initial proof of the existence of God. Descartes, in response to Arnauld in the Replies to Fourth Objections, is the first to introduce this line. (See 7: 245–46, 2: 171.) Descartes is here drawing on what he has written both in the Fifth Meditation (7: 69–70, 2: 48), and in the Replies to Second Objections (7: 158–59, 2: 112), where he acknowledges that doubt can undermine the confidence we have in our memory of having perceived a truth clearly and distinctly, provided we have not yet validated our rational faculties. See Doney (1955) and Frankfurt (1962) for the beginnings of the more recent discussions.

[13] See 7: 36, 2: 25. Newman (1994) notes the changes in the meditator's conception of his nature.

any certainty can be achieved regarding material objects" (7: 63, 2: 44), and in the Sixth Meditation again the meditator begins by setting a forward course: "It remains for me to examine whether material things exist" (7: 71, 2: 50). However, after the false start of looking to the imagination for proof of the existence of bodies, the meditator once again turns to his memory (7: 74, 2: 51). What we might expect is a review of the First Meditation, and we do get that in a certain sense. Nonetheless, the differences between this Sixth Meditation synopsis and the First Meditation are striking, much more than are the subtle differences already noted in the Third. The paradigm examples of sensory perception here are those of our own body and of how external bodies affect our body "in favorable and unfavorable ways." While the former figure in a small way in the First Meditation, the latter, along with the sensations of "hunger, thirst, and other such appetites, and also of physical propensities towards cheerfulness, sadness, anger and similar emotions" the meditator goes on to mention, do not (7: 74, 2: 52). Equally, she focuses here on her sensations coming to her without her consent, but this feature is mentioned only in passing in the Third Meditation, and it does not seem that there is any earlier mention of the special way in which her body is her own, something highlighted in this part of the Sixth Meditation. Indeed in light of this reconstruction of her previous beliefs about the senses, the meditator raises a new skeptical argument about our sensory knowledge – the argument from cases of phantom limbs.

It should be clear that memory is central to the meditator's intellectual development in the *Meditations*. Recalling past mistakes motivates the meditator to move forward to try to find at least one thing that is certain. Recalling what she has found to be certain allows her to leverage that initial knowledge to further certainties. Recollection of her chain of reasoning enables her to resolve the problem she posed for herself – her skeptical doubts. Memory thus serves both to chart her next steps and to unify her thoughts. Any account of the Cartesian self must be able to explain this role of memory. However, it must also be able to explain the very peculiar way that memory works in the *Meditations*. For at two crucial moments – the beginning of the Third Meditation and the first part of the Sixth Meditation – the meditator takes herself to be remembering what has come before when in fact she reconceives her prior results in ways that importantly move the argument of the work forward.

Taking the Cartesian self to consist of a thinking substance faces a challenge in accounting for memory and the unifying role it plays in the *Meditations*. An initially plausible line of approach involves taking memory to be a mode of a thinking substance, so let me consider each of the possible understandings of the relation between substance and mode in a thinking thing outlined in the previous section.[14] On the first option, the meditator's changing thoughts are to be understood as modes bound together by their co-location, in the same substance. How could this view account for memory of a thought? As a first pass, we might think of a memory simply as the persistence of the modification that is the prior thought. However, it cannot be that we continue to have that prior thought before us all along, for then there would be no difference between an occurrent thought and a memory. Rather, the view must be something like this: there is a sense in which the prior thought persists, but it does so in such a way that we do not attend to it. Memory involves a renewed attention to the prior idea. This line has some promise in that it reflects the work of memory in the *Meditations*. The meditator does not simply remember that she reached a conclusion earlier. In remembering her prior conclusions, she brings that prior conclusion to mind once again. That is, she is once again aware of that idea, attending to it.[15] This renewed awareness moves the argument forward, just as much as does the content of which the meditator is aware. Despite its drawing attention to this feature of memory, it is not clear how a substance as simply the locus where thoughts are bound together can do the work that is needed to make good on this feature of memory, for we also require an explanation of how we come to have renewed awareness of our prior conclusions. A substance which simply serves as the site of co-location would not seem to have resources to provide that explanation.

Perhaps the alternative way of understanding the relation between substance and mode can do better. On this view, a substance is a determinable and modes are determinations of that substance. As a determinable, the thinking substance constituting the self is more that a simple locus for modes, but has the power of actualizing one thought or another. It

---

[14] Despite this line seeming initially plausible, it is worth noting that Descartes never lists memory, or remembering, as a mode of thinking substance (in contrast with willing, doubting, understanding, imagining, sensing, and so on). This might seem to indicate that he takes memory to be an essentially bodily matter – there is discussion of the role of brain traces in recollection (11: 177f., 1: 106f.; 6: 55, 1: 139) and the bodily memory of a lute player (3: 48, 3: 146), for instance. The instances of what I am calling memory here, however, are clearly intellectual. Descartes does suggest that memory figures in geometrical deductions in the Fifth Meditation (7: 69–70, 2: 48) and in the *Principles* (8A: 9, 1: 197), and explicitly countenances a distinct intellectual memory that "depends on the soul alone" (3: 48, 3: 146).

[15] Indeed, that memory involves this awareness is critical for our confidence in the conclusions of geometrical proofs as discussed in the Fifth Meditation (7: 69–70, 2: 48) and *Principles* (8A, 9, 1: 197).

can thus explain how thoughts can come into awareness anew. Memory, on this view, would consist in a re-actualization of a thought that, though once actualized, has become potential again. But it would also seem on this view that prior thoughts do not persist in actuality once we are no longer aware of them. And this leaves the view with a bit of a puzzle. For the determination of substance to actualize anew its prior thoughts must be caused either externally or internally. Since it is intellectual memory that is involved, rather than bodily memory (see note 14), that determination is presumed not be caused externally. However, if thinking substance is to determine itself to actualize prior thoughts, then it would seem to require some access to those prior thoughts that have returned to potentiality. It is not clear what this access could consist in.

There is, however, a more pressing issue particular to the context of the *Meditations*. It is hard to see how either conception of the relation between a substance and its modes can accommodate the meditator's inaccuracies or embellishments of memory. Recall that in the Third Meditation, and especially in the Sixth Meditation, the meditator's memory of her past reasoning and conclusions seems to involve somewhat creative retellings of her past intellectual activity. Recollection thus seems to be modeled *not* as a simple reactualization or retrieval of past thoughts. To address this concern, while preserving the standard reading, one might try to understand memory as a second-order thought: a memory would be an actualization of a new thought, one with a prior idea as its object. Such an account might be able to account for the meditator's embellishments, but then it would seem that these would have to be couched as misrepresentations of the original thought. Seeing memory in this way does not adequately reflect the role of memory in the *Meditations*. Memory as exercised in the work, *especially* when embellished, drives the argument forward and as such can hardly be false.

Memory, as exercised in the *Meditations*, brings to awareness anew thoughts the meditator had previously. This remembering is not a matter of simple retrieval or reactivation of the prior thought, for the work of memory invokes a prior thought while at the same time reshaping it in important ways. This reshaping is a kind of appropriation rather than a second-order thought about the prior thought. How is this reshaping of a prior thought a kind of appropriation? In remembering, the meditator's renewed awareness also serves to bring past thoughts to mind in such a way as to move the meditator forward in his reasoning, but it does so by affecting the meditator's awareness of his present thoughts; that present awareness shapes the thoughts the meditator will go on to have. Thus, through this appropriation, there is a constructive element in the meditator's memory. Memory unifies the meditator's thoughts by effecting a continuity of the awareness of those thoughts. And in providing this unity, memory further helps make the meditator the thinking thing – that is, the self – she is.

What then are we to make of the standard view of the Cartesian self? It seems incontrovertible that Descartes takes the self to be a thinking substance. But what makes that substance the same substance at different times? I am suggesting that the meditator's memory involves a kind of appropriation of his prior thoughts, and that these acts of memory serve to constitute the meditator as the same thing over time. For what is central to thinking is awareness, being the subject of thinking. In memory, episodes of awareness are linked together, not in virtue of their being discrete experiences of the same thinking thing but rather in virtue of the way the character of the awareness is itself in part constituted by its previous experiences of itself as a subject. In this way, there is an irreducibly psychological dimension to what makes the meditator the same self at different times.

While I cannot argue fully for this claim here, I am suggesting that Descartes' differences with the view that Locke lays out in his *Essay Concerning Human Understanding* is more subtle than it is usually taken to be. Descartes still holds that what it is to be a self is to be a thinking substance, and in this regard Locke does seem to part company with him and maintain that this self does not depend on any one particular substance (though it does depend on some substance or another). However, both take it to be that it is "being the same consciousness that makes a Man be himself to himself" (*Essay Concerning Human Understanding*, 2.27.10), that is, that there is an irreducibly psychological dimension to a self's being the same self over time.

Progress towards epistemic virtue

In addition to developing intellectually, the meditator also undergoes a kind of epistemic moral development from the beginning to the end of the *Meditations*. While the received account of the 'Cartesian' self has had little to say about this, it is worth probing, for the role of this progress of the meditator can tell us a bit more about Descartes' conception of self.

To see that an epistemic moral development does figure in *Meditations* and how it does so, it is helpful to look first at the *Discourse on the Method for Rightly Conducting Reason*. The title of that work is suggestive of an aim of cultivating in its readers an epistemic virtue, and in the opening paragraph of the work Descartes makes it clear that he is principally concerned with how we *use* our faculty of reason: "For it is not enough to have a good mind; the main thing is to apply it well" (6: 2, 1: 111). And as Part I of the *Discourse* continues, Descartes presents his own life and intellectual pursuits as a kind of morality tale, "a history or, if you prefer, a fable in which, among certain examples worthy of imitation, you will perhaps also find many others that would be right not to follow" (6: 4, 1: 112). The morality tale functions to cultivate epistemic virtue in an interesting way, for Descartes encourages his readers to take up a skeptical attitude towards his own choices rather than model themselves uncritically on his character. The idea seems to be that in adopting this critical perspective, readers must begin to use their reason; the exercise of reason implies its being directed towards the true, and the search for truth in turn leads to an articulation of rules for reasoning well so as to best achieve that end – according to Descartes, the method outlined in the Part II of the work. The *Discourse* is thus committed to the idea that human reason is governed by internal norms that we can discover and resolve to follow.

The *Meditations* is not framed in the same way as the *Discourse*; the work opens with a series of skeptical arguments rather than a morality tale. Nonetheless there are similarities between the two works. Just as is the *Discourse*, the *Meditations* is framed by the overarching end of the search for truth (7: 17, 2: 12).[16] Moreover, the meditator tries not only to discover truths but also to cultivate those dispositions that will afford him those discoveries. The Fourth Meditation, where the meditator hits upon the method for avoiding error, makes this clear. At this point, he not only grasps what it is to use his will well (7: 59, 2: 41), he also recognizes that sometimes (indeed most times) he will not attend to that understanding. In those cases, he can still avoid error by cultivating in himself the *habit* of judging well (7: 62, 2: 43). The meditator thus aims not only to find certainty of belief, but also discovers norms of thought to ensure that certainty, and in light of that discovery strives to instill proper epistemic habits; such good habits, adopted, as his are, for the right reasons, constitute epistemic virtue.[17]

---

[16] See also the way that the search for true beliefs explicitly informs the moves of the meditator in the other five meditations (7: 24, 2: 16; 7: 36, 2: 25; 7: 53, 2: 37, 7: 63, 2: 44; 7: 74, 2: 51; and 7: 89, 2: 61).

[17] Further evidence that the project of the *Meditations* is one of cultivating a virtue can be drawn from the language of the passions in that work. Elsewhere, I have called attention to the pervasiveness of the passions throughout the *Meditations* and suggested that in meditating, the

At the very least, the received view of the 'Cartesian' self makes no mention of any possibility for this kind of epistemic moral development, for a thinking thing's cultivation of epistemic virtue. But notice the challenge of trying to make sense of a 'Cartesian' self that undergoes this cultivation of virtue. How is a meditator who is only a thinking substance to be understood as starting out with bad epistemic habits but capable of acquiring good ones through reform? How are epistemic habits at all in concert with the standard view's conception of a thinking thing?

Recognizing the irreducibly psychological dimension of Descartes' account of self can help us make sense of the cultivation of epistemic virtue evidenced in the *Meditations*. On the reading that I have been suggesting, through the renewed attention of memory the self of the meditator is constructed. Prior thoughts are appropriated as the meditator's own and inform his occurrent awareness, and that occurrent awareness in turn helps shape awareness in the future. The progress of the meditator towards epistemic virtue brings out that this process of shaping our awareness, our capacity of thinking, is not unconstrained but rather is guided by norms of rationality. Insofar as our thinking is properly guided by reason, the construction of Descartes' self is also constrained. To fully realize our selves as selves, we ought not to link up our thoughts at random, or by some sort of association. Rather, our attention ought to be renewed in memory to those thoughts that further us in our pursuit of the truth, and it is this aim that explains the shifts of emphasis and focus that characterize the meditator's appropriation of prior thoughts. Equally, the movement forward in thought is also directed by these norms of rationality. The meditator's awareness of his thoughts as his own, the focus of his memory, and his movement forward, that is, the meditator's continuity as the same thinking thing over time, is constrained by the aim of reasoning well. The norms of rationality, serve to ensure that the episodes of thought that constitute a thinking thing are well integrated into something that can properly be called a self that persists over time.[18]

---

meditator regulates his passions, and in particular his desire for knowledge, as much as he develops a metaphysics and epistemology that can set him on course to achieve certainty (Shapiro [2005]). Efforts to regulate the passions are traditionally aligned with the cultivation of virtue, for that which guides the regulation of the passions is simply the human good. So, if that reading is indeed viable, then we can see that a concern with cultivating virtue pervades the *Meditations*, as much as it frames the work.

[18] On this point, Descartes' and Locke's account of personal identity diverge from each other, for it does not seem that any epistemic norms are contained in Lockean consciousness in the way that I am suggesting they are for Descartes.

Thus, a consideration of the one self we are presented with – the meditator – exposes two features of Descartes' conception of self not typically included in the account he is usually assigned. First, for the 'I' of the meditations, memory plays a central role in connecting the meditator's thoughts at different moments in the *Meditations* with one another and moving the meditator to develop intellectually. Equally, the meditator's intellectual development is intertwined with an epistemic moral development in which the 'I', through the cultivation of appropriate epistemic dispositions, comes to have a more virtuous epistemic character. The received view of the 'Cartesian' self fails to attend to either of these features, and so fails to note that there are some aspects of a proper Cartesian self that are irreducibly psychological.

v

Understanding Descartes' conception of self as having this irreducibly psychological dimension can help address two other challenges that the standard reading of the Cartesian self faces. Recall that on the standard reading, the Cartesian self is disembodied. The meditator identifies himself as a thinking thing in the Second Meditation, and thinking things are really distinct from extended things, that is, from any body, and can exist independently of them. So, the story continues, if the Cartesian self is constituted by a thinking substance, it can exist without any body at all. Nonetheless, the Sixth Meditation presents a somewhat different view of the self. As the meditator reviews his previous conception of himself, he notes that he understood his self to comprise, at least in part, his body, and indeed, as he recalls, he was willing to countenance the idea that he – his self – consisted entirely of his body (7: 74, 2: 52). While it is clear that the reflections of the Second Meditation have undermined that former self-conception, the meditator still recognizes that his view that there is a body "which by some special right I call 'mine' … had some justification" (7: 76, 2: 52). Once he has affirmed that mind and body are really distinct things and establishes that the material world exists as the cause of his sensations, he turns to retrieve the kernel of truth in his former self-conception, and remarks that "nature teaches him" that he is a mind "closely joined" with a body, "intermingled" so as to form a unit, so that there is one body that properly speaking belongs to him (7: 81, 2: 56). Moreover, he notes that "the fact that some of the [sensory] perceptions are agreeable to me while others are disagreeable makes it quite certain that my body, or rather *my whole self*, insofar as I am a combination of body and mind, can be affected by the various beneficial or harmful bodies which surround it" (7: 81, 2: 56; emphasis added). The view of the self being put forward in the Sixth Meditation thus departs quite dramatically from the standard interpretation of the Cartesian self. There, the meditator expressly identifies her whole self as a union of mind and body, and it is that self that has the capacity to interact with the world around her, and to gain some knowledge of that world.

One might worry about how this conception of the self can be consistent with the contention of the Second Meditation that the self is just a thinking thing. The temptation can be to dismiss this remark as simply a *façon de parler*. Understanding Descartes' conception of the self to have an irreducibly psychological dimension, however, can help both to explain this remark and to allow for it to be taken seriously. For we can understand the meditator's mind's union with her body as informing the meditator's awareness in a similar way to that her prior thoughts inform her occurrent thinking. A mind united with its body experiences a whole new range of thoughts, passions, and sensations, a set of experiences which can only affect what and how we attend to things. The meditator's awareness, then, becomes that of an embodied thinking thing, and in that respect it makes sense to speak of his 'whole self' as the union of mind and body.

The second challenge concerns the apparent isolation of the individual that is the Cartesian self. It is certainly not difficult to see why one might be inclined to read Descartes in this way, for the meditator meditates in solitude, and it would seem that he is able to recognize and so constitute himself as himself all on his own, so long as he is granted his rationality. A more attentive reading of the work, however, does not sustain this interpretation. Annette Baier, in her "Cartesian Persons",[19] draws attention to the various ways in which the Cartesian meditator depends on others. In the Third Meditation, the existence of God is established by the meditator's remarking his dependence on God for his existence as a being with the idea of God, and his having the idea of God is crucial to the possibility of his recognizing and correcting his errors and so for his improvement. For the idea of an infinite and perfect being provides the standard through which the meditator can understand that which he lacks. The meditator cannot recognize the norms of rationality as norms on his own; he is dependent on another. This "dependency on another for standards of correctness," Baier argues, extends more generally to

[19] Baier (1985).

Descartes' view of persons (Baier 1985, p. 79).[20] We can also see an engagement with others as integral to Descartes' own efforts in developing his first philosophy, and so his self-understanding. As already noted, in the *Discourse*, Descartes engages in conversations with his readers, much like those he describes himself as having with authors of the past in a complicated dynamic designed to cultivate well-directed rational faculty. The dynamic is alluded to at the outset of the *Meditations*, for we are presented with a meditator who was taught by others, in his childhood. As a final consideration on this issue, in Part VI of the *Discourse*, Descartes gestures towards the collective nature of the project of scientific inquiry. And this sociable aspect of the pursuit of knowledge is also alluded to in the *Meditations*, for Descartes did not originally publish the six meditations alone. They were circulated in advance to potential critics, who wrote up their objections, to which the author replied. These three elements were then packaged together in the original publication. Descartes as author of the work engages intimately with others, and defends and develops his thoughts through that engagement. We can see these interactions with others as importantly informing what the meditator is, his self, insofar as through our interactions with others we are introduced to the norms of rationality. It is through others that we come to be acquainted with different points of view from our own, and so to see that things might be otherwise. The possibility of choice in turn raises the problem of what the right choice is, whether it is a matter of practical action or of what to believe. Here others can help us in evaluating the options, to see more clearly what we have reason to do or to think.

VI

As we have seen, the Second Meditation provides compelling evidence that Descartes does take the meditator to be a substance, and it is easy to take the relation between a substance and its modes to explain the meditator's continuity as the same thing over the course of the *Meditations*. I have been offering a set of considerations that problematize this reading. The role of memory in unifying the meditator's thoughts through his meditations suggests that the meditator is constituted in part through his own awareness of his thoughts at different times. Similarly, the meditator's cultivation of epistemic habits suggests there are norms of rationality

---

[20] Baier focuses on the ways in which other persons figure in our learning of a language, a defining capacity of human beings for Descartes, as well as our representations of space and time.

guiding not only the meditator's project but also his self-constitution through memory. These considerations both involve taking the Cartesian self to be something that develops. This developmental aspect of the Cartesian self is further complicated by the impact of the mind's union with the body to form a 'whole self' and the way in which the *Meditations* is bracketed by the meditator's engagement with others, be it by his initial education on which the *Meditations* critically reflects, or by his engagement with interlocutors about the conclusions of his meditations. As an embodied social being, the meditator continues to develop as the thinking thing he is.

Can recognizing the nature of a self as comprising this irreducibly psychological dimension – awareness – realize those features that many of Descartes' contemporaries found so powerful: the theological advantages that were so central in the seventeenth century, and the sexlessness of cognitive capacities that had a significant impact on the promotion of women's education and political equality in the seventeenth and eighteenth centuries? With regard to the former consideration, I suggest that we look to Locke's defense of his account of persons, for Locke thinks that considering the self as consciousness makes better sense of the doctrine of resurrection than anything else, for what we are aware of constrains that for which we can be properly praised or blamed, or generally, that for which we can be held responsible. Equally, we should only be saved or damned for those actions for which we are properly responsible. With regard to the latter, on the reading I have been suggesting, while the particulars of our embodiment and social situation can inform our awareness, our capacity for thinking in a way that is guided by considerations of the true remains independent of those contingencies. Indeed, it is not difficult to see how one could argue from this point of view that institutions that inhibit women from their natural pursuit of truth are unjust.[21]

[21] Dai Heide, Simon Pollon, and Karen Detlefsen provided helpful comments on earlier versions of this chapter. An audience at Cornell University, along with the comments of Nathan Birch, were also very helpful. Support from the Social Sciences and Humanities Research Council of Canada facilitated work on this chapter.

Bibliography

Ablondi, Fred. 2007. "Why It Matters that I'm Not Insane: The Role of the Madness Argument in Descartes's First Meditation," *International Philosophical Quarterly* 7 (1): 79–89.

Alanen, Lilli. 1994. "Sensory Ideas, Objective Reality, and Material Falsity," in Cottingham (ed.), pp. 229–50.

1999. "Intuition, Assent and Necessity," in T. Aho and M. Yrjönsuuri (eds.), *Norms and Modes of Thinking in Descartes, Acta Philosophica Fennica* 64: 97–121.

2003. *Descartes's Concept of Mind*. Cambridge, MA: Harvard University Press.

2008a. "Omnipotence, Modality and Conceivability," in Broughton and Carriero (eds.), pp. 353–71.

2008b. "Cartesian *Scientia* and the Human Soul," in Dominik Perler (ed.), *Transformations of the Soul: Aristotelian Psychology 1250–1650*, special offprint of *Vivarium*. Leiden: Brill, pp. 418–42.

2009. "The Metaphysics of Error and Will," in A. Kemmerling (ed.), *René Descartes: Meditationen über die Erste Philosophie, Klassiker Auslegen*. Berlin: Academie Verlag, pp. 81–100.

2011. "Spinoza on the Human Mind," *Midwest Studies of Philosophy* 35: 4–25.

Almog, Joseph. 2002. *Who Am I? Descartes and the Mind–Body Problem*. Oxford University Press.

Aquinas, Thomas. [1265–72] 1952–54. *Truth*, trans. Robert W. Mulligan, SJ, James V. McGlynn, SJ, and Robert W. Schmidt, SJ,. Chicago: Henry Regnery Co.

1964–81. *Summa Theologiae*, Blackfriars edn., 61 vols. New York: McGraw-Hill.

Ariew, Roger. 1983. "Mind–Body Interaction in Cartesian Philosophy: A Reply to Garber," *Southern Journal of Philosophy*, 21 (supplement): 33–37.

Ariew, R., Cottingham, J., and Sorrell, T. 1998. *Descartes' Meditations: Background Source Materials*. Cambridge University Press.

Ariew, Roger and Grene, Marjorie (eds.). 1995. *Descartes and His Contemporaries: Meditations, Objections, and Replies*. University of Chicago Press.

Aristotle. 1995. *The Complete Works of Aristotle*, 2 vols. Various translators and edited by Jonathan Barnes. Princeton University Press (*Phys.* = *Physics*; *EE* = *Eudemian Ethics*; *Post.* = *Posterior Analytics*, cited by Bekker numbers).

Armogathe, Jean-Robert and Belgioioso, Giulia (eds.). 1996. *Descartes:* Principia Philosophiae *(1644–1994)*. Naples: Vivarium.

Arnauld, Antoine. 1990. "New Objections to Descartes' Meditations," in *On True and False Ideas, New Objections to Descartes' Meditations*, trans. Elmar J. Kremer. Studies in the History of Philosophy 7. Lewiston, UK: Edwin Mellen Press, pp. 185–96.

Arnauld, Antoine and Nicole, Pierre. [1664] 1970. *La Logique ou L'Art de Penser*, intro. Louis Marin. Paris: Flammarion.

Augustine, St. 1841, *Soliloquies* (PL 32). Paris: J-P. Migne. (Abbreviated as *sol.*)

1970. *Contra Academicos* (PL 32). Corpus Christianorum, Series Latina, 29. Turnhout: Brepols. (Abbreviated as *c. Acad.*)

1992. *Confessions*, trans. F. J. Sheed. Indianapolis and Cambridge: Hackett.

1993. *On the Free Choice of the Will*, trans. T. Williams. Indianapolis: Hackett.

Baier, Annette. 1985. "Cartesian Persons," in *Postures of the Mind: Essays on Mind and Morals*. Minneapolis: University of Minnesota Press, pp. 74–92.

Beck, L. J. 1965. *The Metaphysics of Descartes*. Oxford: Clarendon Press.

Bennett, Jonathan. 1984. *A Study of Spinoza's Ethics*. Indianapolis: Hackett.

Beyssade, Jean-Marie. 1996. "La théoric cartésienne de la substance: Equivocité ou analogie?," *Revue Internationale de Philosophie* 195: 51–72.

Beyssade, Michelle. 1994. "Descartes's Doctrine of Freedom: Differences between the French and the Latin Texts of the Fourth Meditation," in Cottingham (ed.), pp. 191–208.

Biard, Joël and Rashed, Roshdi (eds.). 1997. *Descartes et le Moyen Âge*. Paris: Vrin.

Bolton, Martha. 1986. "Confused and Obscure Ideas of Sense," in Rorty (ed.), pp. 389–403.

Brewer, Talbot. 2009. *The Retrieval of Ethics*. New York: Oxford University Press.

Broughton, Janet. 2002. *Descartes's Method of Doubt*. Princeton University Press.

2005. "Dreamers and Madmen," in Christia Mercer and Eileen O'Neill (eds.), *Early Modern Philosophy: Mind, Matter, Metaphysics*. Oxford and New York: Oxford University Press, pp. 9–23.

Broughton, Janet and Carriero, John (eds.). 2008. *A Companion to Descartes*. Malden, MA, Oxford, and Carleton, Victoria: Blackwell.

Brown, Deborah J. 2008. "Descartes on True and False Ideas," in Broughton and Carriero (eds.), pp. 196–215.

Burnyeat, M. F. 1982. "Idealism and Greek Philosophy: What Descartes Saw and Berkeley Missed," *Philosophical Review* 91: 3–40.

1983. "Can the Skeptic Live His Skepticism?," in Burnyeat (ed.), *The Skeptical Tradition*. Berkeley: University of California Press, pp. 117–48.

Cargile, James. 1975. "The Ontological Argument," *Philosophy* 50: 69–80.

Carlin, Laurence. 2006. "Leibniz on Final Causes," *Journal of the History of Philosophy* 44 (2): 217–33.

Carraud, Vincent. 2002. *Causa sive ratio. La raison de la cause, de Suarez à Leibniz*. Paris: Presses Universitaires de France.

Carriero, John. 2003. "Berkeley, Resemblance, and Sensible Things," *Philosophical Topics* 31: 21–46.

2005. "Spinoza on Final Causality," *Oxford Studies in Early Modern Philosophy* 2: 105–47.

2009. *Between Two Worlds: A Reading of Descartes's "Meditations"*. Princeton University Press.

Carriero, John and Hoffman, Paul. 1990. "Review of *The Philosophical Writings of Descartes*," *Philosophical Review* 99: 93–104.

Cassam, Quassim. 1997: *Self and World*. Oxford University Press.

Chappell, Vere. 1986. "The Theory of Ideas," in Rorty (ed.), pp. 9–23.

1997. "Descartes' Ontology," *Topoi* 16: 111–27.

Cicero, M. T. 1967. *Academica*, ed. and trans. H. Rackham. Cambridge, MA: Harvard University Press.

Clark, S. R. L. 1995. "Objective Values, Final Causes: Stoics, Epicureans, and Platonists," *Electronic Journal of Analytic Philosophy* 3, http://ejap.louisiana.edu/EJAP/1995.spring/clark.1995.spring.html. Last accessed on 15 September 2011.

Clatterbaugh, Kenneth. 1980. "Descartes's Likeness Principle," *Philosophical Review* 89: 379–402.

Cottingham, J. (ed.). 1994. *Reason, Will, and Sensation. Studies in Descartes's Metaphysics*. Oxford University Press.

Cress, Donald. 1994. "Truth, Error, and the Order of Reasons: Descartes's Puzzling Synopsis of the Fourth Meditation," in Cottingham (ed.), pp. 141–55.

Curley, E. 1978. *Descartes against the Skeptics*. Cambridge, MA: Harvard University Press.

1995. "Hobbes versus Descartes," in Ariew and Grene (eds.), pp. 97–109.

Deferrari, Roy J. and Barry, Sister M. Inviolata, with collaboration of Ignatius McGuiness. 1948. *Lexicon of St. Thomas Aquinas*. Baltimore: Catholic University of America Press.

Delaporte, François. [1979] 1982. *Nature's Second Kingdom: Explorations of Vegetality in the Eighteenth Century*, trans. Arthur Goldhammer. Cambridge, MA: MIT Press.

Della Rocca, Michael. 2003. "The Power of an Idea: Spinoza's Critique of Pure Will," *Noûs* 37: 200–31.

2005. "Judgment and Will," in Gaukroger (ed.), pp. 142–59.

De Rosa, Raffaella. 2007. "A Teleological Account of Cartesian Sensations?," *Synthese* 156: 311–36.

2010. *Descartes and the Puzzle of Sensory Representation*. Oxford University Press.

Des Chene, Dennis. 1996. *Physiologia: Natural Philosophy in Late Aristotelian and Cartesian Thought*. Ithaca, NY: Cornell University Press.

  2001. *Spirits and Clocks: Machine and Organism in Descartes*. Ithaca, NY: Cornell University Press.

  2010. "Sensation and Natural Philosophy: On Carriero's *Between Two Worlds*," presented at an author-meets-critics session at the 2010 Pacific APA, 3 April, San Francisco.

Devillairs, Laurence. 2004. *Descartes et la connaissance de Dieu*. Paris: Vrin.

Dicker, George. 1993. *Descartes: An Analytical and Historical Introduction*. New York: Oxford University Press.

Doney, Willis. 1955. "The Cartesian Circle," *Journal of the History of Ideas* 16 (3): 324–38.

Duns Scotus, John. 1986. *On the Will and Morality*, select. and trans. A. B. Wolter. Washington, DC: Catholic University of America Press.

Dutton, Blake. 2003. "Descartes's Dualism and the One Principal Attribute Rule," *British Journal for the History of Philosophy* 11: 395–415.

Eliot, T. S. 1971. *Four Quartets*. Orlando, FL: Harcourt.

Evans, Gareth. 1982. *The Varieties of Reference*, ed. John McDowell. Oxford University Press.

Fine, Gail. 2000. "Descartes and Ancient Skepticism: 'Reheated Cabbage?,'" *Philosophical Review* 109: 194–234.

Foster, John. 1991: *The Immaterial Self: A Defense of the Cartesian Dualist Conception of the Mind*. London: Routledge.

Frankfurt, Harry. 1962. "Memory and the Cartesian Circle," *Philosophical Review* 71 (4): 504–11.

  1970. *Demons, Dreamers, and Madmen: The Defense of Reason in Descartes's Meditations*. Indianapolis and New York: Bobbs-Merrill.

  1978. "Descartes on the Consistency of Reason," in Hooker (ed.), pp. 26–39.

Gabbey, Alan. 1980. "Force and Inertia in the Seventeenth Century: Descartes and Newton," in S. Gaukroger (ed.), *Descartes: Philosophy, Mathematics and Physics*. Brighton: Harvester Press, pp. 230–320.

Galonnier, Alain. 1997. "Descartes et Saint Anselme: du *Proslogion* à *Meditatio tertia*," in Biard and Rashed (eds.), pp. 293–306.

Garber, Daniel. 1995. "J.-B. Morin and the *Second Objections*," in Ariew and Grene (eds.), pp. 63–82.

  1986. "Semel in vita: The Scientific Background to Descartes' *Meditations*," in Rorty (ed.), pp. 81–116.

Garcia, Jorge. 1982. *Suarez on Identity and Individuation: Metaphysic disputation V*. Milwaukee: Marquette University Press.

Garin, Eugenio. 1984. *Vita e opere di Cartesio*. Rome: Laterza, Rome: Laterza.

Garrett, Don. 1999. "Teleology in Spinoza and Early Modern Rationalism," in Rocco J. Gennaro and Charles Huenemann (eds.), *New Essays on the Rationalists*. New York: Oxford University Press, pp. 310–35.

Gaukroger, Stephen. 2000. "The Resources of Descartes' Mechanist Physiology and the Problem of Goal-Directed Processes," in Gaukroger, Schuster, and Sutton (eds.), pp. 383–400.

2010. "Descartes' Theory of Perceptual Cognition and the Question of Moral Sensibility," in John Cottingham and Peter Hacker (eds.) *Mind, Method and Morality: Essays in Honour of Anthony Kenny*. Oxford University Press, pp. 230–51.

Gaukroger, Stephen (ed.). 2005. *The Blackwell Guide to Descartes'* Meditations. Malden MA, Oxford, and Carleton, Victoria: Blackwell.

Gaukroger, Stephen, Schuster, John, and Sutton, John (eds.). 2000. *Descartes' Natural Philosophy*. London: Routledge.

Gilson, Étienne. 1925. *René Descartes: Discours de la méthode, texte et commentaire*. Paris: Vrin.

1975. *Études sur le rôle de la pensée mediévale dans la formation du système cartésien*. Paris: Vrin.

Glouberman, M. 1978. "Cartesian Substances as Modal Totalities," *Dialogue* 17: 320–43.

Gombay, André. 2007. *Descartes*. Malden, MA: Blackwell Publishing.

Gorham, Geoffrey. 2003. "Descartes's Dilemma of Eminent Containment," *Dialogue* 42: 3–25.

Gouhier, Henri. 1962. *La pensée métaphysique de Descartes*. Paris: J. Vrin.

Grene, Marjorie. 1986. "Die Einheit des Menschen: Descartes unter den Scholastikern," *Dialectica* 40: 309–22.

1991. *Descartes among the Scholastics*. Milwaukee: Marquette University Press.

1999. "Descartes and Ancient Skepticism," *Review of Metaphysics* 52: 533–71.

Groarke, L. 1984. "Descartes' First Meditation: Something Old, Something New, Something Borrowed," *Journal of the History of Philosophy* 22 (2): 281–301.

Gueroult, Martial. 1953. *Descartes selon l'ordre des raisons*, 2 vols. Paris: Aubier.

2005. *Descartes según el orden de las razones*, trans. Francisco Bravo and intro. Jorge Secada, 2 vols. Caracas: Monte Avila Editores.

Haldane, E. and Ross, G. (trans.). 1979. *The Philosophical Works of Descartes*, 2 vols. Cambridge University Press.

Hatfield, Gary. 1985. "Descartes's Meditations as Cognitive Exercises," *Philosophy and Literature* 19: 41–58.

1986. "The Senses and the Fleshless Eye," in Rorty (ed.), pp. 45–80.

1992. "Descartes's Physiology and Its Relation to His Psychology," in John Cottingham (ed.), *The Cambridge Companion to Descartes*. Cambridge University Press, pp. 335–70.

1993. "Reason, Nature, and God in Descartes," in Voss (ed.), pp. 259–87.

1998. "The Cognitive Faculties," in Michael Ayers and Daniel Garber (eds.), *The Cambridge History of Seventeenth-Century Philosophy*. Cambridge University Press, pp. 953–1002.

2000. "Descartes' Naturalism about the Mental," in Gaukroger, Schuster, and Sutton (eds.), pp. 630–58.

2002. *Descartes and the Meditations*. New York: Routledge.

2003. *Descartes and the Meditations*. London: Routledge.

2008. "Animals," in Broughton and Carriero (eds.), pp. 404–25.

Hatfield, Gary and Epstein, William. 1979. "The Sensory Core and the Medieval Foundations of Early Modern Perceptual Theory," *Isis* 70: 363–84.

Hwang, Joseph. 2008. "Descartes on the Metaphysics of Sensory Perception." Unpublished dissertation, UCLA.

Hobbes, Thomas. [1651] 1994. *Leviathan*, ed. E. M. Curley. Indianapolis: Hackett.

Hoffman, Paul. 1986. "The Unity of Descartes's Man," *Philosophical Review* 45 (3): 339–70.

  1991. "Cartesian Composites," *Journal of the History of Philosophy* 37: 251–70.

  2009a. *Essays on Descartes*. Oxford University Press.

  2009b. "Does Efficient Causation Presuppose Final Causation? Aquinas vs. Early Modern Mechanism," in Samuel Newlands and Larry M. Jorgensen (eds.), *Metaphysics and the Good: Themes from the Philosophy of Robert Merrihew Adams*. Oxford University Press, pp. 295–312.

Hooker, Michael (ed.). 1978. *Descartes: Critical and Interpretative Essays*. Baltimore: Johns Hopkins University Press.

Hume, David. [1739] 2007. *Treatise on Human Nature*, ed. David Norton and Mary Norton. Oxford University Press.

  1975. *A Treatise of Human Nature*, ed. L. A. Selby-Bigge, with text revision and notes by P.H. Nidditch. Oxford University Press.

Inwood, B. and Gerson, L. 1997. *Hellenistic Philosophy*. Indianapolis: Hackett.

Janowski, Zbigniew. 2000. *Index Augustino-Cartésien. Textes et commentaire*. Paris: Vrin.

Johnson, Monte Ransome. 2005. *Aristotle on Teleology*. Oxford University Press.

Johnson, Monte Ransome and Wilson, Catherine. 2007. "Lucretius and the History of Science," in Stuart Gillespie and Philip Hardie (eds.), *The Cambridge Companion to Lucretius*. Cambridge University Press, pp. 131–48.

Johnson, W. E. 1921. *Logic*, 3 vols. Cambridge University Press.

Kambouchner, Denis. 2008. "Liberté et structure de l'âme," in *Descartes et la philosophie morale*. Paris: Hermann Éditeurs, pp. 25–75.

Kant, Immanuel. [1790] 1987. *Critique of Judgment*, trans. and intro. Werner S. Pluhar. Indianapolis: Hackett.

  1965. *Critique of Pure Reason*, trans. Norman Kemp Smith. New York: St. Martin's Press (cited by page reference to the second, "B" edition).

Kaufman, Daniel. 2000. "Descartes on the Objective Reality of Materially False Ideas," *Pacific Philosophical Quarterly* 81: 385–408.

Keating, Laura. 1999. "Mechanism and the Representational Nature of Sensation in Descartes," *Canadian Journal of Philosophy* 29: 411–30.

Kenny, Anthony. 1973. "Descartes on the Will," in *The Anatomy of the Soul*. Oxford: Basil Blackwell, pp. 105–9.

Kent, Bonnie. 1995. *Virtues of the Will: The Transformation of Ethics in the Late Thirteenth Century*. Washington, DC: Catholic University of America Press.

Kitcher, Philip. 1998. "Function and Design," in Colin Allen, Marc Bekoff, and George Lauder (eds.), *Nature's Purposes: Analyses of Function and Design in Biology*. Cambridge, MA: MIT Press, pp. 479–503.

Kosman, Aryeh. 1986. "The Naive Narrator: Meditation in Descartes' *Meditations*," in Rorty (ed.), pp. 21–44.

Koyré, Alexandre [1950] 1965. "The Significance of the Newtonian Synthesis," *Archives Internationales d'Histoire des Sciences* 3: 291–311. Reprinted in *Newtonian Studies*. London: Chapman & Hall.

La Porte, Jean. 1928. "La finalité chez Descartes," *Revue d'Histoire de la Philosophie* 2 (4): 366–96.

Leibniz, G. W. [1875–90] 1965. *Die philosophischen Schriften von Gottfried Wilhelm Leibniz*, 7 vols., ed. C. I. Gerhardt. Berlin: Weidman. Reprinted, Hildesheim: Georg Olms, 1978.

  1956. *Philosophical Papers and Letters*, trans. and ed. Leroy E. Loemker. Dordrecht: Reidel.

Lennon, Thomas M. 2008. *The Plain Truth: Descartes, Huet, and Skepticism*. Leiden: Brill.

Lennox, James. 1985. "Plato's Unnatural Teleology," in Dominic J. O'Meara (ed.), *Studies in Philosophy and the History of Philosophy*, vol. xiii. Washington: Catholic University of America Press, pp. 195–218.

  1992. "Teleology," in Evelyn Fox Keller and Elisabeth A. Lloyd (eds.), *Keywords in Evolutionary Biology*. Cambridge, MA: Harvard University Press.

  2001. *Aristotle's Philosophy of Biology: Studies in the Origins of Life Science*. Cambridge University Press.

Lin, Martin. 2004. "Spinoza and Descartes on Judgment," in Antonella Del Prete (ed.), *Il Seicento e Descartes: Dibattiti cartesiani*. Florence: Le Monnier, pp. 269–91.

Locke, John. [1690] 1979. *Essay Concerning Human Understanding*, ed. P. H. Nidditch. Oxford University Press.

Loeb, Louis. 1981. *From Descartes to Hume*. Ithaca, NY: Cornell University Press.

  1985. "Replies to Daisie Radner's 'Is There a Problem of Cartesian Interaction?'," *Journal of the History of Philosophy* 23: 227–31.

Loemker, Leroy (ed.). 1989. *Leibniz. Philosophical Papers and Letters*, 2nd edn. Dordrecht: Kluwer.

LoLordo, Antonia. 2007. *Pierre Gassendi and the Birth of Early Modern Philosophy*. Cambridge University Press.

Machamer, Peter and J. E. McGuire. 2009. *Descartes's Changing Mind*. Princeton University Press.

MacKenzie, Ann Wilbur. 1994. "The Reconfiguration of Sensory Experience," in Cottingham (ed.), pp. 251–72.

Mackie, P. J. 1995. "Final Causes," in Ted Honderich (ed.), *The Oxford Companion to Philosophy*. Oxford University Press, pp. 280–81.

Malebranche, Nicolas. 1967. *De la recherche de la verité*, vol. ii, ed. Geneviève Rodis-Lewis. Paris: Vrin.

1980a. *Entretiens sur la métaphysique. Dialogues on Metaphysics*, trans. Willis Doney. New York: Abaris.

1980b. *The Search after Truth* and *Elucidations of the Search after Truth*, trans. Thomas M. Lennon and Paul J. Olscamp. Columbus: Ohio University Press.

1991. *De la recherche de la verité*, vol. 1, ed. Geneviève Rodis-Lewis. Paris: Vrin.

Marignac, Pascal. 1980. "Descartes et ses concepts de la substance," *Revue de Métaphysique et de Morale* 85: 298–314.

Marion, Jean-Luc. 1986. *Sur le prisme métaphysique de Descartes*. Paris: Presses Universitaires de France.

1996. "Sostanza e sussistenza Suárez e il trattato dela *substantia* nei *Principia, I, 51–54*," in Armogathe and Belgioioso (eds.), pp. 203–29.

Marlies, Mike. 1978. "Doubt, Reason, and Cartesian Therapy," in Hooker (ed). pp. 89–113.

Marshall, John. 1998. *Descartes's Moral Theory*. Ithaca, NY: Cornell University Press.

Matthews, G. 1992. *Thought's Ego*. Ithaca, NY: Cornell University Press.

McDonough, Jeffery. 2009. "Leibniz on Natural Teleology and the Laws of Optics," *Philosophy and Phenomenological Research* 78 (3): 505–44.

Menn, S. 1998. *Descartes and Augustine*. Cambridge University Press.

Meyer, Susan Sauvé. 1992. "Aristotle, Teleology, and Reduction," *Philosophical Review* 101 (4): 791–823.

Miles, Murray. 1999. *Insight and Inference: Descartes's Founding Principle and Modern Philosophy*. University of Toronto Press.

Naaman-Zauderer, Noa. 2010. *Descartes' Deontological Turn: Reason, Will, and Virtue in the Later Writings*. Cambridge University Press.

Newman, Lex. 1994: "Descartes on Unknown Faculties and our Knowledge of the External World," *Philosophical Review* 103 (3): 489–531.

2005. "Descartes's Epistemology," in Edward N. Zalta (ed.), *Stanford Encyclopedia of Philosophy* (Fall 2008 edn.), http://plato.stanford.edu/archives/fall2008/entries/descartes-epistemology/. Last accessed 29 September 2009.

2008. "Descartes on Will in Judgment," in Broughton and Carriero (eds.), pp. 334–52.

Newman, Lex and Alan Nelson. 1999. "Circumventing Cartesian Circles," *Noûs* 33: 370–404.

Nolan, Lawrence. 1997. "Reduction and Nominalism in Descartes' Theory of Attributes," *Topoi* 16: 129–40.

2005. "The Ontological Argument as an Exercise in Cartesian Therapy," *Canadian Journal of Philosophy* 35: 521–62.

Nolan, Lawrence and Alan Nelson. 2005. "Proofs of the Existence of God," in Gaukroger (ed.), pp. 104–21.

Normore, Calvin. 1986. "Meaning and Objective Being: Descartes and His Sources," in Rorty (ed.), pp. 223–41.

1998. "Picking or Choosing: Anselm and Ockham on Choice," *Vivarium* 36: 23–29.

2008. "Descartes and the Metaphysics of Extension," in Broughton and Carriero (eds.), pp. 271–87.

O'Neill, Eileen. 1987. "Mind–Body Interaction and Metaphysical Consistency: A Defense of Descartes," *Journal of the History of Philosophy* 25: 227–45.

Osler, Margaret J. 1996. "From Immanent Natures to Nature as Artifice: The Reinterpretation of Final Causes in Seventeenth-Century Natural Philosophy," *The Monist* 79 (3): 388–407.

Ott, Walter. 2009. *Causation and Laws of Nature in Early Modern Philosophy*. New York: Oxford University Press.

Parfit, Derek. 1971. "Personal Identity," *Philosophical Review* 80 (1): 3–27.

Patterson, Sarah. "Nature and Habit: The Case for Mechanism in Descartes' *Meditations*." Unpublished manuscript.

Peacocke, Christopher. 1992. "Scenarios, Concepts and Perceptions," in Tim Crane (ed.), *The Contents of Experience: Essays on Perception*. Cambridge University Press, pp. 105–35.

Plato. 1997. *Timeaus*. In *Plato: Complete Works*, ed. John Cooper and D. S. Hutchinson. Indianapolis: Hackett. Cited by the abbreviation *Tim.* and page number corresponding to Stephanus number.

Popkin, R. 1979. *The History of Skepticism from Erasmus to Spinoza*. Berkeley: University of California Press.

2003. *The History of Scepticism from Savonarola to Bayle*. New York: Oxford University Press.

Radner, Daisie. 1985a. "Is There a Problem of Cartesian Interaction?," *Journal of the History of Philosophy* 23: 35–50.

1985b. "Rejoinder to Richardson and Loeb," *Journal of the History of Philosophy* 23: 232–36.

Ragland, Clyde Prescott. 2006. "Is Descartes a Libertarian?," *Oxford Studies in Early Modern Philosophy* (3): 57–90.

Richardson, Robert. 1982. "The 'Scandal' of Cartesian Interactionism," *Mind* 91: 20–37.

1985. "Replies to Daisie Radner's 'Is There a Problem of Cartesian Interaction?'," *Journal of the History of Philosophy* 23: 221–26.

Rodis-Lewis, Geneviève. 1950. *L'individualité selon Descartes*. Paris: Vrin.

1998. *Descartes: His Life and Thought*, trans. J. Todd. Ithaca, NY: Cornell University Press.

Rodriguez-Pereyra, Gonzalo. 2008. "Descartes's Substance Dualism and His Independence Conception of Substance," *Journal of the History of Philosophy* 46: 69–90.

Rorty, Amélie Oksenberg (ed.). 1986a. *Essays on Descartes' Meditations*. Berkeley: University of California Press.

1986b: "The Structure of Descartes' *Meditations*," in Rorty (ed.), pp. 1–20.

Rosenthal, David M. 1986. "Will and the Theory of Judgment," in Rorty (ed.), pp. 405–34.

Rozemond, Marleen. 1998. *Descartes's Dualism*. Cambridge, MA: Harvard University Press.

Rubin, Ronald. 2008. *Silencing the Demon's Advocate. The Strategy of Descartes' Meditations*. Stanford University Press.

Rudder Baker, Lynne. 2011. "Beyond the Cartesian Self," *Phenomenology and Mind* 1 (5): 48–57.

Sancto Paulo, Eustachius a. 1648. *Summa philosophiae quadripartita, etc. Tertia part. Physica*. Cambridge: Roger Daniel.

Schmaltz, Tad M. 2008. *Descartes on Causation*. Oxford University Press.

2011. "*Causa Sui* and Created Truth in Descartes," in J. Wippel (ed.), *The Ultimate Why Question: Why Is There Anything at All Rather than Nothing Whatsoever*. Washington, DC: Catholic University Press of America, pp. 109–24.

Schussler, Rudolf. Forthcoming. "Descartes's Doxastic Voluntarism," *Archiv fur Geschichte der Philosophie*.

Scott, David. 2009. "Descartes, Madness and Method: A Reply to Ablondi," *International Philosophical Quarterly* 49 (2): 153–71.

Scotus, John Duns. 1966. *A Treatise on God as First Principle*, ed. Allan B. Wolter. Chicago: Franciscan Herald Press.

Secada, Jorge. 2000. *Cartesian Metaphysics: The Scholastic Origins of Modern Philosophy*. Cambridge University Press.

2005. "The Doctrine of Substance," in Gaukroger (ed.), pp. 67–85.

2009. "Review of Ronald Rubin, *Silencing the Demon's Advocate. The Strategy of Descartes' Meditations*," *Notre Dame Philosophical Reviews*, http://ndpr.nd.edu/news/23981-silencing-the-demon-s-advocate-the-strategy-of-descartes-meditations/. Last accessed 31 October 2012.

Sextus Empiricus. 2000. *Outlines of Skepticism*, 2nd edn., trans. and ed. J. Annas, and J. Barnes. Cambridge University Press (cited as PH in the text, by book and section).

Shapiro, Lisa. 2003. "The Health of the Body-Machine? Seventeenth-Century Mechanism and the Concept of Health," *Perspectives on Science* 11: 421–42.

2005. "What are the Passions Doing in the *Meditations*?," in Joyce Jenkins, Jennifer Whiting, and Chris Williams (eds.), *Persons and Passions: Essays in Honor of Annette Baier*. University of Notre Dame Press, pp. 14–33.

2008. "Turn My Will in Completely the Opposite Direction: Radical Doubt and Descartes' Account of Free Will," in Paul Hoffman, David Owen and Gideon Yaffe (eds.), *Contemporary Perspectives on Early Modern Philosophy: Essays in Honour of Vere Chappell*, Peterborough, ON: Broadview Press, pp. 21–39.

Silhon, Jean. 1991. *Les deux véritez … l'une de Dieu et de sa providence, l'autre de l'immortalité de l'âme*. Paris: Fayard.

Simmons, Alison. 1999. "Are Cartesian Sensations Representational?," *Noûs* 33: 347–69.

2001. "Sensible Ends: Latent Teleology in Descartes' Account of Sensation," *Journal of the History of Philosophy* 39 (1): 49–75.

2003. "Descartes on the Cognitive Structure of Sensory Experience," *Philosophy and Phenomenological Research* 67: 549–79.

Slezak, Peter. 2000. "Descartes' Startling Doctrine of the Reverse-Sign Relation," in Gaukroger, Schuster, and Sutton (eds.), pp. 542–56.

Sorell, Tom. 1995. "Hobbes's Objections and Hobbes's System," in Ariew and Grene (eds.), pp. 63–96.

Spinoza, Benedict. 1925. *Spinoza Opera*, ed. C. Gebhardt, 4 vols. Heidelberg: Carl Winter.

Stalnaker, R. 1984. *Inquiry*. Cambridge, MA: MIT Press.

Suárez, Francisco. 1960–66. *Disputaciones metafísicas*, ed. Sergio Rábade Romeo, Salvador Caballero Sánchez, and Antonio Puigcerver Zanón, 7 vols. Madrid: Gredos.

1965. *Disputationes Metaphysicae*, 2 vols. Reprinted, Hildesheim: Georg Olms.

Svensson, Frans. 2011. "Happiness, Wellbeing, and Their Relation to Virtue in Descartes' Ethics," *Theoria* 77 (3): 238–60.

Taylor, R. 1967. "Causation," in Paul Edwards (ed.), *Encyclopedia of Philosophy*, vol. 11. New York: Macmillan.

Tye, Michael. 1995. "A Representational Theory of Pains and Their Phenomenal Character," *Philosophical Perspectives* 9: 223–39.

van Inwagen, Peter. 2009. *Metaphysics*, 3rd edn. Boulder: Westview Press.

Vendler, Zeno. 1989. "Descartes' Exercises," *Canadian Journal of Philosophy* 19: 193–224.

Vinci, Thomas C. 1998. *Cartesian Truth*. New York: Oxford.

Voss, Stephen (ed.). 1993. *Essays on the Philosophy and Science of Descartes*. New York: Oxford University Press.

Wee, Cecilia. 2006: *Material Falsity and Error in Descartes' Meditations*. London: Routledge.

Wells, Norman J. 1984. "Material Falsity in Descartes, Arnauld, and Suarez," *Journal of the History of Philosophy* 22: 25–50.

1990. "Objective Reality of Ideas in Descartes, Caterus, and Suárez," *Journal of the History of Philosophy* 28: 33–61.

Wickes, Howard. 1994. "Descartes's Denial of the Autonomy of Reason," in Cottingham (ed.), pp. 111–39.

Williams, Bernard. 1970. "Deciding to Believe," in H. Kiefer and M. Munitz (eds.), *Language, Belief and Metaphysics*. Albany: State University of New York Press, pp. 95–111.

1978. *Descartes: The Project of Pure Enquiry*. Harmondsworth: Penguin Books.

1983. "Descartes's Use of Skepticism," in Burnyeat (ed.), pp. 337–52.

Wilson, Catherine. 2005. "What is the Importance of Descartes's Meditation Six?," *Philosophica* 76: 67–90.

Wilson, Margaret D. 1978. *Descartes*. London: Routledge and Kegan Paul.

    1990. "Descartes on the Representationality of Sensation," in J. A. Cover and Mark Kulstad (eds.), *Central Themes in Early Modern Philosophy*. Indianapolis: Hackett, pp. 1–22.

    1993. "Descartes on the Perception of Primary Qualities," in Voss (ed.), pp. 162–76.

    1999. *Ideas and Mechanism: Essays on Early Modern Philosophy*. Princeton University Press.

Wippel, J. and Wolter, A. B. 1969. *Medieval Philosophy*. New York: Free Press.

Wolf-Devine, Celia. 1993. *Descartes on Seeing: Epistemology and Visual Perception*. Carbondale: Southern Illinois University Press.

Wolff, Christian. [1728] 1983. *Philosophia rationalis sive logica*. Verona. Reprinted, Hildesheim and New York: Georg Olms.

Yolton, John W. 1984. *Perceptual Acquaintance from Descartes to Reid*. Minneapolis: University of Minnesota Press.

Index

Spinoza, Baruch, 100, 158, 178, 179, 195–6, 199
Stalnaker, Robert, 29, 30
Stoics/Stoicism, 27, 195
Suárez, Francisco, 4, 82, 95, 97, 213, 218
   and Causal Containment Axiom (CCA), 84
   on creation and conservation, 93
   on eminent containment, 88, 90–2
   on formal containment, 85
   on objective reality of ideas, 86
subject/substance, *see also* substance
   and accident/faculty/mode, 46–8, 50, 52–3, 55
substance, 3, 45, *see also* being; body; mind;
      matter; soul; thinking
   as bare substratum, 60, 63
   as capacity for independent existence, 48–9,
      57, 58, 61–2
   common concept of, 49, 52, 62–3
   conception of
      in Fourth Set of Objections and Replies,
      57–8
      in *Meditations*, 49–50, 51–2, 57
      in *Principles*, 48, 50, 58–62
      in Second Set of Objections and Replies,
      50–2
   essence/nature of, 59–60, 65, 66–7, 75, 81
   extended, 49, 50, 51, 60–1, 65
   finite vs. infinite, 49, 64
   functional-causal view, 74–5
   as general rule, 78–9
   knowledge of
      by intellect, 66–7
      exhausted by knowledge of principal
      attribute, 57–8, 59–60, 62
      no immediate, 51, 52, 54–5, 57, 58–9, 66
   as "modal totality", 77–9
   and modes, 79–81
      how to account for memory as thoughts/
      modes, 233–6
      and inaccuracies/embellishments of
      memory as thoughts/modes, 235–6
      inherence relation, 65, 76–7, 229
   and principal attribute
      mere distinction of reason, 59–61,
      69–70
   and principal attribute and modes, 48, 50,
      59–62, 75–6
   as ultimate subject, 48, 51–6, 58, 60–1
   thinking, 3–4, 49–50, 51, 60

teachings of nature, 109, 127, 144, 149,
      see also doubt; resemblance; teleology
   apparent vs. actual, 130
   and truth, 129–30
   vs. truth revealed by natural light, 109–10, 129
   and will and free decision/judgment, 41–2

teleology, *see also* animals/living things;
      natures
   Aristotelian/natural, 157; *see also* Aristotle
      Descartes' rejection of, 160
   and/vs. chance, 158
   divine, 155–6
   and explanation, 153, 155, 157, 159–60, 161,
      163–5, 168
   and explanation in the life sciences, 153, 169
   intrinsic vs. incidental ends, 158–9, 163–5
      and scientific explanation, 170–2
   and living things without souls, 169, 173–4
   and mechanism, 160
   and mind–body composite, 153, 154–6
   natural, 155–6
   and natures, 158–9, 161–2
   and non-living things, 154
   non-Platonic and non-Aristotelian, 174–5
   Platonic/unnatural, 157, 168, 174–5;
      see also Plato
      Descartes' acceptance of, 161
      Descartes' rejection of, 160–1
   rational, 155
   and teachings of nature, 154
things
   simple vs. composite, 32–3
thinking, *see also* knowledge; mind; substance;
      thoughts
   and/vs. acts of thought, 65, 71
   as changing vs. unchanging, 72
   as faculty/power of thinking, 69–70
   qua nature of a substance, 69, 79, 81
Third Set of Objections and Replies (Hobbes),
      45, 46–8, 52–4, 69–70
Thomistic philosophy, 86
thoughts
   as modes bound together by their
      co-location in the same substance
      and memory, 234
   as modes that determine a determinable
      substance
      and memory, 234–5
time
   nature of, 92
true and immutable natures, 35, *see also* essence;
      God's existence, arguments for;
      natures
truth, *see also* eternal truths; falsity; ideas;
      judgment; material falsity; passions;
      skepticism; teachings of nature
   and adequacy of intellect with reality,
      180–1
   and appearance, 26, 29–30
   conception of, 18, 180–1
   and falsity require judgment, 180

CPSIA information can be obtained
at www.ICGtesting.com
Printed in the USA
LVHW071032290623
751112LV00003B/145